The Middle Path in Math Instruction

Solutions for Improving Math Education

Shuhua An

ScarecrowEducation
Lanham, Maryland • Toronto • Oxford
2004

Published in the United States of America
by ScarecrowEducation
An imprint of The Rowman & Littlefield Publishing Group, Inc.
4501 Forbes Boulevard, Suite 200, Lanham, Maryland 20706
www.scaroweducation.com

PO Box 317
Oxford
OX2 9RU, UK

British Library Cataloguing in Publication Information Available

Library of Congress Cataloging-in-Publication Data

An, Shuhua, 1957–
    The middle path in math instruction : solutions for improving math educa-
tion / Shuhua An.
        p. cm.
    Includes bibliographical references.
    ISBN 1-57886-089-X (pbk. : alk. paper)
    1. Mathematics—Study and teaching—China. 2. Mathematics—Study and
teaching—United States. 3. Comparative education. I. Title.
QA14.C6 A5 2004
510'.71'051—dc22

                                                      2003020559

To my parents,
Hongzhang An and Xiangwen Chu.
Your love, encouragement, and support
I will always treasure.

Contents

Foreword

The practice of comparing the mathematics achievement of U.S. students with that of other countries has become commonplace in the past several years. The Second International Mathematics and Science Study, in which U.S. students placed near the bottom, initiated an intensive period of concern about our system of mathematics education. The nation's governors exhorted educators to make improvements, setting the goal of being first in the world in mathematics achievement by the turn of the century. Somewhat naively, many policy makers concluded that borrowing perceived good practices from top-ranked countries was the answer to improving mathematics achievement. Even though some of the key reasons for the low performance of U.S. students have been clearly outlined (McKnight et al. 1987), many politicians and educators ignored the important effects of mathematics curriculum and teaching practices in favor of other less relevant factors. For example, a great deal of attention was focused on the amount of time students, especially those in Asian countries, spent in mathematics class. School districts invested significantly to increase the number of hours students spent in school by extending the length of class periods or days in the school year.

The comparative study of mathematics education has become more sophisticated in the past few years. The Third International Mathematics and Science Study (TIMSS) included direct attention to the curriculum and teaching. Textbooks were compared, with the general finding that U.S. mathematics textbooks attempted to cover significantly more topics than did other countries, resulting in the characterization of the curriculum as "a mile wide and an inch deep" (Schmidt, McKnight, and Raizen 1997). Analyses of videotaped lessons of eighth grade teachers in the United States, Japan, and Germany revealed teacher-centered classes in the United States devoted mainly to transmitting information. Mathematics teaching in Japan provided in-depth work with problems and allowed students to work together and then share and present their work and thinking. Implications and ideas drawn from the TIMSS findings include attention to teachers' professional development, focusing on the connection of mathematics and teaching knowledge (Stigler and Hiebert 1999).

The ability to teach mathematics effectively depends on a combination of mathematical knowledge, a set of beliefs about mathematics and how children learn, and an in-depth understanding of the teaching process. This set of factors has been called "pedagogical content knowledge." Each of the factors that make up pedagogical content knowledge interacts in complex ways and each is heavily influenced by the expectations and cultural history of a country. One's experiences as a student learning mathematics, as well as experiences as a teacher, also have significant influences on a person's effectiveness as a teacher.

The potential for comparative studies to contribute to the improvement of mathematics education for any country lies in the possibility of having an impact on teachers' pedagogical content knowledge. At issue is the extent to which attempts to enhance this special type of teacher knowledge can transcend cultural, political, and institutional factors. Can a careful analysis of mathematics teachers' beliefs and pedagogical content knowledge in different countries identify areas in which one country can learn and benefit from another? The work reported in this book suggests that the United States and China can indeed improve mathematics education by attending to some important areas of pedagogical content knowledge. The author's recommendations are concrete and useful ideas for teacher education in both countries.

Gerald Kulm
Curtis D. Robert Professor, Mathematics Education
Texas A&M University
November 10, 2003

REFERENCES

McKnight, C. C., Crosswhite, F. J., Dossey, J. A., Kifer, E., Swafford, J. O., Travers, K. J., and Cooney, T. J. 1987. *The underachieving curriculum: Assessing U.S. mathematics from an international perspective.* Champaign, Ill.: Stipes.

Schmidt, W. H., McKnight, C. C., and Raizen, S. A. 1997. *A splintered vision: An investigation of U.S. science and mathematics education.* East Lansing, Mich.: U.S. National Research Center for the Third International Mathematics and Science Study.

Stigler, J. W. and Hiebert, J. 1999. *The teaching gap: Best ideas from the world's teachers for improving education in the classroom.* New York: Free Press.

Acknowledgments

Writing a book is a challenging endeavor, and without many people's support, it is not possible. This book began as my doctoral dissertation at Texas A&M University. My first thanks go to all the members of my doctoral committee for their support and advice along the way: Gerald Kulm, Charles Lamb, Gaile Cannella, and Stephanie L. Knight. I am grateful to the chair of my doctoral committee, Gerald Kulm, Curtis D. Robert Professor, for his endless support, advice, and encouragement throughout my study and beyond.

I want to express my appreciation to all my friends and colleagues for their support and encouragement. My thanks go to my colleague Marina Krause for taking time to read my chapters. I owe special thanks to my friend Nelson Bank, whose help and editing made my book-writing endeavor go smoothly. My appreciation goes to my friends Dong Qian and Xinjian Yan, whose care encouraged me to meet challenges during my study.

I also wish to thank all the teachers in both China and the United States for their participation in this study. The group of people who deserve recognition in China includes Fu Ma and Lin Wang, who helped me contact teachers in China. Without their help, my study would have been limited.

I would also like to thank the staff at ScarecrowEducation for their professional support. In particular, I would like to thank Thomas F. Koerner, vice president and editorial director, for his constructive suggestions on my original manuscript and detailed guidance in the process of publication, as well as Cindy Tursman, managing editor, and Amos Z. Guinan, associate editor, for their positive editorial work. My special appreciation goes to Jessica McCleary, associate editor, for her thoughtful editorial guidance and the effort to ensure a quality manuscript with Chinese characters. In addition, I wish to thank Chrisona Schmidt, copyeditor, for her hard work on editing my manuscript.

Most of all, I am grateful for my family's endless support and encouragement. My husband, colleague, and best friend, Zhonghe Wu, has been involved in this study from the beginning to the end of writing this book, and he has provided valuable suggestions and insights. I thank my son, Andy Wu, for his help during my study and for his patience and understanding with my busy schedule for this study.

CHAPTER 1

Dilemmas in Mathematics Education: Opposite Directions

The more we know of Chinese art, Chinese literature, and Chinese philosophy of life, the more we admire the height to which that civilization attained.

—Whitehead 1925, 6

When I was a little schoolgirl in China, I dreamed of being a scientist like Madame Marie Curie, a Frenchwoman who dedicated her life to science. During the Cultural Revolution, we did not have many books to read. Curie's story inspired my interest in science and she became my heroine and role model. However, my dream was lost when I could not attend the university I hoped to attend. During that time, students in China did not have many choices in the admission process; often they were recruited by universities not according to grades and personal choices, but other factors. I had to study mathematics education while at Nanjing Normal University, one of the top teacher universities now in China. My students frequently ask me why I chose an education major. I always reply that it was not my primary goal; it was an accidental decision. However, I appreciated the opportunity to be an educator once I was enrolled in the education program. Although I could not be an engineer in the natural sciences, I am proud to be an "engineer of the human soul," as I help students design and grow in their future lives.

I have taught mathematics at various levels for 15 years—9 years at the college level in China and 6 years at the secondary level in Texas. After years of teaching experience, I can say that teaching K–12 mathematics is a rewarding career. This reward comes from observing my students' growing ability and confidence in their learning. It comes from the realization that I have sparked my students' interest in mathematics, have touched their hearts, and have exerted a positive influence in their lives. My teaching practices have enriched my knowledge, enhanced my ability to teach effectively, and, most importantly, have increased my interest in devoting myself to mathematics education. Through teaching mathematics I realize that an effective mathematics teacher not only teaches students mathematics content, but also teaches students how to develop their minds to think intellectually and critically and to gain knowledge and skills to survive in an ever-changing society.

As a mathematics teacher with 16 years of experience in both China and the United States, I was alarmed by the weak mathematics ability of students entering high school. For example, at least one-third of my students often made the following mistake when adding fractions in Algebra I and II: $3/4 + 4/5 = 7/9$. Also I was surprised to discover that my high school students were not familiar with basic mathematical facts. For example, they did not know $\sqrt{2} \approx 1.414$, $\sqrt{3} \approx 1.732$.

Some of them did not remember the squares of numbers from 1 to 20, which are basic facts for Chinese elementary students. Furthermore, teachers were required to often use a TI-82 or TI-83 calculator and manipulatives to help students understand algebraic reasoning. When I became a faculty member at the university level, I realized that my graduate students who teach at the elementary school level barely knew the above facts. Many students from high school could not pass the state end-of-year exam for Algebra I in Texas. How could this happen? And what is missing in teaching and learning mathematics in the United States? I was deeply concerned about my students' progress and concerned about middle school mathematics teaching in this country. These concerns inspired me to find a way to raise the low achievement level in mathematics of my high school students and led me to pursue a Ph.D. in the field of mathematics education.

Teaching experiences in both China and the United States made me ponder teaching problems in the United States from a different angle and to cross the threshold from an outsider to an insider. The Chinese traditional perspective enables me, as an outsider, to reflect on the loopholes in U.S. teaching; my U.S. teaching experience enables me, as an insider, to enjoy rich resources and a variety of new teaching approaches. Furthermore, I understand the reality and necessity of using manipulatives and concrete models to reach all students and realize how difficult and challenging teaching mathematics in the United States is compared to teaching in China. My teaching experience in both cultures has motivated me to pursue and conduct comparative studies in mathematics education between the two countries.

From conducting a series of comparative studies of mathematics education in recent years, I have come to realize that with comparison studies, teachers reflect on their own traditional teaching practices and become aware of better choices in constructing the teaching and learning process. Moreover, comparative studies can inspire teachers to apply different approaches used by other systems to solve a similar problem. They can also stimulate debate and discussion, and they can help teachers understand common contemporary issues and problems in mathematics education.

According to the Third International Mathematics and Science Study (TIMSS), U.S. middle school students score below average in mathematics among 42 nations (National Center for Education Statistics 1999). Since middle school mathematics builds a connection between arithmetic and algebraic thinking, it plays an important transitional role into high-level mathematics. However, middle school mathematics is not strong in the United States. Most schools devote three or four years from fifth through eighth grades teaching fractions, decimals, percentages, and so on according to a spiral curriculum. Despite the repetitive method, students show a lack of basic knowledge in mathematics when they study algebra at the beginning of high school. Furthermore, in some states, not all high school students were required to take algebra before 2002. In contrast, in China, all students have to take algebra from seventh grade through ninth grade.

Since November 1999, a "math war" has been provoking sharp debate in the United States. Mathematicians and educators look for new approaches to improve mathematics education and address the lack of strong basic conceptual understanding and skills. A rigorous testing system for K–12 has become a major trend in mathematics education. My experiences in both cultures and my professional responsibility have motivated me to caution educators that the new testing system could place much pressure on U.S. students and teachers. Teachers may forgo providing concrete models and meaningful activities in the interest of time "to teach to the test," with the result that the United States may lose its advantage in the areas of inquiry and creativity.

My concerns about mathematics education led me to conduct a comparative study on teachers' knowledge. With my educational background and teaching experience, I understand the needs in mathematics education in both China and the United States, and I am highly motivated to find solutions for improving mathematics education. I believe that the problems in mathematics education can be solved though understanding the components and construction of teachers' knowledge, investigating the impacts of pedagogical content knowledge on the effectiveness of teaching and learning, and exploring how to develop strong pedagogical content knowledge. Teachers' pedagogical content knowledge is defined as the knowledge of subject matter being taught and how this subject matter is transformed through the teaching and learning process. It includes teachers' knowledge of students' cognition and is influenced by teachers' beliefs about education.

DILEMMA 1: SHIFTING THE DIRECTION TO THE WESTERN WAY IN CHINA

High Achievement of Chinese Students

China's 5,000-year-old civilization is greatly respected and admired all over the world. According to Ashmore and Cao, "To the Westerner, trying to understand China is a bit like being Alice in Wonderland: Everything strikes one as being 'curiouser and curiouser'" (1997, 1). For many years mathematics learning in China was a mystery to the West, but more recently researchers in international studies have sought to investigate how Chinese students learn mathematics effectively and differently. This mystery has "raised the eyebrows of sociologists, educators and psychologists" in recent decades (Wong and Wong 2002, 1).

In general, when cross-national studies in mathematics education have included samples of Chinese and U.S. students, the findings show that mathematical performance of Chinese students is higher than that of their U.S. counterparts (Lapointe, Mead, and Askew 1992; Stevenson et al. 1990). In particular, Chinese students are good at computation skills (Cai 2000, 2001). This phenomenon is described by Wong and Wong (2002) in their study of Confucian heritage culture:

- Hong Kong scored the highest and Japan achieved second place in the second International Association for the Evaluation of Educational Achievement (IAEEA) mathematics study.
- China scored first in the 1992 International Assessment of Education Progress (IAEP) mathematics study, and Taiwan and Korea were tied for second place.
- Japan, South Korea, Singapore, and Hong Kong, known as the "Four Little Dragons," ranked as the top four in the Third International Mathematics and Science Study held recently.
- The Chinese team ranked first on the medal chart in 1990, 1992, 1993, 1995, 1997, 1998, 2000, and 2001, and runner-up in 1991 and 1994 in the International Mathematical Olympiads.

Learning from Western Culture:
Inviting U.S. Educators

In 1999, as an experienced high school math teacher in Texas, a former college mathematics instructor in China, and a doctoral candidate in math education, I, along with my professor and a colleague, was invited by the Education Department of China to share U.S. mathematics teaching experiences with a group of Chinese teachers. We showed Chinese teachers how to use manipulatives in a mathematics classroom, including a fraction kit and a statistical survey project. Chinese teachers were surprised to learn that fraction kit activities were interesting and helpful for understanding fractions. Our workshop drew 200 Chinese educators from different cities and regions. In the next two years, other U.S. scholars and I went to China to hold workshops and presentations for a group of Chinese educators and researchers about the reform of U.S. mathematics education, new approaches to teaching and learning, and alternative assessments. This might be puzzling to many people in the United States because, in general, the United States has viewed Asian countries, including China, as having a superior educational system, especially in mathematics. Many of my American colleagues and even my college students wonder why Chinese math educators would want to learn from U.S. math education and educators.

Global Perspectives in Mathematics Education

During our visits to China, we were struck by the global outlook of Chinese educators. For example, in order to reform the national curriculum for mathematics, the Department of Education in China formed research groups to study the mathematics curricula of particular countries—including Russia, Germany, Australia, Great Britain, and the United States—in order to find what each country is doing successfully in its mathematics education and how China can adopt parts of those programs to improve its mathematics curriculum. I helped one of the groups study National Council of Teachers of Mathematics (NCTM) standards. My study, which was used by the Chinese research group, not only examined NCTM standards but also revealed the reasons for revision of the NCTM standards and explored NCTM standards developmental trends in the 21st century. Learning from other countries, China has developed new mathematics curriculum standards, integrating ideas similar to those of NCTM. In recent years, a set of unified traditional math textbooks has been replaced by a variety of new texts in different provinces and regions, with features of constructivism focusing on inquiry and creative, hands-on activities. Interestingly, colorful pictures and charts and tables are replacing black-and-white printing in mathematics texts. With new curricula and textbooks, China is reforming its examination system as well. In spring 2000, the State Education Commission of China issued a document to abolish middle school entrance examinations in the whole nation. In summer 2001, I made a presentation on how to use alternative assessments in math classrooms, for Chinese math educators and researchers in Beijing, China. Chinese math teachers especially are interested in portfolio assessment to improve the portfolio system that they have been using. Chinese teachers call portfolios "learning growth records" in order to encourage students to make progress and avoid negative impact. The Chinese mathematics education system is now looking for new ways to shift its emphasis away from reliance on traditional and rigid procedural development toward inquiry practices and creative learning processes by focusing on both conceptual understanding and procedural development.

Chinese math reform raised the first dilemma: Why is Chinese mathematics education reform moving toward the Western way? If the Chinese traditional educational system could produce high-achieving students, why is China now trying to reduce its traditional educational curriculum, which was successful in practice for decades? These questions raised concerns and cautions among scholars. Today "the most important dilemma for China is how to adopt Western ideas in order to compete economically, while at the same time not lose a culture that has survived for thousands of years" (An 2000, 133).

DILEMMA 2: STRENGTHENING THE TESTING SYSTEM IN THE UNITED STATES

The Myth of the Math War

For several decades, U.S. mathematics education swung widely under the influence of social, cultural, and political changes. Since 1989, NCTM has proposed sets of standards for curriculum, teaching, and assessment. Classroom teachers have worked hard to create various new approaches to help students learn mathematics, such as using manipulatives, using cooperative groups, making connections, and using technology. In 2000, the new *Principles and Standards for School Mathematics* from NCTM further updated mathematics standards and continued to guide U.S. mathematics education toward the direction of inquiry, creativity, and problem solving.

In January 2000, the *Washington Post* printed a letter opposing mathematics reform, signed by over 200 leading mathematicians and scientists. This letter sparked a math war in the United States. The reformed mathematics has been characterized as "fuzzy math" and has been charged with lacking mathematical depth and rigor and promoting watered-down mathematics. What is the reality of reformed mathematics? Constructivism is the philosophical and theoretic base for reformed math, which argues that children create their own knowledge by seeing, doing, and connecting in the learning process. In the reformed math classroom, a student-centered approach is often used to direct students to discover math concepts from their prior knowledge and experience. Teachers use concrete examples and manipulatives to make math visual, meaningful, and understandable. However, in many mathematics classrooms this approach is often accompanied by de-emphasizing proficiency, fluency, accuracy, and competence in basic procedures and skills.

What do the opponents of reformers propose to take the place of the reform approach? In the traditional math classroom, instruction is usually approached in a teacher-centered way. Teachers introduce definitions, formulas, and algorithms, focusing on procedure and skill development. Students are expected to do extensive drills in order to master concepts and skills, and achieve proficiency and competency. The opponents of reform suggest that states and school boards abolish reform curricula and implement new curricula that emphasize mathematical fundamentals, which are defined as fostering proficiency and competency in basic procedures and skills.

Which side is right? Who is going to win the math war? According to a Chinese saying, one cannot see the real face (whole picture) of a mountain if one is inside the mountain. Although I am an insider in mathematics education in the United States, I am Chinese and was exposed to Chinese cultural influence. So I am also an outsider. I can see a clear picture of this math war. Both sides seem to be going to extreme ends and do not recognize any middle option. Actually, reform and traditional approaches have advantages and disadvantages. The solution to the math war is to find a middle road. This book is going to explore a possible middle way that might bring new inspiration to math education in the United States.

The TIMSS Study and Other National Reports

The Third International Mathematics and Science Study, conducted in 1995, examined mathematics and science achievement of students in 42 countries at three grade levels (fourth, eighth, and twelfth grade levels). This study found that U.S. students scored above the international average in mathematics at the fourth grade level. At the eighth grade level, U.S. students performed below the international average. By the twelfth grade, U.S. performance was among the lowest in mathematics (National Center for Education Statistics 1999). Mathematics educators were shocked by these findings. TIMSS was like an alarm that woke up

U.S. mathematics education and provoked debates and fighting between those advocating reformed mathematics education and supporters of the traditional approach.

The Third International Mathematics and Science Study–Repeat (TIMSS-R) collected data in 38 countries at the eighth grade level. The findings from TIMSS-R revealed that U.S. eighth graders exceeded the international average in 38 nations in mathematics, but there were no changes in mathematics achievement for U.S. eighth graders between 1995 and 1999 (Mullis et al. 2000).

Since 1969, the National Assessment of Educational Progress (NAEP) has conducted ongoing nationwide assessments of student achievement in various subjects. The NAEP report *Trends in Academic Progress: Three Decades of Student Performance* (Campbell, Hombor, and Mazzeo 2000) presents the results of long-term NAEP trend assessments in reading, mathematics, and science administered in 1999 to students aged 9, 13, and 17. Although NAEP shows that U.S. students have made steady progress in mathematics achievement since 1973, it also indicates some areas of weakness that must be improved (National Center for Education Statistics 2000).

A report from the National Research Council (2001), *Adding It Up: Helping Children Learn Mathematics,* further indicates that in the United States, too few children are leaving elementary and middle school with adequate mathematics skills and understanding. The report urges that for mathematics education in this nation to be satisfactory, major reforms are needed in mathematics instruction, curricula, and assessment from prekindergarten through grade 8.

Overall, evidence from the TIMSS and other national reports provides a warning that U.S. students still do not rank well compared to students of other nations with which the United States competes economically. To compete internationally in mathematics education, much should be done to improve mathematics achievement. The No Child Left Behind Act of 2002 aims to foster an environment in which every child can learn and succeed. It provides direction about how to educate our children and how the federal government supports elementary and secondary education. Additionally, it provides more options for parents so that their children can get the best possible education. However, it sets standards for student achievement and for holding students and educators accountable for their results. This may pressure teachers and students and, in particular, it may promote teaching and learning for tests.

SOLUTION OF DILEMMAS

Why do these dilemmas exist in the mathematics education field? How do we view them? Through what lens can we obtain a clear view of the right direction for mathematics education? This book intends to provide a different point of view that may help us to clear up the dilemmas.

Both China and the United States are reforming mathematics education; ironically, both sides are trying to adopt "a new approach" that the other side is giving up or reducing. Most importantly, U.S. mathematics education, under the influence of new federal policy, is framing a circle of reform, turning away from constructivism of inquiry and creativity and back to the old path of traditional pedagogy. Why is the United States reforming math education? What can it gain from the reform? What is missing in the reform of mathematics education in the United States? Neither the United States nor China seems to know what their real aims are and what their final directions are. Notably, both sides ignore the negative consequences of reform. In the United States, the strengthening of the testing system promotes teaching and learning for tests. Under this system, students may learn fragments of math knowledge and skills without really understanding mathematics. In the long run, the deficits in learning will show up. These deficits could be a mirror of Chinese mathematics education. For many years in China, people have complained that the examination system killed children's creativity and ability. No Chinese person has obtained a Nobel Prize on Chinese soil, but Chinese scholars have been awarded the Nobel under the U.S. educational system. This is a part of the reason China wants to learn from the U.S. system. However, using new approaches learned from the West without examining their validity in Chinese cultural traditions may cause the same problems that the United States has had for decades. Eventually China may lose its advantages: a strong foundation in the basic concepts and skills in math and high performance internationally.

To thoroughly understand why opposite directions have existed in the East and West, to find a solution to the dilemmas, to wake others up to the math war, this book presents a foundational component in mathematics education for both cultures and suggests new directions for mathematics education. There is a Chinese saying "to throw a brick to attract gold" (抛砖引玉), which means to serve as a spark of exploration. The book begins with a philosophical and historical overview of Chinese and U.S. mathematics education and examines in depth the philosophy underlying each system. This examination leads to a discussion of finding a common base that is the foundation for successful teaching and learning mathematics in all systems. The foundation for teaching and learning in this book refers to pedagogical content knowledge. After an analysis of research in this field, a framework of teachers' pedagogical content knowledge is then constructed and key components of it are addressed. Based on the criteria of pedagogical content knowledge, the book examines differences in teachers' pedagogical content knowledge in mathematics at the middle school level, between China and the United States. The book addresses how teachers' beliefs, classroom teaching, and teaching preparation impact the differences. This book posits that no matter how math education is reformed, teachers' pedagogical content knowledge always plays a vital role in students' successful learning. Consequently, enhancing teachers' pedagogical content knowledge is the key to the direction of mathematics education in both China and the United States.

CHAPTER 2

Philosophical and Historical Overview of Mathematics Education

Philosophers of education are interested in analyzing and clarifying concepts and questions central to education.

—Noddings 1995, 4

By examining the prevailing thought of an age, one can discover its patterns of education.

—Gutek 1995, 11

THE NATURE OF MATHEMATICS AND MATHEMATICS EDUCATION

The Nature of Mathematics

According to Dossey (1992), "Perceptions of the nature and role of mathematics held by different societies have a major impact on the development of school mathematics curricula, instruction, and research" (39). Mathematics development is closely related to the development of human history and reflects its degree of civilization. Different eras have different perceptions and beliefs about the role and nature of mathematics. As we examine the philosophy and history of the development of mathematics, many perspectives emerge.

Before 6 B.C., under the influence of mathematical development in Egypt, Babylonia, India, and China, mathematics study focused on numbers and computations, which were used to solve real-world problems for human survival. Between 6 B.C. and A.D. 6, mathematics

developed based on the logic and reasoning of ancient Greek mathematicians such as Pythagoras, Plato, and Aristotle. In this period, mathematics no longer related only to numbers and computations; it also focused on the study of spatial relationships. Plato claimed that the objects
of mathematics had an existence of their own beyond the mind in the external world, while Aristotle, a student of Plato, viewed mathematics as
the basis of experienced reality, where knowledge is obtained from experimentation, observation, and abstraction (Dossey 1992).

From the 13th to the 15th centuries, Eastern mathematics (e.g., in
China and India) developed toward more complex computation and generalization, with an integrating induction process (Li 1999). For example,
the strategies of solving systems of equations and the introduction of in-
tegers in the Chinese book *Arithmetic of Nine Chapters* provided evidence of applying reasoning and logical thinking to computations. Between the 15th and 16th centuries, the combination of Eastern and
Ancient Greek mathematics disseminated in Europe by Egyptian mathematicians had an impact on the birth of modern mathematics (Li 1999).

In the early 1500s Francis Bacon separated mathematics into pure
and applied forms. He defined pure mathematics as a field of quantity
study that is completely separated from substance and natural philosophical, universally accepted truth. In the 17th century, Descartes argued that any field can be related to mathematics if its purpose is to
study order and measurement. After the calculus of Newton and Leib-
niz, the role of mathematics was expanded to study movement and
changes (Li 1999). The debate between the rationalists and experimen-
talists influenced all developments in mathematics and science from
the 17th and 18th centuries (Dossey 1992).

In the 19th century, there were three views about the nature of mathematics: logicism, intuitionism, and formalism. Logicism viewed the
content of mathematics as the elements of the body of classical mathematics with definitions, postulates, and theorems; intuitionism considered the content of mathematics to be the theorems that had been constructed through logical patterns of reasoning; formalism considered
mathematics to be made up of the formal axiomatic structures developed to relieve classical mathematics of its shortcomings (Dossey
1992). Dossey argues that all three philosophies ended up viewing the
content of mathematics as a product rather than a process.

In the late 20th century, an era termed the information or digital age, the nature and role of mathematics faced further challenges to meet the needs of technology development. The nature of mathematics is still debated among mathematicians and mathematics educators. Traditionally, mathematics is seen as a well-defined, static discipline that has a set of concepts, procedures, formulas, principles, and skills with an infallible reasoning process (Fisher 1990; Tymoczko 1986). "This view of mathematics provides a sense of security and certainty" (Cooney and Shealy 1997, 89). In contrast, many studies of the reform movement in mathematics and science education consider mathematics a living, dynamic, growing field of study (American Association for the Advancement of Science [AAAS] 1989; Mathematical Sciences Education Board [MSEB] 1989, 1990; National Council of Teachers of Mathematics [NCTM] 1989, 2000; Romberg and Kaput 1999). This view introduces uncertainty and constant change into the nature and role of mathematics. This reconceptualization of mathematics changes our view of the nature of mathematics and the external world, and it also provides insights on how mathematics learning and teaching should take place.

The Nature of Mathematics Education

Noddings (1995) states, "Philosophers of education are interested in analyzing and clarifying concepts and questions central to education" (4). In order to define the nature of mathematics education, we need to answer the following questions: What is the purpose of mathematics education? How do teachers teach mathematics? What knowledge is essential for teachers to teach mathematics effectively? What primary mathematical skills should students learn? How do students learn mathematics and why? The answers to these questions reflect our belief system of teaching and learning, and determine the nature of mathematics education.

Tymoczko (1986) describes the central component of the philosophy of mathematics as the pedagogy of mathematics. Cooney and Shealy (1997) believe that mathematics and mathematics pedagogy are closely intertwined philosophically. However, the pedagogy of mathematics is often neglected by the philosophers of mathematics (Tymoczko 1986).

The NCTM standards (1989, 2000) and other studies present important challenges and new views regarding mathematics education in recent years. In order to understand the impact of perceptions about the nature of mathematics on learning and teaching mathematics, many researchers have explored the relationship between beliefs about the nature of mathematics and beliefs about teaching mathematics (Cooney 1985; Dossey 1992; Ernest 1989; Thompson 1992). Dossey's (1992) observation indicates that most professional mathematicians think little about the nature of mathematics. Yet a teacher's conception of mathematics has a strong impact on the way in which mathematics is approached in the classroom (Cooney 1985). Classroom teachers hold three key views about the nature of mathematics, as Paul Ernest (1989) observed:

> First of all, there is the instrumentalist view that mathematics is an accumulation of facts, rules and skills to be used in the pursuance of some external end. Thus mathematics is a set of unrelated but utilitarian rules and facts. Secondly, there is the Platonist view of mathematics as a static but unified body of certain knowledge. Mathematics is discovered, not created. Thirdly, there is the problem-solving view of mathematics as a dynamic, continually expanding field of human creation in invention, a cultural product. Mathematics is a process of inquiry and coming to know, not a finished product, for its results remain open to revision. (250)

These three views have far-reaching consequences for mathematics pedagogy, curriculum, and assessment. With the instrumentalist and Platonist perspectives, teachers view mathematics as a well-defined accumulation of static facts; therefore, "assessing achievement is simply a matter of assessing product-oriented outcomes" (Cooney and Shealy 1997, 90). With the problem-solving view of mathematics, teachers need to consider mathematics learning as a dynamic process that is connected in a social and cultural context. Teachers know that students' understanding is more complex in a multifaceted learning process, and various assessments should be used to probe student understanding. The highest level of these three philosophies of mathematics is the problem-solving view, which considers mathematics teaching and learning a dynamic process and structure that is connected in a social and cultural context. Through education, students are brought into social processes and the cultural context; they will be able to connect and apply their knowledge to solve problems in the real world.

Principles and Standards for School Mathematics (NCTM 2000) states that all students should learn important mathematical concepts and processes with understanding, and all students should have access to high-quality, engaging mathematics instruction. This vision provides a direction for developing mathematics education through the K–12 levels.

THE DEVELOPMENT OF MATHEMATICS EDUCATION IN THE UNITED STATES AND CHINA

United States: The Development of Mathematics Education

Although mathematics has developed and has been institutionalized in schools for thousands of years around the world, U.S. mathematics education has been influenced by European philosophers and mathematicians with a variety of beliefs for only decades. Mathematics education has been influenced by U.S. culture, though the goal of mathematics education in general is to develop students' ability in reasoning and problem solving. According to Kilpatrick (1994), primary mathematics education has attempted to prepare children for their future by teaching mathematics as a tool for solving practical problems, while secondary and college mathematics teaching has aimed at the appreciation of deductive reasoning and axiomatic structure.

U.S. mathematics education as an academic field began only at the end of the 19th century, even though the development of mathematics has a long history. Mathematics educators began teacher education programs in universities, and mathematicians reformed secondary curriculum (Kilpatrick 1994). After World War II, influenced by economic and political events, the United States began to restructure the educational system (Smith 1994). A second reform of mathematics education emerged. New concerns with science and mathematics education led to two international conferences in the 1950s and the 1960s. Both conferences proposed a restructuring of mathematics curriculum as the solution for problems in teaching and learning; students should be learning organized concepts and not drilling in specific and arbitrary material (Smith 1994). This revolution of learning mathematics with an emphasis on the basic concepts of mathematics, programmed learning, and discovery learning was called the "new math" movement. However, it failed. Willoughby (1990) revealed that the major failure of new math was in its direction: "The overformalism and the lack of any obvious connections to the real world strengthened opponents of the movement when nostalgic, unenlightened pedants took us squarely back into the 19th century with the back-to-basics movement" (7). In 1983, *A Nation at Risk* (National Commission on Excellence in Education 1983) alarmed the country with a report on problems in the U.S. educational system. *Everybody Counts* (Mathematical Sciences Education Board 1989), produced by the National Research Council, called for reformulating the mathematics curriculum and teacher preparation to focus on reasoning and problem solving and to completely change the way mathematics was taught and learned.

The standards produced by NCTM in the past decade include *The Curriculum and Evaluation Standards for School Mathematics* (1989), the *Professional Standards for Teaching Mathematics* (1991), and the *Assessment Standards for School Mathematics* (1995). These standards have had a deep impact on the development of mathematics education in the past decade. In order to ensure continued quality, provide goals, and promote positive change in mathematics education in grades pre-K–12 in the 21st century, NCTM (2000) has developed a revised *Principles and Standards for School Mathematics,* aiming to build a solid foundation with a set of principles and standards that are focused, coherent, responsive, and grounded. Two key issues are addressed in the new standards. First, they address the characteristics of a mathematics instructional program that will provide all students with high-quality mathematics education experiences across the grades. Second, they propose mathematical content and processes that students should master as they progress through school. *Principles and Standards for School Mathematics* (NCTM 2000) plays an important role in the guidance of mathematics instructional programs with its experimentation, implementation, and periodic updating.

China: Historical and Modern Perspectives

Chinese civilization has had a great impact on education in China. For more than 2,000 years the Chinese have been following Confucius (551–479 B.C.) as the "father of Chinese education" (Ashmore and Cao

1997). Confucianism plays an important role in both historic and modern education in China as well as other Asian countries. Spring (1998) observed that under traditional Confucianism, the school system becomes authoritarian, rigid, and antidemocratic. The successful education systems in Asian countries are based on Confucianism.

For many centuries, Chinese education was characterized as scholar-nurturing education. Under the influence of Confucian philosophy, education was equated with moral superiority that justified political power and high social status. People believed that highly educated people are honorable. According to Chinese sayings, the golden room comes with books (书中自有黄金屋), and people with mental jobs rule and people with physical jobs are ruled (劳心者治人，劳力者治于人). Thus one has to be a scholar to be at the top of society. A distinctive feature of this scholar-nurturing education was dominance by the state, which grew steadily with the elaboration of the examination system (Pepper 1996). Since the Sui dynasty, about 1,300 years ago, government officials have been chosen on the basis of scholarly "imperial examinations" (Ashmore and Cao 1997).

During the early developmental period (200 B.C.), traditional mathematics was listed as the sixth of six skills for scholars in China. It was considered a "tool" for all areas. It was used as a method to select officials in government, as a tool in management, as a necessary educational course for the noble elite, and as a day-to-day tool for farmers, workers, and traders. Therefore, the famous Chinese mathematicians came from different levels of society. Some of them were government officials who specialized in mathematics education and the computation of astronomy, such as Zhang Heng and Zhu Chongzi. They were high-level officers of the government or scholars, and their objective in the study of mathematics was to know the truth and serve the emperor. Some of them worked in different levels of government management, such as tax collection, creation of budgets, and construction. Some of them were also ordinary intellectuals, such as Mo Zi, who treated mathematics as a special area of research, and Zhou Shuang, who used mathematics as a tool of astronomy (Li 1999).

Because of the various roles of mathematicians in Chinese society, mathematicians were more interested in developing mathematical computations to solve real-world problems. For example, in the Tang dynasty the official school created a computation course. The main purpose of this course was to apply mathematics to solve real-world problems, and *Arithmetic of Nine Chapters* was used as the textbook, the classic work that has exerted the greatest influence on mathematics learning and teaching in China. It determined the traditional mathematics style that is widely used in calculation and application (Li and Chen 1995). It includes 246 application problems covering the measuring and dividing of fields, growth and depreciation, division, balance, equations, and Pythagorean calculations related to daily life. The book is organized through a sequence of questions, answers, and principles. Specifically, the procedure of this model of education is to pose a question, find the solution for the question, use the principle to explain the problem, and to apply it in the real world. Questions and emphasis on proficiency in computation are at the center of this instructional model. Since mathematicians focused on application of mathematics, they tried to generalize real-world situations in patterns and find a unified way to solve various kinds of problems. The key to this generalization is to find an accurate and efficient means of computation. That is why the Chinese have called elementary mathematics the "Suan Shu" (算术) and secondary and higher-level mathematics the "Shu Xue" (数学) throughout history. "Suan Shu" means "the skill of computation" and "Shu Xue" means "the study of numeration system." The main characteristic of Chinese mathematics is to teach computational skills and achieve proficiency in computation in order to develop efficient methods for solving problems and building models of real-world situations (Wang 1994).

At the beginning of the 19th century, Chinese intellectuals recognized the necessity of learning Western science and technology and new ideas to reform the old education system. Western mathematics, including algebra, analytic geometry, and calculus, was introduced in China. However, under the influence of the examination system, mathematical problem solving became equivalent to problem answering on examinations, and mathematics teaching and learning mainly focused on the preparation for the exam.

In the 1950s, the Chinese mathematics curriculum and textbooks were influenced by the Soviet Union. The curriculum was rigorous, logical, and purely deductive. Mathematics teaching and learning emphasized strong skill and accuracy in computation and the rigor of deduction to meet the high competition of the examination. This exam-driven system isolated mathematics learning from the process of inquiry and creativity. It also disconnected mathematics learning from applications, modeling, and problem solving in real-world situations.

During the Cultural Revolution (1966–1976), mathematics education went in the opposite direction under the influence of Chairman Mao's philosophy: theory should be connected with practice in the real world. Mathematics teaching and learning focused only on solving practical and real-world problems, ignoring the basic knowledge of conceptual understanding and reasoning and procedural development. Students were sent to the countryside and factories to reflect on and connect their learning.

After the Cultural Revolution, China opened its doors to the world and established many educational exchange programs with the West. The central government has focused on education reform as one of the key components in achieving the goal of the four modernizations—agriculture, industry, science and technology, and defense (Ashmore and Cao 1997). Both policy makers and intellectuals have realized that China should absorb the richest ideas, knowledge, and skills from the West and search for an ideology that would direct China into a definite and better future (Su 1995). Since 1986, the National Center for Education Development Research (NCEDR) in the Department of Education in China has formed the Research Division of Comparative Education to prepare for education reform. Its objectives are (1) to conduct research and analysis in comparative education, and undertake studies on lessons of experiences and trends in the development and reform of international education, in connection with research for macro educational policy making; (2) to pay close attention to and study the latest developments and reform of education in selected countries, including the United States, the United Kingdom, France, Japan, Germany, and other industrialized countries; and (3) to undertake and engage in international academic exchange and collaboration (NCEDR 1999).

In order to increase the pace of globalization in education and to achieve success in the high competition of global economies in the 21st century, China is reforming the national curriculum in the perspective of globalization. For instance, in the past few decades, China has had one national curriculum and one unified set of textbooks. However, through the influence of global education, China began the process of reforming curricula for K–12 in the following ways:

1. Various textbooks are available under a national curriculum: China has allowed textbooks to be published by different provinces or cities, guided by the national curriculum. A commission to evaluate textbooks was founded to examine and approve the textbooks.
2. Curriculum planning and decision making are becoming democratic. In curriculum planning, there are two levels of planning, the national level and the local level. At the national level, curriculum planning determines the major courses, hours, content, and requirements of instruction. This shows the basic requirements of compulsory education from the government and ensures the quality of education. At the local level, states and cities may adjust curriculum plans according to their needs and then report to the central government for the record.
3. The process of curriculum writing becomes more democratic. The Law of Compulsory Education of the People's Republic of China of 1992 shows an example of this new trend. In 1985, the education commission formed a team to produce the first draft curriculum plan, which was called the suggestions draft. It was sent to education departments of provinces, cities, and schools all over the country for feedback. In 1986, a draft trial edition of the curriculum plan was issued. Several research symposiums were held to debate the draft trial edition curriculum plan. Research institutions studied and examined it. Conferences among principals, teachers, and specialists were held to discuss it. Finally, the draft was extended to the whole country to encourage more input to the plan. The trial edition curriculum plan of compulsory education was promulgated in 1992.

In recent years, the Department of Education in China has formed research groups to study the mathematics curricula in different countries in order to reform the national curriculum for mathematics. By learning from other countries, China created a new mathematics curriculum in 2001 with Chinese educational characteristics.

CHAPTER 3

Understanding Teachers' Pedagogical Content Knowledge

> What is also needed is knowledge of the most useful forms of representation of those ideas, the most powerful analogies, illustrations, examples, explanations, and demonstrations—in a word, the ways of representing and formulating the subject that make it comprehensible to others.
>
> —Shulman 1986, 9

THE PRIMARY KNOWLEDGE BASE: PEDAGOGICAL CONTENT KNOWLEDGE

The Connection and Balance of Teachers' Knowledge

According to an old Chinese saying, if you want to give the students one cup of water, you (the teacher) should have one bucket of water of your own. This belief is also held by many Western educators. Shulman (1985) stated that "to be a teacher requires extensive and highly organized bodies of knowledge" (447). Elbaz (1983) had the same view: "The single factor which we see to have the greatest power to carry forward our understanding of the teacher's role is the phenomenon of teachers' knowledge" (45).

Although teachers' knowledge has been recognized as a key component in effective teaching, many studies have focused on only one of the two separate aspects of teachers' knowledge: content knowledge and pedagogical knowledge. For example, Ma (1999) focused on the mathematical content knowledge of the elementary teacher and advocated that elementary teachers should have profound mathematics knowledge, while Darling-Hammond (2000) supports enhancing teachers' pedagogical knowledge and preparation program. The debates in the "math war" in the United States is based upon the distinction between content and pedagogy. Despite the effort and evidence of both sides, teachers and teaching are still found to be one of the major factors related to students' achievement in TIMSS and other studies. What is missing in the network of teachers' knowledge? What is a primary base of teachers' knowledge?

The National Council of Teachers of Mathematics (2000) states that "teaching mathematics well is a complex endeavor, and there are no easy recipes for helping all learn or for helping all teachers become effective" (17). For mathematics teachers, knowledge is more complex and dynamic (Fennema and Franke 1992), and also increasingly uncertain, problematic, and difficult to master. In a time of rapid technological adaptation, mathematics teachers are challenged to have more knowledge. Teachers must know new aspects of teaching, such as integrating technology into teaching and learning. At the same time, teachers must be able to meet the needs of students from multicultural and diverse backgrounds. However, no matter how much teachers' knowledge changes, the connection of pedagogy and content knowledge should be the most important element in the domain of mathematics teachers' knowledge, which has been termed pedagogical content knowledge (Pinar et al. 1995; Shulman 1987). Pedagogical content knowledge addresses how to teach mathematics content and how to understand students' thinking. It considers the cultural background of the student as well as the student's preference for various teaching and learning styles (An, Kulm, and Wu 2004). Pedagogical content knowledge makes a connection between teachers' content knowledge and pedagogical knowledge. This connection includes transforming content knowledge into a simple and understandable language for students, structuring lessons from easy to difficult levels in a sequential and logical order, and focusing lessons on both conceptual understanding and procedural development with carefully designed layered questions and practices to promote thinking and reinforce understanding.

Shulman's Model

Shulman (1987) identifies the following categories of teachers' knowledge base: (1) content knowledge, which is the subject discipline area; (2) pedagogical knowledge, which refers to principles and methods of classroom management and organization; (3) curriculum knowledge, which is knowledge about the materials and program; and (4) pedagogical content knowledge, which combines content and pedagogy, including knowledge of learners and their characteristics; knowledge of educational contexts; knowledge of educational ends, purposes, and values; and their philosophical and historical bases. Among these categories, Shulman considers pedagogical content knowledge an important component in teachers' knowledge base. Shulman (1986) explains the meanings and functions of pedagogical content knowledge as follows:

> Within the category of pedagogical content knowledge I include, for the most regularly taught topics in one's subject area, knowledge of the most useful forms of representations of those ideas, the most powerful analogies, illustrations, examples, explanations, and demonstrations—in a word, the ways of representing and formulating the subject that make it comprehensible to others. . . . Pedagogical content knowledge also includes an understanding of what makes the learning of specific topics easy or difficult: the concepts and preconceptions that students of different ages and backgrounds bring with them to the learning of those topics. If those preconceptions are misconceptions, which they so often are, teachers need knowledge of the strategies most likely to be fruitful in reorganizing the understanding of learners, because those learners are unlikely to appear before them as blank slates. (9)

He defines pedagogical content knowledge as the teacher's ability to transform the content knowledge in a way that is "pedagogically powerful and yet adaptive to the variations in ability and background presented by the students" (Shulman 1987, 15). Pedagogical content knowledge allows a teacher "eventually to lift the curriculum away from texts and materials to give it an independent existence" (Doyle 1992, 499).

Fennema and Franke's Model

Using Shulman's model as a base, Fennema and Franke (1992) identify five components of teachers' knowledge: the knowledge of the content of mathematics, knowledge of pedagogy, knowledge of students' cognitions, context-specific knowledge, and teachers' beliefs.

The content of mathematics component includes teachers' knowledge of the concepts, procedures, and problem-solving processes of the domain in which they teach. Pedagogical knowledge is knowledge of teaching procedures, including planning, organization, management, and motivation. The learners' cognitions component includes knowledge of how students think and learn. Fennema and Franke's model illustrates the complex and dynamic nature of teachers' knowledge. Placing teachers' knowledge and beliefs in context demonstrates the interactive relationship between components of knowledge and beliefs. Furthermore, "within a given context, teachers' knowledge of content interacts with knowledge of pedagogy and students' cognitions and combines with beliefs to create a unique set of knowledge that drives classroom behavior" (Fennema and Franke 1992, 162).

Fennema and Franke (1992) consider all aspects of teacher knowledge and beliefs as a system in which teachers' knowledge will be transformed and developed into new knowledge. Their model challenges researchers to explain "the relationship between the components of knowledge as new knowledge develops in teaching" and "the parameters of knowledge being transformed through teacher implementation" (163).

THE ROLE OF PEDAGOGICAL CONTENT KNOWLEDGE IN EFFECTIVE TEACHING

The Network of Pedagogical Content Knowledge

According to NCTM (2000), "Effective teaching requires knowing and understanding mathematics, students as learners, and pedagogical strategies" (17). However, it is not sufficient for a mathematics teacher to have only content and pedagogical knowledge of mathematics. To teach effectively, a mathematics teacher should have a kind of knowledge that enables the teacher to connect and balance both knowledge of content and pedagogy. This knowledge is pedagogical content knowledge, which is a key component in teachers' knowledge base.

In this study, the knowledge base for teachers consists of three major components: knowledge of content, knowledge of curriculum, and knowledge of teaching. Knowledge of content consists of broad mathematics knowledge as well as specific mathematics content knowledge for the grade level being taught. Knowledge of curriculum includes selecting suitable curriculum materials and fully understanding the goals and key ideas of textbooks and curricula (NCTM 2000). Knowledge of effective teaching is referred to as pedagogical content knowledge. Although all of these components are very important in constructing a solid base for teachers' knowledge, the core component is knowledge of effective teaching. It consists of knowing students' thinking, preparing instruction, and mastering instruction delivery. Figure 3.1 illustrates the interactive relationship among the three components that come into play and shows that pedagogical content knowledge can be enhanced

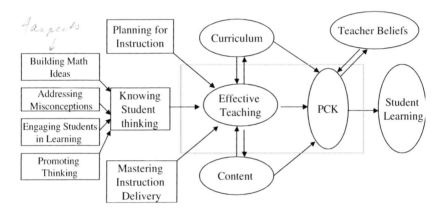

Figure 3.1. *The Network of Pedagogical Content Knowledge*

by content and curriculum knowledge. Ma's study (1999) calls for teachers to have "profound understanding of fundamental mathematics." However, figure 3.1 indicates that profound content knowledge alone is not sufficient for effective teaching. An effective teacher must also possess a deep and broad knowledge of teaching and curriculum. Connecting these three aspects of knowledge—content, curriculum, and teaching—in a dynamic and supportive network is a base on which a teacher can teach effectively. This means that teachers with profound pedagogical content knowledge are able to make a connection between content and pedagogy and to balance the focus on either end. They must know students' thinking in order to build math ideas on prior knowledge, address and correct misconceptions, and engage students in learning lessons with a logical and sequential structure.

In this network of teachers' pedagogical content knowledge, three types of knowledge interact with one another and produce transformations from one form to another around the central task of effective teaching. Ultimately, these components enhance student learning. Figure 3.1 also shows that teachers' beliefs impact this network of knowledge (Ernest 1989; Fennema and Franke 1992). Different educational belief systems produce different attributes of pedagogical content knowledge. In turn, profound pedagogical content knowledge plays an important role in shaping teachers' beliefs and in determining the effectiveness of their mathematics teaching (An et al. 2002).

Four Aspects of Pedagogical Content Knowledge

In order to address and measure teachers' pedagogical content knowledge, the framework in this study categorizes mathematics teachers' pedagogical content knowledge into four key aspects: (1) building on students' mathematics ideas and understanding, (2) addressing students' misconceptions, (3) engaging students in mathematics learning, and (4) promoting and supporting students' thinking about mathematics. Each aspect consists of essential components derived from mathematics teachers' responses to the questionnaire (see table 4.2).

To build on students' mathematics ideas and understanding, a teacher must know students' thinking and be able to connect their prior knowledge, and then construct students' concrete understanding by connecting to models, pictures, or tables at the beginning of the new lesson. To reach abstract understanding, the teacher needs to develop students' abstract thinking using concepts or definitions and procedural development.

During the lesson, a teacher with pedagogical content knowledge is able to identify students' misconceptions from questions and tasks. After addressing the misconceptions, the teacher needs to correct errors to the entire class immediately.

To engage students in mathematics learning, a teacher must carefully design activities to connect prior knowledge and concrete models using manipulatives, pictures, or tables, as well as examples that focus on students' thinking. Furthermore, the teacher must be able to engage students in exploring various representations to express mathematical ideas in a simple and highly structured lesson.

To promote students' thinking about mathematics, teachers must use a variety of activities to determine what is students' thinking at first, and then use different levels of questions and tasks to elicit and help students progress in their ideas. Teachers must also provide opportunities and strategies for students to reflect on their thinking.

The Role of Pedagogical Content Knowledge in Effective Teaching

Effective teaching can be a divergent or a convergent process. A divergent process of teaching is based on content and curriculum knowledge without focus. It ignores students' mathematical thinking and ignores the connection between content and pedagogy. A convergent process of teaching focuses on the connection between content and pedagogy and focuses on understanding students' thinking. This process consists of four aspects of pedagogical content knowledge: building on students' math ideas, addressing and correcting students' misconceptions, engaging students in mathematics learning, and promoting and supporting students' thinking mathematically. Together, these four aspects of convergent teaching constitute the notion of teaching with understanding (Carpenter and Lehrer 1999). Under a convergent process, students, not textbooks and the curriculum, are the center of teaching. An effective teacher with pedagogical content knowledge attends to students' mathematical thinking throughout the convergent teaching process by preparing instruction according to students' needs, delivering instruction consistent with students' levels of understanding, addressing and correcting students' misconceptions with specific strategies, engaging students in activities and problems that focus on important mathematical ideas, and providing opportunities for students to revise and extend their mathematical ideas (Kulm et al. 2001).

Teachers' beliefs about their students' learning can be categorized as either learning as knowing or learning as understanding. Lacking pedagogical content knowledge, teachers who understand learning as knowing often assume that mathematics is learned and understood if a concept or skill is taught. This type of learning usually is achieved at a surface level. Teachers are often satisfied with students' knowing or re-membering facts and skills but are not aware of students' thinking or misconceptions about mathematics. This divergent teaching process often results in fragmented and disconnected knowledge. In contrast, teachers with deep and broad pedagogical content knowledge, who recognize learning as understanding, realize that knowing is not sufficient and that understanding is achieved at the level of internalizing knowledge by connecting prior knowledge through a convergent process. In this process, the teacher focuses on not only conceptual understanding but also procedural development in which the teacher consistently inquires about students' thinking and makes sure students fully grasp the knowledge and are able to apply the concepts and skills.

Teachers using the convergent process develop systematic and effective ways to identify and support their students' thinking. Figure 3.2 indicates that with profound knowledge of students' thinking, a teacher can enhance students' learning substantially, leading to content mastery.

Comparative Study of Teachers' Knowledge

During the past several decades, there has been increased attention to cross-national comparisons of education; especially, there is remarkable growth in the international dimension in mathematics education (Bishop 1992). Comparative study can increase our understanding of how to educate effectively and enhance our understanding of our own education and society (Kaiser 1999). Specifically, comparative studies can illuminate procedures used by different systems to solve the

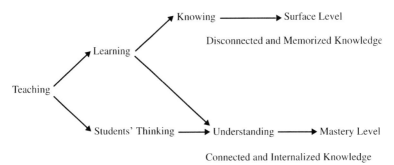

Figure 3.2. *Two Types of Learning*

same problems, and can reinforce the understanding of common contemporary problems in education (Romberg and Kaput 1999).

Although there has been some research comparing Chinese and U.S. mathematics teachers' content knowledge (e.g., Ma 1999), there is no research comparing teachers' pedagogical content knowledge in these two countries, and no research comparing how mathematical and pedagogical knowledge was integrated into knowledge of students' thinking.

Many studies show that there are problems in mathematics education in both China and the United States. China needs to reduce the high pressure of the exam-driven system, develop multiple teaching strategies such as hands-on activities to help different levels of students, apply new technology in teaching and learning mathematics, connect other subjects such as science and real-world problem solving to mathematics teaching and learning, and explore new approaches to enhance students' abilities in inquiry and creativity, without losing their strong foundation of basic concepts and skills. On the other hand, the United States needs to strengthen basic conceptual understanding and skills and to achieve proficiency and fluency in mathematics. Solving these problems challenges educators in both countries to understand the components and construction of teachers' knowledge, investigate the impacts of pedagogical content knowledge on the effectiveness of teaching and learning, and develop strong pedagogical content knowledge for teachers. Teachers' knowledge is not isolated from its effects on teaching in the classroom and student learning (Fennema and Franke 1992); teacher pedagogical content knowledge is closely connected to the subject matter, and how this subject matter achieves the transformation through the learning process in which teachers know how the students think.

Jiang and Eggleton (1995) state, "Now is the time for mathematics educators to learn from cultural differences and gain insight into cross-cultural practices" (193). Comparative studies can help the effort in the United States to improve mathematics and science achievement in order for students to achieve higher rankings internationally. Comparative studies can also help China learn the Western educational system, reconstruct the exam-driven system into a multiple-assessment and teaching system, and make the best use of its advantages. This study investigates the differences between the pedagogical content knowledge of middle school mathematics teachers in the United States and China, and attempts to discover how these differences are revealed in teachers' beliefs, planning, learners' cognition, and teaching methods. In addition, this study advocates the idea that a connection is needed between teachers' content knowledge and pedagogical knowledge to counterbalance the emphasis on teachers' knowledge. Furthermore, both countries need to balance mathematical procedural development and conceptual understanding of mathematics. Importantly, more attention needs to be given to learners' cognitions, preparation of instruction, teaching methods, and teachers' beliefs.

CHAPTER 4

Teachers' Pedagogical Content Knowledge in Mathematics Teaching

Cross-cultural comparison also leads researchers and educators to a more explicit understanding of their own implicit theories about how children learn mathematics.

Stigler and Perry 1988, 199

DEMOGRAPHIC INFORMATION OF PARTICIPANTS AND BACKGROUND OF THE STUDY

In order to explore and identify differences in pedagogical content knowledge between the United States and China, as well as their impact on mathematics education programs, this chapter compares mathematics teachers' pedagogical content knowledge in American and Chinese middle schools and examines differences in these two mathematics programs according to teachers' beliefs, plans for instruction, learners' cognition, and teaching methods. This chapter focuses on the middle school, addresses mathematics teachers' pedagogical content knowledge within a cultural context, and explores how this knowledge is used by teachers to understand and develop students' mathematical thinking and learning.

The participants were 28 mathematics teachers in fifth to eighth grades from 12 schools in four school districts in a large metropolitan area in Texas, and 33 mathematics teachers in fifth and sixth grade levels from 22 schools in four school districts in a large city in Jiansu province in China. In order to examine the teachers' pedagogical content knowledge at the middle school level (particularly in the area of fractions, ratios, and proportions), this study included U.S. teachers in a wide range from fifth to eighth grades, considering U.S. mathematics curricula in fifth to eighth as similar to those in fifth to sixth grades in China (seventh and eighth graders in China have already learned Algebra I).

All participants from the United States had bachelor's degrees; three had master's degrees with an average of 24 hours of mathematics course work and 13 years' teaching experience. Among the U.S. participants, one teacher taught fifth grade mathematics, 14 of them taught sixth grade, 7 of them were seventh grade teachers, and 6 of them were eighth grade teachers. The U.S. teachers who participated in this study only teach mathematics. All Chinese participants had three-year education degrees at normal schools after ninth grade; 23 of them also had three-year university degrees, including 10 who majored in fields other than mathematics. The average number of hours in mathematics courses for the Chinese teachers was 15. For example, with a three-year degree from a university, a teacher had calculus, modern algebra, elementary mathematics methods, history of elementary mathematics education, and Olympic elementary mathematics. Their average teaching experience was nine years. Six of them were fifth grade teachers, and 27 of them taught sixth grade. Like the U.S. teachers, all Chinese teachers in this study teach only mathematics.

The U.S. schools were located in both urban and suburban areas, and the school populations ranged from 800 to 1,300 students. The schools were similar in ethnic makeup and, on average, consisted of 30 percent African American, 27 percent Caucasian, 27 percent Hispanic, and 16 percent Asian. The schools in China were located in urban areas and the number of students in each school ranged from 1,000 to 1,200. All students were from the same ethnic group.

In this study, data were collected via an author-constructed mathematics teaching questionnaire, an author-constructed teachers' beliefs about mathematics teaching and learning questionnaire, and interviews and observations with selected teachers. Both questionnaires were prepared in English and then translated into Chinese.

The questionnaire consisted of four problems designed to examine teachers' pedagogical content knowledge in topics of fractions, ratios, and proportions. The questionnaire focused on teachers' knowledge of students' cognition, with attention to assessing teachers' knowledge and strategies for building on students' mathematics ideas, identifying and correcting students' misconceptions, engaging students in learning, and promoting and supporting student thinking.

After the responses to the questionnaires were reviewed and analyzed, five teachers from each country were selected to represent a range of education backgrounds, length of teaching experience, levels of responses to the questionnaires, and classroom observations to confirm that their teaching matched their responses on the questionnaires. The observations were conducted on a prearranged date and time. Field notes and audiotape recordings were made during the classroom observations. An instructional criteria observation checklist was used, which was constructed as a guide for classroom observations. The checklist was adapted from criteria used for analyzing the instructional quality of mathematics textbooks (AAAS 2000). The observation criteria included specific activities in the following categories: building on student ideas in mathematics, being alert to students' ideas, identifying students' ideas, addressing students' misconceptions, engaging students in mathematics learning, providing firsthand experiences, promoting student thinking about mathematics, guiding interpretation and reasoning, and encouraging students to think about what they've learned.

After each observation, an interview was conducted using a set of interview questions. The objective of the interviews was to examine teachers' beliefs about the goals of mathematics education and the impact of their beliefs on their teaching practices, to investigate the teaching approaches they use in the classrooms, to learn how the teachers prepare for instruction and how they determine their students' thinking. The interview questions further explored the teachers' pedagogical content knowledge and its importance in their teaching.

The data was analyzed to answer the following research questions: What are the differences between the pedagogical content knowledge of middle school mathematics teachers in the United States and China? How are these differences revealed in their beliefs, planning, knowledge of learners' cognition, and teaching methods?

In this study, four problems were designed to examine the understanding of the role of teachers' pedagogical content knowledge in topics of fractions, ratios, and proportions. The teachers' responses to four problems on the mathematics teaching questionnaire were coded and grouped into 18 categories. These 18 categories were sorted into groups and assigned descriptive codes. Table 4.1 lists the categories and their definitions. In table 4.2, the 18 categories (except for incorrect or unintelligible responses) are grouped according to the four components of pedagogical content knowledge in the conceptual framework in chapter 3.

The presentation of data for each problem and question takes three forms: statement of the problem, table of codes for responses and their

Table 4.1.   Categories for Describing Teachers' Responses to Pedagogical Content Knowledge Questions

Category	Brief Definition
1	Connect to prior knowledge: Know students' prior knowledge and connect it to new knowledge
2	Use concept or definition: Use concept or definition to build math ideas and promote understanding
3	Focus on rules and procedure: Focus on rules and procedure to reinforce the knowledge
4	Draw picture or table: Use picture or table to show a mathematical idea
5	Give example: Address a mathematical idea through examples
6	Use estimation: Solve problems using estimation
7	Connect to concrete model: Use concrete model to demonstrate mathematical idea
8	Misunderstanding of prior knowledge: Students lack understanding of prior knowledge
9	Provide students opportunity to think and respond: Promote students' thinking on problems and give them chances to answer questions
10	Use manipulative activity: Provide hands-on activities for students to learn mathematics
11	Attempt to address students' misconceptions: Identify students' misconceptions
12	Use questions or tasks to correct misconceptions: Pose questions or provide activities to correct misconceptions.
13	Use questions or tasks to help students' progress in their ideas: Pose questions or provide activities to increase the level of understanding for students
14	Provide activities and examples that focus on student thinking: Create activities and examples that encourage students to ponder questions
15	Use one representation to illustrate concepts: Apply repeated addition to address the meaning of fraction multiplication, or use area to address the geometrical meaning of fraction multiplication
16	Use two representations to illustrate concepts: Apply both repeated addition and area to address the meaning of fraction multiplication
17	Unintelligible response: Provide response that is not relevant to the question
18	Incorrect: Provide a wrong answer

Table 4.2. Categories for Describing Four Aspects of Teaching in Response to Pedagogical Content Knowledge Questions

Pedagogical Content Knowledge	Essential Components	Category Number
Building on students' mathematics ideas and understanding	Know students' thinking on prior knowledge	
	1. Forget prior knowledge	1
	2. Do not understand prior knowledge	8
	Construct concrete understanding	
	1. Use concrete model and manipulatives	7, 10
	2. Draw picture or table	4
	Develop abstract thinking	
	1. Use concept or definition	2
	• Concept	
	• Unit fraction	
	2. Use rule and procedure	3
	3. Promote thinking	9
Addressing and correcting students' misconceptions	Identify misconceptions	
	1. Address students' misconceptions	11
	2. Use questions or tasks to find misconceptions	12
	Make correction for errors	
	1. Use rule and procedure	3
	2. Draw picture or table	4
	3. Connect to concrete model	7
Engaging students in math learning	Design introductory activities	
	1. Connect to prior knowledge	1
	2. Connect to concrete model	7
	3. Use manipulatives	10
	4. Draw picture or table	4
	5. Give examples	5
	6. Provide activities focused on students' thinking	14
	Use various representations	
	1. Use one representation (area or repeated addition)	15
	2. Use both representations (area and repeated addition)	16
	Provide various activities	
	1. Provide activities focused on students' thinking	14
	2. Give examples	5
	3. Use manipulatives	10
	4. Use area to illustrate fraction multiplication	15
	5. Connect to prior knowledge	1
Promoting and supporting students' thinking about mathematics	Use activities to promote students' thinking	
	1. Provide activities focused on students' thinking	14
	2. Draw picture or table	4
	3. Connect to concrete model	7
	4. Use manipulatives	10
	5. Give examples	5
	Provide suggestions and questions to support thinking	
	1. Use questions or tasks to help students to progress in their ideas	13
	2. Use estimation	6
	Use strategies to encourage reflective thinking	
	1. Provide activities focused on students' thinking	14
	2. Draw picture or table	4
	3. Connect to concrete model	7
	4. Use estimation	6

measurement in percent from the U.S. teachers and the Chinese teachers, and a summary and analysis of responses for both groups of teachers.

BUILDING ON STUDENTS' MATHEMATICS IDEAS

About 46 percent of the U.S. teachers believed that Adam (see problem 1 below) forgot prior knowledge of finding the common denominators, while 55 percent of Chinese teachers said that Adam did not understand the meaning of fractions. Thirty-six percent of the U.S. teachers connected to a concrete model and manipulative activities to assist students in understanding the meaning of adding fractions, while only 9 percent of Chinese teachers' responses focused on concrete models and manipulatives. Thirty-nine percent of the U.S. teachers mentioned the importance of the "rule" of adding fractions, while 79 percent of Chinese teachers mentioned this.

PROBLEM 1

Adam is a 10-year-old student in fifth grade who has average ability. His grade on the last test was 82 percent. Look at Adam's written work for these problems:

a. What prerequisite knowledge might Adam not understand or be forgetting?

$$\frac{3}{4} + \frac{4}{5} = \frac{7}{9}$$

$$2\frac{1}{3} + 1\frac{1}{2} = 3\frac{2}{5}$$

b. What questions or tasks would you ask Adam in order to determine what he understands about the meaning of fraction addition?

c. What real-world example of fractions is Adam likely to be familiar with that you could use to help him?

These three questions were designed to investigate teachers' knowledge of students' thinking and to explore teaching approaches of building on students' mathematics ideas and understanding.

Know Students' Thinking on Prior Knowledge

All U.S. teachers in this study stated that the prerequisites for adding fractions include finding the common denominators. Table 4.3 shows that 46 percent of the U.S. teachers believed that Adam forgot prior knowledge for finding the common denominators. For example, Ms. Ross mentioned things that Adam forgot: "Adam does not remember that to add, you must add like denominators, and fourths and fifths are not alike. He does not remember to make equivalent fractions using the lowest common denominator."

Table 4.3.   Percentage of U.S. and Chinese Teachers' Response for Each Component of Response of Problem 1

Pedagogical Content Knowledge	Essential Components	Problem Number	Category Number	U.S. %	China %
Building on students' mathematics ideas and understanding	Know students' thinking on prior knowledge				
	1. Forget prior knowledge	1.a	1	46	27
	2. Do not understand prior knowledge	1.a	8	11	55
	Construct concrete understanding				
	1. Use concrete model and manipulatives	1.a	7, 10	11	0
		1.b	7, 10	36	9
	Real World	1.c	7,10	97	48
	2. Draw picture or table	1.b	4	7	42
		1.c	4	93	82
	Develop abstract thinking				
	1. Use concept or definition				
	• Concept	1.a	2	14	9
		1.b	2	29	21
		1.c	2	4	7
	• Unit fraction	1.a	2	0	21
		1.b	2	0	30
		1.c	2	0	30
	2. Use rule and procedure	1.a	3	39	79
		1.b	3	25	76
		1.c	3	4	36
	3. Promote thinking	1.b	9	61	79
		1.c	9	4	24
	Unintelligible response	1.a	17	7	0
		1.b	17	12	3
		1.c	17	0	3

Note: N = 28 for each type of response for the U.S. teachers. N = 33 for each type of response for the Chinese teachers. Each individual teacher response could be coded more than once, resulting in total percentages greater than 100 for each problem.

Only 11 percent of the U.S. teachers indicated that Adam did not understand the prerequisite knowledge of finding common denominators. Ms. Griffin, a sixth grade teacher with nine years' experience, realized that Adam did not have a concrete understanding of fraction common denominators:

> Fraction pieces must be the same size before they can be combined in an addition problem. He doesn't have a concrete understanding of fractions because he would be able to see that fourths and fifths cannot be combined to create ninths. The concrete understanding was not fully formed.

Ms. William, who has taught mathematics for nine years, also described this concrete understanding for addition of fractions, saying that he "must have like-sized pieces to combine groups." Ms. Reed considered equal denominators as "equal parts," so she expected students to "not add unequal parts; they must change to equal parts first."

In contrast, 55 percent of Chinese teachers said that Adam did not understand the meaning of fractions, and he did not understand that only two numbers with like units could be added. Ms. Wang pointed out that Adam did not understand the fraction because he seemed to separate numerator and denominator into independent parts. For teachers like Ms. Wang, the concept of fraction is one number; the numerator and denominator cannot be separated from this number. Sowder and colleagues (1998) agree that the notion of a fraction as a quantity, as a number, is important for understanding. Kerslake (1986) observes that some teachers and children have difficulty conceiving of a fraction as a number and consider it either as two numbers or not a number. Some Chinese teachers in this study also believe that a student might not think of a fraction as a number at all. But this misconception of fraction can be corrected by understanding the *unit fraction concept,* as the Chinese teachers suggested.

To understand the concept of a unit fraction, it is interesting to learn how the Chinese define the concept of fraction. *Chinese Mathematics Textbook,* volume 10 (fifth grade) (State Education Commission, People's Republic of China 1989) defines the fraction in the following way: to equally divide the unit "1" into several parts, the number represented as one or more such parts is called a fraction. This definition describes a fraction as a number. In this number, the denominator tells how many equal-sized parts the unit "1" is divided into; the numerator tells how many such parts to take. One of the parts is called the "unit fraction." Here the unit "1" represents an object, a unit of measurement, a group, or the whole of some objects, such as a field, a class of students, or a box of toys. For example, 3/5 means to equally divide unit "1" into five parts, where three of the five parts are considered. The "unit of fraction" of 3/5 is 1/5.

To add fractions, the Chinese teachers Ms. Sheng, Ms. Wang, and Mr. He suggested using the unit fraction concept and connecting it to the whole number: only with like units can two numbers be added, such as 3 books + 5 books = 8 books. Three books cannot be added to four desks because "book" and "desk" are different units. A fraction is a number, so only with like unit fractions can two fractions be added; therefore with unlike unit fractions, two fractions cannot be added. Chinese teachers realized that Adam's mistake indicated that he did not understand the concept of like units and could not see the connection between whole number and fraction addition, which may misdirect him to think of a fraction as something other than a number.

Here "forgot" and "did not understand" indicate the different understandings of students' thinking and have two distinct meanings for the teachers. According to An, Kulm, and Wu (2004), the teachers who said the student "forgot" did not know their students' thinking about fraction addition and did not understand the challenges students are likely to encounter in learning fraction addition. They appeared to believe that learning simply consists of knowing or not knowing; that is, remembering or forgetting if the material has already been taught. In contrast, teachers who said that the student "did not understand" showed evidence of knowing students' thinking about fraction addition. A large percentage of Chinese teachers connected prior knowledge of whole number addition to fraction addition: numbers with like units can be added. This means that no matter what numbers they are (such as whole numbers, decimals, and fractions), as long as the numbers have the same unit, they can be added together. This connection not only helps students to see a fraction as a number, but also helps students understand and use the rule of fraction addition easily. Understanding also means that students are able to internalize a concept and use it in different situations, such as understanding like units in whole number addition and applying like units in fraction addition. Internalizing and connecting knowledge about like units into a coherent whole provides a close link that makes learning easier and leads to mastery.

Construct Concrete Understanding

As shown in table 4.3, to determine students' understanding of the meaning of fraction addition in problem 1.b, 36 percent of the U.S. teachers first connected to a concrete model and manipulative activities, then asked specific questions to determine what Adam understood about the meaning of adding fractions. In contrast, only 9 percent of Chinese teachers' responses focused on concrete models and manipulatives. Most of the Chinese teachers related it to the concept of fraction (30 percent to unit fraction and 21 percent to the concept of fraction) or rules and procedures (76 percent) by asking layered and conceptual questions.

The following examples showed that the U.S. teachers' responses focused on connections with concrete materials and manipulatives. Ms. Griffin explained the approach to help Adam and to determine what Adam understood about the meaning of fractions:

> First, I would have him display the two fractions using fraction circles or fraction pieces. Then I would have him combine the two fractional parts. Finally, I would have him state the number of whole items and then find a piece or pieces that would exactly cover the remaining part. The smallest number of parts he could use would be 11/12. I would start out with problems with a lower common denominator first.

Ms. William had the same approach to help Adam. She said:

> Have Adam use fraction pieces to show 3/4 and 4/5 and ask him: What must we do in order to combine
>
> $$\frac{3}{4} + \frac{4}{5}$$
>
> Work together to find what size pieces fourths and fifths share; then find equivalent fractions and add.

Although the above two teachers were able to use fraction models to build the problem so that Adam "could concretely see the correct answer," they did not connect concrete fraction models to conceptual understanding. In contrast, although two Chinese teachers used concrete approaches to help Adam in problem 1.b, they were able to connect the fraction model to the concept of unit fraction. For example, Mr. Zhou would give Adam two equal circle pieces, have him divide them into four and five parts separately, and then take three parts from the first circle and four parts from the second circle. He would then have him compare these three and four parts; although there are seven parts, they are not all equal-sized, which means the units of fraction are unlike. Adam would then know that with different units (i.e., unlike denominators), fractions couldn't be added directly.

To visualize how and why adding fractions without finding the common denominator does not work, 7 percent of the U.S. teachers suggested drawing pictures of 3/4 and 4/5 to help Adam understand, while 42 percent of Chinese teachers used pictures. Ms. Hanks explained: "First I would give him an addition problem where the denominators are the same. Let him add and possibly draw a picture for it. Then give him an addition problem where denominators are different. Draw a picture to help." Ms. Scott would ask Adam to draw pictures of 3/4 and 4/5 first and then ask him questions: "Is 3/4 + 4/5 more or less than a whole? Is 3/4 almost a whole? Is 3/4 more than 1/2? Is 4/5 almost a whole? More than 1/2?" These questions encouraged Adam to estimate a fraction. Ms. Ross would also ask Adam to round and estimate and ask him, "What does each fraction mean?" "Could 3/4 and 4/5, or almost a whole, add up to almost a whole, possibly less than a whole?" She expected Adam to explain in his own words what he did. It is interesting to note that about 14 percent of the U.S. teachers suggested using estimation to assist Adam's thinking while no Chinese teachers made this suggestion in problem 1.b.

In problem 1.c, table 4.3 indicates that 97 percent of the U.S. teachers gave some real-world examples that Adam would be familiar with, and they expected that these examples would help Adam understand fraction addition. The examples teachers used included pizzas, pies and cakes, a Hershey's bar, an egg carton, crayon boxes, measuring cups, sports, statistics, money, time, and fraction pieces. For instance, Ms. Baker described how she would set up examples for Adam: "I would ask him if he had ever shared anything with a relative. If so how did he divide it, or I would give Adam a cookie and ask him to share it with another classmate equally."

Seven U.S. teachers mentioned the use of money to help Adam. Mr. Davis "always uses money as an example if possible." He gave an example:

$$3/4 \text{ of a } \$1.00 = \$0.75$$
$$+4/5 \text{ of a } \$1.00 = \$0.80$$
$$31/20 = \$1.55. \; \$1.55 \text{ is more than a whole.}$$

He said, "Common sense should tell you the answer should be more than a whole, not 7/9." Ms. Thomas agreed with him, changing 3/4 + 4/5 to decimal parts of a dollar.

Besides adding money as an example, Ms. Larson also suggested using hundreds grids and tens grids for fractions and decimals. Ms. Madison and Ms. Flores suggested using time, such as 1/2, 1/4, and 1/60 of an hour. Ms. Elliott would make fraction books, and also use fraction pieces to make fraction pizzas and color fraction cars.

In contrast, table 4.3 shows that only 48 percent of Chinese teachers suggested real-world examples related to Adam's experience, and 9 percent of Chinese teachers referred to manipulative activities. These real-world examples are showing pictures, dividing an apple or a watermelon, cutting a cake, and cutting a rope. For example, Mr. Zhou would put some pictures of rectangles and circles in the classroom so the students could visualize the fractions. Ms. Chen would show Adam an example of eating cake: If you eat 1/4 of the cake, then eat 1/2 of the cake, how much did you eat in all? Ms. Zhang would use manipulative activities to help Adam:

Give Adam three paper circles. Have him divide two circles into equal-sized parts with the same number of parts and divide the third circle into equal parts with a different number. Have Adam color one part in each circle using three colors and cut them off, then compare the colored parts to see which one adds *directly*. This activity could help Adam understand that only with equal-sized parts, i.e., with common denominator–like unit fractions, can fractions be directly added.

Here Ms. Zhang not only used a concrete model but also used the concept of unit fraction to help students understand fraction addition.

Develop Abstract Thinking

On developing students' abstract understanding, table 4.3 shows that in problem 1.a, 39 percent of the U.S. teachers mentioned the importance of the "rule" of adding fractions, while 79 percent of Chinese teachers mentioned it: to add fractions with like denominators, add the numerators; the denominator stays the same. To add fractions with unlike denominators, find a common denominator first, and then apply the same rule as for like denominators. To Chinese teachers, once students understand why like unit fractions are needed to add fractions, students would firmly remember the rules and also know how to use the rules flexibly in various situations.

Table 4.3 shows that 51 percent of Chinese teachers referred to the concept of fraction when they asked questions in problem 1.b. Since the "unit fraction" is a very important concept in Chinese textbooks, 30 percent of Chinese teachers focused on this concept when they formed the questions for Adam.

In problem 1.c, using the concept of unit fraction to help students understand fraction addition, 39 percent of Chinese teachers referred to the term "unit fraction" or to the concept of fraction in their examples. Thirty-six percent of teachers expected their students to know fraction addition through mastering the procedure or the rule for adding fractions. This consists of 75 percent of these teachers referring to definition and rules compared to 8 percent of the U.S. teachers mentioning definition and rules.

The ability to design questions and use the questions to determine students' thinking is basic and important for effective teaching. Proper and focused questions will provide students opportunities to think and ponder the relationships and connections among mathematics ideas, and to engage in the process of internalizing and abstract thinking. A total of 61 percent of the U.S. teachers asked questions that provided students opportunities to think and respond. For example, Ms. Parker was able to relate the questions to real-life experience: "How would you add slices of two pizzas? Should you first cut all of them to the same size?" Ms. Nelson focused more on the concept of fraction; she asked Adam, "What is the difference between 1/2 and 1/3? When you add 1/2 + 1/2 what do you get? How could we add 1/2 + 1/3 of a candy bar?"

These questions would encourage Adam to think about the meaning of a fraction, which could help him understand how to add two fractions with unlike denominators. However, compared to Chinese teachers' questions, the U.S. teachers' questions seem too general and less focused. For example, Ms. Li, a sixth grade Chinese teacher, asked the following questions:

1. What is the unit of the fraction?
2. What fractions can be added directly? Give the problems $1/5 + 2/5$, $1/3 + 2/3$, and $5/6 - 1/6$ to Adam. Can you give picture problems for this?
3. What does it mean to find the common denominator? Why do you need to find the common denominator? And how do you find the common denominator?
4. Look at the example $1/3 + 1/2$: it does not have a common denominator; in other words, the unit fractions are unlike, so numerators cannot be added directly. In order to add the two fractions, transfer unlike unit fractions $1/3$ and $1/2$ to like unit fraction $1/6$. From figure 4.1 we can see that they do not have equal-sized parts.

Figure 4.1.   *Circles for Comparing Unit Fractions*

To divide the unit "1," a circle, into six equal-sized parts, the unit fraction becomes $1/6$ for both circles. The unit fraction is now the same.

Figure 4.2.   *Circles for Like Unit Fractions*

5. How do you add fractions with unlike denominators?

To help Adam fully understand the concept of fraction, Ms. Wang asked the following questions and provided more fraction addition problems:

1. What does 3/4 represent? What does 4/5 represent?
2. What is the unit fraction of 3/4? What is the unit fraction of 4/5? How many units are in each fraction? Which is larger, 1/4 or 1/5?
3. Can 3/4 and 4/5 be added directly? Why?

Problem 1: 1/4 + 3/4 =? 1/5 + 3/5 =?
Problem 2: Find the common denominator, then compare which is larger: 3/4 and 4/5, 1/3 and 1/2.

Four teachers considered an understanding of the addition of whole numbers as the basis for understanding fractions. They asked questions relating to whole numbers: What is the meaning of the addition of whole numbers? What is the meaning of fraction addition? What is the difference between these two? For instance, Ms. Zhang asked the following question with examples of whole number, decimals, and fractions: When we add fractions with unlike denominators, why do we find the common denominator first?

1. $2315 + 42 = 2357$ Whole numbers with like units can be added.
2. $0.60 - 0.04 = 0.56$ Decimals with like units can be subtracted.
3. $1/8 + 3/8 = 4/8 = 1/2$ Fractions with a common denominator or like unit fractions can be added.
4. $1/2 + 1/3 = 2/6 + 3/6 = 5/6$ Fractions with unlike denominators should be changed to like unit fractions in order to add.

From these four examples, Adam should be able to understand that two numbers can be added or subtracted only when there are like units.

Table 4.3 shows that in problem 1.b, 76 percent of Chinese teachers focused on the procedure or the rule of fraction addition when they developed the questions or tasks to help Adam understand the meaning of fraction addition. A total of 79 percent of Chinese teachers were able to use questions or tasks to provide students an opportunity to think and respond. However, Ms. Wood, a U.S. teacher who has been teaching for many years at both elementary and middle school levels, indicated the problems in teaching the procedure of finding common denominators.

> There is another skill that needs to be addressed in finding common multiples. Very often students are taught to "cross multiply" in finding common denominators. Although this technique "works," it does not promote number sense and leaves students with very large numbers to simplify in order to express the sum in lowest terms.

It is true that simply "cross multiplying" will create difficulties for students in simplifying fractions.

In conclusion, both the U.S. and Chinese teachers were able to apply various methods to build on students' ideas and understanding about fractions. However, the U.S. teachers focused more on connecting concrete models and manipulatives to build on students' ideas and understanding in fractions, while Chinese teachers used the unit fraction concept to build on understanding of fractions, and emphasized rules and procedures of fractions.

ADDRESSING AND CORRECTING STUDENTS' MISCONCEPTIONS

About 18 percent of the U.S. teachers used questions or tasks to help understand students' misconceptions, while 61 percent of Chinese teachers provided appropriate questions to check students' thinking for misconceptions. Sixty-one percent of the U.S. teachers designed questions and tasks to help students to progress in their ideas compared to 100 percent of Chinese teachers. Furthermore, 42 percent of Chinese teachers would apply a procedure or rule to correct Robert's misconception (see problem 2) compared to 11 percent of the U.S. teachers.

PROBLEM 2

A fifth grade teacher asked her students to write the following three numbers in order from smallest to largest:

$$\frac{3}{8}, \frac{1}{4}, \frac{2}{3}$$

Latoya, Robert, and Sandra placed them in order as follows.

Latoya:

$$\frac{1}{4}, \frac{2}{3}, \frac{3}{8}$$

Robert:

$$\frac{2}{3}, \frac{1}{4}, \frac{3}{8}$$

Sandra:

$$\frac{1}{4}, \frac{3}{8}, \frac{2}{3}$$

a. What might each of the students be thinking?
b. What question would you ask Latoya to find out if your opinion of her thinking is correct?
c. How would you correct Robert's misconception about comparing the size of fractions?

These three questions were designed to examine teachers' understanding of students' misconceptions and to investigate teaching approaches of addressing misconceptions and helping students correct misconceptions in comparing fractions.

Identify Misconceptions

Know Students' Thinking

Table 4.4 shows that in problem 2.a, 86 percent of the U.S. teachers correctly understood each student's thinking on comparison of fractions. Ms. Nelson, like other teachers, indicated the following misconceptions that each student had:

Latoya doesn't understand common denominators and organizes by numerator only without common denominators. Robert organizes by denominators only, ignoring numerators. Sandra seems to understand the value of common denominators.

Ms. Scott had a different view about Sandra's thinking. She thought that Sandra might estimate "which fraction is closer to 0, 1/2, or 1?" This view showed her knowledge of students' thinking on ordering fractions and also expressed her flexible teaching approach.

Table 4.4.   Percentage of U.S. and Chinese Teachers for Each Component of Response of Problem 2

Pedagogical Content Knowledge	Essential Components	Problem Number	Category Number	U.S. %	China %
Addressing and correcting students' misconceptions	Identify misconceptions				
	1. Know students' thinking on misconceptions	2.a	11	86	97
	2. Use questions to verify your thinking on student misconceptions	2.b	12	18	61
	Make corrections for misconceptions				
	1. Connect to concrete model	2.c	7, 10	39	30
	2. Draw picture or table	2.c	4	29	30
	3. Use concept or definition	2.c	2	0	12
	4. Use rule and procedure	2.c	3	11	42
	5. Give example	2.c	5	0	27
	6. Design questions and tasks to help students progress in their ideas	2.b	13	61	100
	7. Provide students opportunity to think and respond	2.c	9	4	6
	8. Stress estimation	2.c	6	4	0
	Unintelligible response	2.a	17	14	3
		2.b	17	79	39
		2.c	17	39	0

Note: N = 28 for each type of response for the U.S. teachers. N = 33 for each type of response for the Chinese teachers. Each individual teacher response could be coded more than once, resulting in total percentages greater than 100 for each problem.

Similar to the U.S. teachers, most Chinese teachers knew students' thinking and misconceptions on ordering of fractions. Table 4.4 shows that in problem 2.a, 97 percent of Chinese teachers knew each student's thinking on comparing fractions. For example, Mr. Wang understood:

> Latoya followed the rule of ordering fractions with common denominators, but she forgot the premise of common denominator and only remembered that the larger fraction is the one with the larger numerator.
> Robert forgot the premise of like numerator; he placed denominators only and thought that small fractions were determined by a small denominator.
> Sandra compared fractions correctly. She might use the following methods:
>
> 1. Find common denominator first, then compare the fractions.
> 2. Find like numerator first, then compare the fractions.

3. Look at the middle number "1/2," then compare three fractions with "1/2."

Based on his response about Sandra's thinking, Mr. Wang has identified all the possible cases of ordering fractions, especially estimation strategy, which is important and makes sense to students. He said that he would teach students to use estimation to order the fractions with this particular problem.

Ask Questions

Table 4.4 shows that only 18 percent of the U.S. teachers used questions or tasks to help students recognize their misconceptions. Questions designed by the U.S. teachers like "Where would 5/11 go in this series of numbers?" and "Do 1/3 and 1/8 have different values?" would encourage Latoya to think about the differences between fractions, which may help her find the error. Questions such as "Do you have your fraction cut into equal parts?" and "How did you order the fractions? Do you know what a lowest common denominator is?" would help Latoya to think about the concept of fraction and the meaning of common denominator, which are the key parts in fraction comparison.

However, table 4.4 indicates that 61 percent of Chinese teachers provided appropriate questions to find out if their opinion of Latoya's thinking is correct. Three teachers designed questions with manipulative activities. Taking an example from Ms. Wu:

> Can you directly order fractions by comparing numerators only while the numerators and denominators are all different? Have Latoya use same-size paper to fold 1/4, 2/3, 3/8, and then compare these three pieces.

Mr. Wang also would have Latoya verify her answers by drawing the graph: From drawing figure 4.3, Latoya would reflect on her thinking and understand the concept of comparison of fractions.

Some questions were related to the concept of unit fractions. Ms. Chu's questions were "Is a 4-unit fraction necessarily larger than a 3-unit fraction? Which is larger: 2/5 or 3/8?"

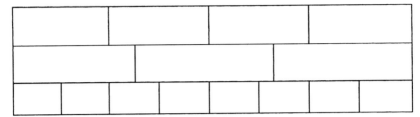

Figure 4.3. *Comparison of Fractions*

Ms. Yian provided three groups of fractions to help Latoya understand how to compare fractions:

1/4, 2/4, 3/4. Fractions with a common denominator
1/5, 1/15, 1/20. Fractions with like numerators
1/4, 2/3, 3/8 → 6/24, 16/24, 9/24. The result of finding a common denominator

These three groups of fractions help students know the rules of comparing fractions:

1. With a common denominator, fractions could be compared by numerators only.
2. With a like numerator, fractions could be ordered by comparing denominators only.
3. With uncommon denominators, one needs to find a common denominator first.

About 79 percent of the U.S. teachers and 39 percent of Chinese teachers tried to provide questions to help students, but these questions seemed too general and did not help Latoya directly identify the misconception. Questions such as "How did you order these?" and "Explain why you put the fraction in that order" would provide a chance for Latoya to think and respond, but did not directly lead her to realize the misconception.

Correct Misconceptions

Connect to Concrete Models and Draw Pictures

Table 4.4 indicates that both the U.S. and Chinese teachers suggested various activities and examples to correct Robert's misconception about comparing the size of fractions. Thirty-nine percent of the U.S. teachers provided activities that connect to concrete models compared to 30 percent of Chinese teachers; 29 percent of the U.S. teachers provided activities that related to pictures or graphs and 30 percent of Chinese teachers took the same approach.

Ms. Griffin presented one of these activities: "I would have him show/draw the fractions for visual comparison and then have him use these visuals to create equivalent fractions with a common denominator. This would take him from concrete to more abstract and numerical."

Ms. Nelson also would show him physical examples of a candy bar. When shown the sections of 2/3, 1/4, and 3/8, Robert would be able to concretely conceptualize each fraction.

Ms. Parker would make visual materials using transparencies. She stated, "Make three circles on three different transparencies, shade the three portions and put the three transparencies on top of each other for comparison."

All of the Chinese teachers presented clear descriptions of how to correct Robert's misconception about comparing the size of fractions. Three Chinese teachers mentioned using paper folding to compare these fractions. Others used different manipulative activities. Ms. Jian presented the following approach:

> Have Robert cut two equal-sized ropes, one in seven pieces, and one in two pieces. Then have him compare a section from each rope to find out which one is longer. Help him summarize the rules: take one part from each rope. The one with the short part has a larger denominator, and the fraction is smaller. Therefore, compare fractions by not only looking at the denominator; a large denominator does not mean the fraction is larger.

Here Ms. Jian would not only help students understand concretely, but also direct students toward abstract understanding by generalizing the rules.

Use Definitions or Rules

Like Ms. Jian, 42 percent of Chinese teachers would apply a procedure or rule to correct Robert's misconception compared to 11 percent of the

U.S. teachers. For example, Ms. Elliott, a U.S. teacher, presented clear descriptions: "I would explain that you must get common denominators and then order the numerators to find the smallest to largest fractions. I have my students do this. Then they can easily put them in order."

Ms. Larson would present the procedure in another way. She would say, "Change fractions to decimals, then compare."

However, using definitions and rules, Chinese teachers were able to help students analyze different situations and use real-world examples to support students' thinking. Ms. Wu's response demonstrated this support:

> First, ask Robert to explain his thinking. Then ask him what two approaches can be used to compare fractions. With common denominators, the order of fractions is determined by the numerators—the larger the numerator, the larger the fraction; with like numerators, the order of fractions is determined by the denominators—the larger the denominator, the smaller the fraction. When can we use the denominator to determine the order of fractions? Do you think your thinking is right? Let us look at the real world to see if your thinking works: Let us cut cakes into 1/4, 2/3, and 3/8.

Mr. Wang pointed out that there are many ways to compare fractions. One basic method is to get like unit fractions:

$2/3 = 16/24$, unit fraction is $1/24$; there are 16 unit fractions
$1/4 = 6/24$, unit fraction is $1/24$; there are 6 unit fractions
$3/8 = 9/24$, unit fraction is $1/24$; there are 9 unit fractions

From comparing the number of unit fractions above, students can see the order of fractions: $2/3 > 3/8 > 1/4$.

Like Mr. Wang, 12 percent of teachers agreed that using definitions like unit fractions was the best approach to correct the misconception on ordering of fraction. Ms. Lu stated, "First Robert should understand that fractions cannot be compared with unlike unit fractions. Further transformation is needed to get like unit fractions. This transformation finds a common denominator. With common denominators, fractions can be compared."

Designing questions and tasks to help students progress in their ideas will help students achieve conceptual understanding. Table 4.4 indicates that 61 percent of the U.S. teachers were able to do so, compared to 100 percent of Chinese teachers.

In summary, the U.S. teachers use activities such as graphs, manipulatives, and procedures to help students correct misconceptions, but focus on concrete models. In contrast, Chinese teachers deal with students' misconceptions by various activities but focus on probing questions.

Comparing fractions can be crucial for students since it relates to students' understanding of the meaning of fraction. In general, there are three methods to compare fractions: (1) comparing fractions with the same denominator—a fraction with greater numerator has greater value; (2) comparing fractions with the same numerator—a fraction with greater denominator has less value; (3) comparing fractions with different denominators and numerators—changing fractions to either common denominator or common numerator using fraction properties and then using method 1 or 2 to compare fractions. In teaching how to compare fractions, teachers need to use concrete models to help students visualize inequality of fractions and develop an abstract understanding of comparing fractions.

ENGAGING STUDENTS IN MATHEMATICS LEARNING

About 64 percent of the U.S. teachers would use area to represent fraction multiplication, 11 percent of them would use repeated addition, and 11 percent of them preferred both methods. In contrast, about 67 percent of Chinese teachers would use both area and repeated addition to represent multiplication, 28 percent of Chinese teachers would like to use area, and 6 percent of teachers would like to use repeated addition.

PROBLEM 3

You are planning to teach procedures for doing the following type of fraction multiplication:

$$\frac{3}{4} \times \frac{2}{3} = \frac{6}{12}$$

  a. Describe an introductory activity that would engage and motivate your students to learn this procedure.

b. Multiplication can be represented by repeated addition, by area, or by a combination of these. Which one of these representations would you use to illustrate fraction multiplication to your students? Why?

c. Describe an activity that would help your students understand the procedure of multiplying fractions.

These three questions were designed to examine teachers' knowledge of engaging students in learning fraction multiplication with multiple representations.

Design Introductory Activities

To design introductory activities, Chinese teachers connected concrete models and stories related to students' lives more frequently than the U.S teachers in problem 3.a. Table 4.5 shows that 85 percent of Chinese teachers could provide an introductory activity to motivate students to learn the procedure of fraction multiplication. Among these activities, 64 percent of them connected to concrete models, and 18 percent of them related to manipulative activities. In addition, 91 percent of teachers gave detailed examples of activities, such as making field trips, eating birthday cakes, distributing class time, and dividing clothing. By providing examples related to students' real lives, manipulatives, and concrete models, Chinese teachers were able to make a connection between manipulatives and problem-solving strategy and to build understanding for students by developing rigorous procedures.

Ms. Wang designed an introductory activity using problem solving:

In the class, 56 students were divided into four groups with 14 students in each group.

The teacher has a student divide a colored paper into 4 pieces, so each group gets 1/4 of the paper. To illustrate the procedure of fraction multiplication, let's use group one as an example first: In order to share 1/4 of the paper among 14 students in group 1, 1/4 of this paper will be divided equally into 14 pieces. How much paper will each student in group 1 get? How do you write this expression? It should be expressed as

$$\frac{1}{4} \times \frac{1}{14}.$$

If all four groups do the same, every student in class will get one part of the paper.

How much paper will each student get? To find 1/14 of 1/4, a student can divide 1/4 into 14 parts, taking one part of it, which means the student divides one paper into 4 × 14 parts and has one of those 4 × 14. The result can be expressed as

$$\frac{1}{4\times14} \times 1 = \frac{1\times1}{4\times14}.$$

Therefore, the answer is

$$\frac{1}{4} \times \frac{1}{14} = \frac{1\times1}{4\times14} = \frac{1}{56}.$$

For two students, they will get 2/14 of 1/4 the paper:

$$\frac{1}{4} \times \frac{1}{14} \times 2 = \frac{1}{4} \times \frac{2}{14} = \frac{2}{56}.$$

So two students get 2/56 of the paper.

Mr. Wang concluded: "Now we can arrive at a conclusion: when multiplying fractions, the numerator will be the product of numerators, and the denominator will be the product of denominators."

$$\frac{1}{4} \times \frac{2}{14} = \frac{1\times2}{4\times14} = \frac{2}{56}.$$

At last, Mr. Wang applied the above conclusion to direct students to solve problem 3:

$$\frac{3}{4} \times \frac{2}{3} = \frac{3\times2}{4\times3} = \frac{6}{12}.$$

This activity visually addressed the connection between a concrete model and procedure of fraction multiplication, which provides clear steps for fraction multiplication and also promotes students' engagement in learning.

The notation here differs from U.S. notation. In Chinese textbooks, the multiplication of fractions is represented differently: dividing 1/4 of the paper into 14 pieces is written the same as "to find 1/4's 1/14" (Chinese language expression) and its expression is 1/4 × 1/14, while in the United States it would be "to find 1/14 of 1/4" and its expression is 1/14 × 1/4.

The Chinese way of defining fraction multiplication seems to have the same order between the meaning and expression (i.e. first having 1/4, and then having 1/4's 1/14.) which complements student thinking more effectively, while the U.S. way of defining fraction multiplication tends to produce confusion for students.

Ms. Yian told a birthday story: "Your mother bought a birthday cake for you. You eat 1/4 of it. Your father came back home and he wanted to eat 2/3 of the leftover cake. How much cake did your father eat?"

Ms. Zhen related the problem to time: "One period of mathematics class is 45 minutes (3/4 hours); students use 1/3 of a period to read the instructions in the book and use 2/3 of a period to make rectangle prism models. How much time do students use to make rectangle prisms?"

Table 4.5 indicates that 79 percent of the U.S. teachers were able to provide activities to encourage students to engage in the learning procedure. Thirty-six percent of teachers designed an introductory activity with concrete models and 39 percent of teachers used manipulative activities to introduce fractions. Some teachers would do this type of manipulative with candy bars. For example, Ms. Griffin said:

> I would hold up an unwrapped Hershey bar. I would tell the kids that I was going to give away 3/4 of my candy bar. Then I would tell the kids that one person could have 2/3 of that 3/4. Using the candy bar lines, we would find 2/3 of the 3/4 and give it away. At that point, we would determine how much that piece was compared to the original candy bar. Then we used the 1/4 left and gave 1/2 of that. This continued until every child got a piece of the candy bar.

Some U.S. teachers were able to connect multiplication with area. For example, three teachers would model multiplication by using geoboards to find area. Ms. Wood described this type of activity as one of her favorite activities in teaching multiplication:

> My favorite teaching tool for multiplying fractions is to use clear transparencies. The students use markers to draw congruent squares or rectangles. Then they divide the rectangles into columns to represent the denominator of each fraction. The numerator is represented by shading in the appropriate columns (the portion being multiplied.) When the two

Table 4.5.   Percentage of U.S. and Chinese Teachers for Each Component of Response of Problem 3

Pedagogical Content Knowledge	Essential Components	Problem Number	Category Number	U.S. %	China %
Engaging students in mathematics learning	Design introductory activities				
	1. Connect to prior knowledge	3.a	1	7	45
	2. Connect to concrete models	3.a	7	36	64
	3. Use manipulative activities	3.a	10	39	18
	4. Draw picture or table	3.a	4	14	15
	5. Give examples	3.a	5	4	91
	6. Provide activities focused on students' thinking	3.a	14	79	85
	Use various representations				
	1. Use one representation (area)	3.b	15	64	28
	Use one representation (repeated addition)	3.b	15	11	6
	2. Use both representations (area and repeated addition)	3.b	16	11	67
	Provide various activities				
	1. Provide activities focused on students' thinking	3.c	14	68	61
	2. Give examples	3.c	5	11	76
	3. Use manipulative activities	3.c	10	29	27
	4. Use area to illustrate fraction multiplication	3.c	15	46	33
	5. Connect to prior knowledge	3.c	1	4	21

Note: N = 28 for each type of response for the U.S. teachers. N = 33 for each type of response for the Chinese teachers. Each individual teacher response could be coded more than once, resulting in total percentages greater than 100 for each problem.

transparencies are crisscrossed (like the multiplication sign) the result is an intersection of the shaded portions, which represents the product.

Ms. Larson would have students sing a fraction song and dance to it: "the top times the top and the bottom times the bottom." This activity makes it fun for students to learn and also helps students remember the rule of multiplication.

Although the U.S. teachers were able to create various activities to make mathematics visual, meaningful, and fun to learn, they often ignored developing the connection between manipulative activities and abstract thinking. For example, Ms. Parker would direct students, "Cut a circle (paper) into three pieces. Take 2/3. Cut each one of these two pieces into four and take three of each one. You have 6 out of 12 pieces." She failed to connect the manipulative explanation and procedure of multiplying fractions. The lack of such a connection would result in failure to build a bridge for students to understand why they use the manipulatives and how activities would help them use the procedure when they are doing multiplication.

In the introduction of new concepts, using prior knowledge not only helps students review and reinforce the knowledge being taught, but also helps them picture mathematics as an integrated whole rather than bits of separate knowledge. Table 4.5 shows that 45 percent of Chinese teachers focused on the importance of determining students' prior knowledge; in contrast, very few U.S. teachers (7 percent) connected students' prior knowledge in learning fraction multiplication. For example, Ms. Zhong presented the following introductory story, which connects addition:

> The monkey's mother bought a watermelon and cut it into 9 pieces; every monkey ate 2/9 of the pieces. How many pieces did four monkeys eat? How do you express this problem in addition? How do you express this problem in multiplication? Which method is easier?

This example helps students transfer prior knowledge of repeated addition to multiplication with better conceptual understanding of fraction multiplication. It also brings students into the problem-solving process and motivates students to ponder strategies and to make choices about the best method.

Use Various Representations

Table 4.5 indicates that 64 percent of the U.S. teachers would use area to represent fraction multiplication, 11 percent would use repeated addition, and 11 percent preferred both methods. In contrast, 67 percent of Chinese teachers would use both area and repeated addition to represent multiplication. Twenty-eight percent of Chinese teachers would use area and 6 percent of Chinese teachers would use repeated addition to represent multiplication. This data indicated that the U.S. teachers liked to use representation with visual and meaningful features, while most Chinese teachers prefer to use both area and repeated addition to illustrate fraction multiplication.

Let's look at the U.S. teachers' responses first. Ms. Scott explained the reason for using area: it is related to life examples, and it also makes the problem meaningful to students. "Students tend to have more real-life examples that relate to area. I think it is also easier for them to visualize area."

Ms. Nelson introduced area to prepare students for learning algebra in the future: "I would use area. This method can be adapted later to understanding the methods of multiplying polynomials (using algebra tiles)."

Three teachers would use the addition method. They think that it is easier for students to understand. Ms. Smith said, "Students can relate more easily to addition."

Three teachers would combine both methods. Ms. Waller explained the reason for using a combination method: "Some students like to relate to something they understand and most seem to understand addition. Others like to broaden to area." Ms. Jenkins said, "Because the more they are able to see combinations [of methods], the more they associate them with other combinations [of methods]."

Most Chinese teachers, however, not only used both area and repeated addition to illustrate fraction multiplication but also understood when and how to use each representation. The response from Ms. Yian provided a clear explanation on how to use different representations for multiplication:

> (1) If a fraction multiplies a whole number, using repeated addition is easier for students to understand. (2) If a fraction multiplies a fraction, using the area graph is better for visualization. (3) For fractions that are mixed numbers, use both methods.

Ms. Wang addressed the repeated addition method with an example and a picture:

> Xiaoxin, her mother, and her father are eating a cake; each one eats 2/9 of the cake. How much cake will three people eat? Show pictures first:

From figure 4.4, students can write the expression

$$\frac{2}{9} + \frac{2}{9} + \frac{2}{9} = \frac{2+2+2}{9} = \frac{6}{9} = \frac{2}{3}.$$

Figure 4.4. *2/9 of Each Piece from a Cake*

Use multiplication:

$$\frac{2}{9} \times 3 = \frac{2 \times 3}{9} = \frac{6}{9} = \frac{2}{3}$$

Conclusion: When a fraction multiplies a whole number, the resulting numerator is the product of the original numerator and the whole number, and the denominator is the same.

Ms. Zhen used the following graph of area to represent the multiplication. Figure 4.5 shows the overlap area for the product of 2/3 and 3/4.

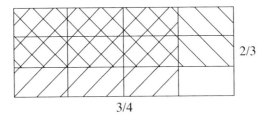

3/4

Figure 4.5. *The Overlap Area for the Product of 2/3 and 3/4*

Provide Various Activities

Table 4.5 shows that 68 percent of the U.S. teachers were able to clearly describe activities to help students understand multiplication of fractions, compared to 61 percent of Chinese teachers. These activities included the area activity and manipulatives. However, only 11 percent of the U.S teachers gave an example of the activities that related to the procedure of multiplying fractions, while 76 percent of Chinese teachers provided a detailed example, focusing on the procedure of multiplying fractions.

For example, the U.S. teacher Ms. Wood would create different activities to help students learn multiplication of fractions:

I prefer to use the area models to represent multiplication of fractions. I also use this method to bring to light the fact that multiplying by a fraction is really more like dividing by a whole number. Using play money, I have students multiply fifty-cent pieces by 1/2. They must, of course, switch to quarters. Thus a half of a dollar multiplied by one half yields one-fourth of a dollar. Then using power of ten rods, I ask them to multiply 5 rods by one-half. Since the children cannot physically break the rods in half, many times the students want to draw a line across the rods at the fifth ridge. Whenever we do a concrete task, the next activity is to draw the picture of the new learning. For multiplication of decimals, we can use grid paper, cut into 10 by 10 squares or for fractions, use plain paper to draw the columns. The models are glued into the math journal. Learning the appropriate use of the terms "half of," or "two thirds of" to denote "a portion of," is also vital for students to grasp the multiplication of fractions concepts.

Most of the U.S. teachers, like Ms. Wood, were able to design activities to engage students in learning. Ms. Larson suggested, "The song and dance really helps create a memory for students to follow the steps." Ms. Jenkins agreed with using a song to help students learn: "We usually make up a rap or song for math concepts, so this is a great area to apply that strategy." Ms. Ross also would have students sing "The Fraction Family."

Ms. Waller used base-ten blocks or graph paper to explain the multiplication of fractions. Drawing a picture of area is one favorite activity for most teachers. Ms. Griffin explained this activity:

Students begin by drawing a rectangle. Give the students this problem: 1/2 of 1/4. Have students show 1/4 on their rectangle. Color in the 1/4 with a colored pencil. Then, show 1/2 of the 1/4 by drawing the 1/2 perpendicular to the 1/4 line. Color this half with a different color. The overlapping colors would demonstrate the product. Show the same problem using pie pieces. Then solve several other problems using the rectangles. After each problem, record the problem and product so the picture can be directly related to the algorithm. The students would then discover that the product is a result of the product of the numerators over the product of the denominators.

Although Ms. Griffin used manipulatives to show the algorithm of multiplication of fractions, she did not clearly address the connection between the manipulatives and the procedural development.

It is interesting to note that five Chinese teachers provided similar manipulatives of coloring folded paper. However, the responses from Chinese teachers, such as Ms. Wang, provided a linkage between manipulatives and procedural development:

Give every student a paper rectangle; have students fold 1/3 of the paper and color this part. Then have students fold a half of the colored portion and color again using another color. The overlapping colors will be the result of multiplication of fractions. The procedure of multiplying 1/3 by 1/2 can be determined by the following: Divide 1/3 into 2 equal parts; each part is

$$\frac{1}{3 \times 2}$$

of unit "1." One of the parts is

$$\frac{1}{3 \times 2} \times 1 = \frac{1 \times 1}{3 \times 2},$$

Therefore, when multiplying fractions, the numerator should multiply the numerator, and the denominator should multiply the denominator.

$$\frac{1}{3 \times 2} \times 1 = \frac{1 \times 1}{3 \times 2} = \frac{1}{6}$$

Ms. Wu used magnet material to make a group of instruction tools for fractions. For example, for 3/4 × 1/2, numerators 3 and 1 will be represented by one group of different magnet forces, and denominators 4 and 2 will be represented by another group of different magnet forces. Put two numbers together. If they attract each other, then they can be multiplied; if they repel each other off, then they cannot be multiplied.

$$\textbf{S pole} \qquad \textbf{N pole}$$
$$\frac{3}{4} \times \frac{1}{2}$$
$$\textbf{N pole} \qquad \textbf{S pole}$$

Figure 4.6. *Magnet Forces for Multiplying Fractions*

This concrete model makes the rule of multiplication vivid and meaningful to students. This model also relates to students' learning experience from science.

In summary, there are differences in engaging students in mathematics learning between U.S. and Chinese teachers. First, most of the U.S. teachers would engage and motivate their students to learn fraction multiplication by concrete materials and manipulatives, while Chinese teachers would engage and motivate their students to learn the procedure of multiplication by examples with prior knowledge and stories. Next, the U.S. teachers would use area to illustrate fraction multiplication; Chinese teachers would use both area and repeated addition to illustrate fraction multiplication. Last, the U.S. teachers would provide various activities to engage students in learning fraction multiplication, while Chinese teachers would provide examples that connected to both manipulatives and procedures of multiplication of fractions.

Multiplication of fractions is an expansion of whole number multiplication. Understanding of multiplication of fractions is based on understanding of fractions and multiplication of whole numbers. For middle school students, this understanding is abstract and sometimes difficult. Ms. Zhen provided a very useful method to help students understand the concept of multiplication. In teaching multiplication fraction, the following steps are helpful: (1) using whole number times fraction, (2) using fraction times fraction, (3) explaining that when multiplying by a fraction less than 1 the result is smaller than the number that it multiplies, and (4) explaining that when multiplying by a fraction more than 1 the result is greater than the number that it multiplies.

PROMOTING AND SUPPORTING STUDENTS' THINKING ABOUT MATHEMATICS

About 52 percent of the U.S. teachers clearly described activities that will help students develop thinking strategies to solve the problem, while 73 percent of Chinese teachers addressed the same approach. About 57 percent of the U.S. teachers were able to clearly use questions to help students justify their answers, while 100 percent of Chinese teachers were able to use questions to help students justify their answer. Sixty-eight percent of the U.S. teachers provided the strategies to help their students to reflect on their answers and solutions compared to 94 percent of Chinese teachers who provided strategies to encourage their students' reflective thinking.

PROBLEM 4

Your students are trying to solve the following proportion problem: The ratio of girls to boys in Math Club is 3:5. If there are 40 students in the Math Club, how many are boys?

 a. Describe an activity that you would use to demonstrate the types of solution strategies your students could use to solve the problem.

Here are two students' solutions to the problem:

June's solution: $\frac{3}{5} = \frac{x}{40}$. There are 24 girls, so there are 16 boys.

Kathy's solution: $\frac{3}{8} = \frac{x}{40}$. There are 15 boys.

 b. What question would you ask Kathy to determine if she could justify her answer and reasoning?
 c. What suggestion would you provide to June that might help her revise her approach?
 d. What strategy would you use to encourage your students to reflect on their answers and solutions?

These three questions were designed to examine teacher's knowledge of promoting and extending students' thinking, and to investigate teaching strategies of supporting students' reflection.

Use Activities to Promote Students' Thinking

Table 4.6 indicates that 52 percent of the U.S. teachers clearly described an activity that will help students develop strategies to solve the problems, while 73 percent of Chinese teachers clearly provided an activity to help students develop thinking strategies to solve the problems. The U.S. teachers would use pictures or tables, connect to concrete models, and apply manipulative activities to teach students how to think about proportion and how to set up a proportion. For example, six teachers designed a role-play activity by using the sample of students in the classroom to solve this problem. Ms. Griffin described her activity in the classroom:

Table 4.6.   Percentage of U.S. and Chinese Teachers for Each Component of Response of Problem 4

Pedagogical Content Knowledge	Essential Components	Problem Number	Category Number	U.S. %	China %
Promoting and supporting students' thinking about mathematics	Use activities to promote students' thinking				
	1. Provide activities focused on students' thinking	4.a	14	52	73
	2. Draw picture or table	4.a	4	14	15
	3. Connect to concrete models	4.a	7	18	3
	4. Use manipulatives	4.a	10	11	24
	5. Give examples	4.a	5	0	18
	Provide suggestions and questions to support thinking				
	1. Use questions to help students	4.b	13	57	100
	to progress in their ideas	4.c	13	68	97
	2. Use estimation	4.b	6	0	9
		4.c	6	4	6
	Use strategies to encourage reflective thinking				
	1. Provide activities focused on students' thinking	4.d	14	68	94
	2. Draw picture or table	4.d	4	7	0
	3. Connect to concrete models	4.d	7	7	0
	4. Use estimation	4.d	6	0	3
	Unintelligible Response	4.a	17	36	21
		4.b	17	43	0
		4.c	17	11	3
		4.d	17	29	6

Note: N = 28 for each type of response for the U.S. teachers. N = 33 for each type of response for the Chinese teachers. Each individual teacher response could be coded more than once, resulting in total percentages greater than 100 for each problem.

Set up a real-life situation in the classroom. Ask three girls and five boys to come to the front. Present the question to the class. They must solve the problem by showing some type of work, graph, etc. They will then be asked to describe their strategy to the class. This verbal or written description would provide information about the thought process used.

Ms. Larson also used students in the classroom as the samples:

We count the number of girls and boys in the class and simplify [fractions]. We have used a chart to write equivalent ratios or proportions. We used a paint problem and demonstration. We graphed proportions. We incorporated some proportionality into our curriculum.

Immersing students in a real problem-solving situation not only motivates students' interests in learning, but also engages students in "doing" mathematics.

The U.S. teachers also would use a chart to write equivalent ratios.
With a chart, students could identify a pattern and understand the problem easily. For example, Ms. Flores displayed her chart for the activity:

Girls: 3   6   9   12   15   18   21   24
Boys: 5   10   15   20   25   30   35   40

Other teachers would use different colors of blocks or cubes to build
a model to solve problems. Ms. Wood shared her activity:

Use different color cubes or counters to represent boys and girls. Add
rows of boys in groups of five and girls in groups of three until a total of
40 children are represented. Create a table of multiples for three and five.
Have students circle the two multiples whose sum equals 40.

In this activity, Ms. Wood was able to connect the proportion to a concrete model and create a chart to show the pattern. She also taught students how to use a total to find the answer.

Table 4.6 shows that 42 percent of Chinese teachers also used manipulative activities and drew pictures or tables. Six Chinese teachers
also applied role-play activities in the classrooms. They selected 40
students in the classroom and distributed girls and boys following the
ratio of 3:5. This activity definitely encourages students to engage in
the learning process and creates a visual model for the proportion.

Other Chinese teachers used activities by distributing pencils, chess
pieces, candy, and cookies. In China, teachers rarely use pattern blocks,
cubes, and other manipulative materials because of teachers' beliefs
about manipulative materials in mathematics learning. However, a
number of Chinese teachers were able to explain activities with abstract
procedures. It is worth noting that simple equations and direct/indirect
variation are introduced in the sixth grade in Chinese elementary math
textbooks, and corresponding content areas are introduced in U.S. sixth
grade textbooks. However, teachers' responses in this study indicated
that Chinese teachers tend to use the algebraic approach more than the
U.S. teachers in solving proportion problems. Ms. Wang described how
to solve this problem by using equations:

The ratio of girls to boys is 3:5, which means the girls are 3/5 of boys and boys are 5/3 of girls. So if the ratio of boys to girls is more than one, it will be a direct variation. Let the number of boys be x; the number of girls will be $(40-x)$, so the ratio of boys to girls = $x:(40-x)$. Therefore, from the proportion

$$\frac{5}{3} = \frac{x}{40-x}$$

we can find the number of boys.

Chinese teachers encourage students to use different ways to solve this problem. Ms. Zhen explained the procedure without using a proportion equation: "Since girls are 3 parts and boys are 5 parts, the total is 8 parts with 40 students. Every part has 40/8 = 5 students. So boys will be 5 parts times 5 students, i.e., 5 × 5 = 25 students."

Provide Suggestions and Questions to Support Thinking

Table 4.6 shows that 57 percent of the U.S. teachers would use questions to help Kathy justify her answers, while 100 percent of Chinese teachers would use questions to help Kathy justify her answer. Although 43 percent of the U.S. teachers in this study provided general questions attempting to provide insight into students' thinking (such as "Do you have the problem set up correctly?") which could prompt a student to look at a problem again, such questions focus less on students' misconceptions. Some U.S. teachers provided very good suggestions to avoid mistakes, for example suggesting that students "label all numbers in a proportion and see if the tops match and the fractions match." Ms. Wood explained the questions and tasks she would ask Kathy:

I would ask Kathy to label her numbers and then look to see if she is comparing the facts that she needs to solve the problem. Kathy's solution uses the concept that 3 girls plus 5 boys makes a total of 8 students. When she sets up the proportion, she uses the number of girls out of the whole group instead of determining the number of boys. In a 3:5 ratio, n:15 would mean that $n = 9$ and 9 + 15 does not equal 40. Kathy's "15" is actually the number of girls in the club. Once she has the correct label on the 15, she would be able to subtract 15 from 40 to find the number of boys, 25. The 15:25 ratio corresponds to the 3:5 ratio of girls to boys listed in the facts of the problem.

U.S. teachers such as Ms. Hanks and Ms. Anderson were able to point out the error directly: "What are there 3 of? Are your numerators referring to the same amount?" "Have her reread the question to make sure she is answering what is being asked. Have her explain what the numbers represent and how she got her answer."

Compared to the U.S. teachers, more Chinese teachers used probing questions at various levels in order to explore students' thinking directly in different ways and encourage students' thinking deeply and critically. In addition, Chinese teachers tended to relate questions to formal definitions and estimation. For example, Ms. Wang would ask her students:

> What measurements are being compared in the ratio of 3:8? Girls are being compared to the whole.
> What measurements are being compared in the ratio of x:40? Boys are being compared to the whole.
> How can we use unequal ratios to make a proportion? How can we make changes in order to get two equivalent ratios?
> Method 1. Let x be the number of boys, so $5/8 = x/40$.
> Method 2. Let x be the number of girls, so $3/8 = x/40$.

Here Ms. Wang focused on the definition of the proportion—an equation stating that two ratios are equivalent. She also used two different methods of problem solving to help students understand an alternative way of solving a problem.

Ms. Bao directed Kathy to estimate: "According to the ratio of boys to girls, who do you think is more? Boys or girls? Why?" This question motivated Kathy to think about and justify her answer using number sense.

Ms. Zhao told Kathy to observe the proportion again and to see if both sides are equal. Ms. Zhen asked questions: "What does x stand for? (number of boys) What does 3 stand for? Does 3 represent the number of boys?" By asking these questions, Ms. Zhen promoted students' thinking and considering the representation of each part.

From Table 4.6, we see that 68 percent of the U.S. teachers would provide suggestions that might help June revise her approach, while 97 percent of Chinese teachers would provide suggestions to help June revise her solution.

Most U.S. teachers suggested that June label the numbers more carefully. Ms. Griffin shared her suggestion: "I would ask her to label the parts in the proportion. The labels of numerators must be alike and the labels of denominators must be alike. This would help her see that the question is being asked from a total of 40 students."

Ms. Hanks also considered the importance of labeling. She would have June "reread the question. Does she have the problem set up correctly? Look at what the numbers represent. Is she consistent in the labeling?"

By focusing on labeling in proportions, the U.S. teachers provided a visual aid to help June identify mistakes and revise the proportion.

Other U.S. teachers suggested June look at the problem backward. Ms. Nelson and Ms. Larson asked June to check the problem with the answer. "Does your ratio of 24 girls to 16 boys mean the same as a 3:5 ratio?" Ms. Nelson asked. Ms. Wood understood June's thinking about the solution; she had the same suggestion for June revising her approach:

June is trying to solve the problem by comparing the number of girls to the total number of students in the club, rather than the ratio of girls to boys. If she thinks that 16 boys are in the club, can she set up a proportion so that 16:40 equals 5:8? No, it is not possible.

In contrast, most Chinese teachers focused on definition of proportion and suggested that June pay attention to the corresponding relationship between the two sides of the equation and that she should understand that two ratios are equivalent and they have corresponding relationships.

Ms. Zheng responded: June did not build the corresponding relationship between the two sides. Three parts and five parts correspond to the number of girls and the number of boys. So the expression should be

$$\frac{3}{5} = \frac{40 - x}{x}, \ or \ \frac{5}{8} = \frac{x}{40}$$

Some Chinese teachers reminded June to estimate and reflect on her answer, asking, "Which represents the greater number, girls or boys?" Other Chinese teachers suggested June check the problem backward. They asked, "Is your result or solution reasonable?" "Reread the problem carefully." Ms. Pan asked directly, "Is the ratio of 24 to 16 equal to the ratio of 3 to 5?" These types of questions would encourage June to justify her answer and to find mistakes in the solution.

Use Strategies to Encourage Reflective Thinking

Table 4.6 shows that 68 percent of the U.S. teachers provided strategies to help their students reflect on their answers and solutions compared to 94 percent of Chinese teachers.

Some U.S. teachers would provide students opportunities to discuss and share their ideas in order to have their students engage in "discussion, reworking, discourse, and remembering and learning from their mistakes." Ms. Baker "always asks students to explain their answers." Ms. William described her strategies:

Have students work in pairs to solve 5 problems. Have volunteers explain how their group solved a problem and have different techniques shown for each problem. I could also have students gather data from a survey question and display in ratio, proportions and percents until they get a total of 40 for boys and girls.

$$\frac{5 \; boys}{8 \; all} = \frac{25 \; boys}{40 \; all}$$

$$\begin{array}{r} 40 \; total \\ -25 \; boys \\ \hline 15 \; girls \end{array}$$

$$\frac{15 \; girls}{25 \; boys} \begin{array}{c} \div 5 \\ \div 5 \end{array} = \frac{3}{5} ratio$$

I would also let students work in pairs to solve the problem before students or teacher modeled the above methods.

Two teachers referred to strategies with pictures or tables and another two teachers referred to strategies with concrete models. Ms.

Caldwell would use concrete models, and she would have students share ideas with peers and have students explain their solution to larger groups. Ms. Knight would also use visual demonstrations to help students reflect on their answers. Ms. Wood agreed that concrete examples could be very helpful:

> Students need to learn to label the numbers so that they know what they are comparing in a proportion or ratio problem. I also think that using concrete examples can be very helpful. For instance, if a company gives a charitable donation of $3 for every $1.00 an employee contributes, how much would the company donate if the employee contributes $14.00? $3/1 = n/14$ is the correct proportion. Is it possible or reasonable for a company to send a donation of $42? Sure, because the amount is larger than the employee's monetary gift. If the student set up the proportion incorrectly, the resulting $4.67 is less than the employee's contribution and would not make sense logically.

Ms. Wood focused on making sense of mathematics to students and also recognized the benefits of labeling the numbers in a proportion. Ms. Griffin noticed the importance of the strategy of labeling the number. She said:

> I always encourage students to label every part of the proportion including the answer. If the labels don't match, the problem is not set up correctly; I also ask them to make a ratio table to check the reasonableness of their answer. They label the rows in the table and only like labels can go in that row.

Ms. Scott noticed that writing words is more visual and powerful than labeling numbers, so she suggested writing the wording of the ratio: "Have them look at the wording and write the wording of the ratio by the problem. I would also have them do a chart if they continued to have difficulty."

Two teachers thought that writing journals is a good approach for students to reflect on their ideas. Ms. Loving reported:

> In the past, my students have recorded problems, solutions, and strategies in a journal I call "Talk about Math." This year my seventh grade GT students will be working in pairs to solve problems available on the

Internet. When they have finished, which includes a written strategy, they will e-mail them to a college where students in the math department will critique their papers and answer by e-mail.

Although most U.S. teachers provided good strategies to encourage students to reflect on their answers and solutions, only 14 percent of the U.S. teachers explicitly suggested their students "go back and see if their answer makes sense." For example, Ms. Parker told students, "substitute your answer and cross multiply it. The results should be equal." Ms. Flores also had students "cross multiply for equivalencies."

Eighty-eight percent of Chinese teachers, however, would encourage their students to substitute their answers into original equations and check to see if they make sense. Mr. Wang said:

First, tell students the importance of reflection and checking answers. Second, teach students the procedure of solving problems and checking answers. Third, encourage and praise students for not making errors in the solution; for example, give those students small gifts or put their name on the bulletin board.

Ms. Yian would take the same approach:

(1) Have students act as a little "doctor" to check the "illness" of their math work. (2) Have students act as a little teacher to grade their math work. (3) Have students substitute answers in the original equation and check it. (4) Give praise to students who do a good job.

Ms. Lu also encouraged her students to check their answers to see if they matched the original problem. In the same way as Ms. Yian, Ms. Lu expected her students to become careful "mathematics doctors."

Mrs. Wang developed the following rules for students to reflect on their answers and solutions:

(1) Both sides of a ratio should have the same relationship. (2) Apply the method of solving proportions and solve correctly. (3) Use the substitution method to check the answer.

Ms. Zhou agreed with Ms. Wang, but she also would have her students play with small sticks and use sticks to set up the right proportion if some students have difficulties understanding. Ms. Jian would also teach students to estimate answers.

Two teachers preferred providing students opportunities to discuss and share their ideas with groups. Ms. Sheng said that having students talk about how they solved a problem would not only promote reflection, but also broaden students' thinking and outlook on mathematics. Ms. Dong shared the following approach:

> (1) Have students explain their methods and compare their methods with others. (2) Have students describe the meaning of each expression when they evaluate their work. (3) Have students compare their answers with the correct answer and find their own strong points and mistakes.

Ms. Dong's approach encourages students to engage in the dynamic process of communication, reasoning, evaluation, and reflection.

In conclusion, there are similarities and differences in promoting students' thinking in mathematics between the U.S. and Chinese teachers. Both groups are able to provide examples and activities that focus on student thinking; however, the U.S. teachers tend to use concrete or pictorial models, charts, pictures, and manipulatives to promote students' thinking; the Chinese teachers tend to encourage students' abstract thinking by developing students' reflection and using procedures and rules. Teachers' responses in this study show that Chinese teachers tend to use the algebraic approach more than U.S. teachers in solving proportion problems.

NCTM (2000) views communication as an essential part of mathematics teaching and learning. "Reflection and communication are intertwined processes in mathematics learning" (NCTM 2000, 61). In this study, the U.S. teachers tended to provide students with opportunities to discuss and share their ideas. Chinese teachers also encouraged students' thinking and communication, but focused on developing students' reflection, where students check and analyze their work and thinking. Indeed, reflection helps students reorganize knowledge and find their errors by themselves. Importantly, reflection develops a deep understanding and fosters good learning habits. Chinese teachers encourage their students to think about problem solving, to substitute their answers into the original equations, and to check answers to see if they make sense. Reflection has been viewed as a critical learning strategy constantly taught in mathematics classrooms in China. The importance of reflection was noted by Fennema and Romberg (1999), who state that reflection plays an important role in solving problems, and a critical factor of reflection is that teachers recognize and value reflection. Chinese teachers like Ms. Wang and Ms. Lu in this study encouraged students to be a "mathematics doctor," which means to reflect and to examine the errors in problem solving. They also value reflection by rewarding students who do well in checking procedures and answers.

CHAPTER 5

Teachers' Beliefs about Mathematics Teaching and Learning

I feel that if children know how and why a concept works, they can discover the procedure using conceptual understanding.

—Ms. Griffin, U.S. teacher

Explaining well on the typical problem will help students gain a thorough understanding. It seems that the students only solve one problem, but actually students master the method of one whole type of problem.

—Ms. Gao, Chinese teacher

Mathematics education in different countries is strongly influenced by cultural and social factors and philosophies, which result in different educational systems. These factors and philosophies build the foundation of teaching goals, beliefs, expectations, and methods, and they are influenced by one another. As Thompson (1992) suggested, complex relationship between beliefs and teaching in the social context embeds values, beliefs, and philosophical leanings in the educational system.

Many countries view the beliefs of mathematics teachers as having a powerful impact on their teaching (Ernest 1989). To discover the major influence in teaching, researchers in the United States have focused since 1980 on the beliefs of teachers about mathematics teaching and learning. Researchers believe that understanding teaching from the teacher's perspective is to understand teachers' beliefs about education with which they define their work (Nespor 1987).

For more than 2,000 years the Chinese have followed Confucius (551–479 B.C.) as the father of Chinese education (Ashmore and Cao 1997). One belief of Confucianism in learning is that to acquire knowledge, one needs to ask questions (学问), and to gain new knowledge, one needs to review prior knowledge (问故而知新). For example, the whole classic work of *Arithmetic of Nine Chapters* in the Tang dynasty (A.D. 618–907) shows the characteristics of a sequencing of questions, answers, and principles. The center of this instructional model consists of the questions, and the emphasis is on the computations, which has had a significant influence on mathematics education in China. In contrast, U.S. mathematics education has been influenced by European philosophers and mathematicians with a variety of beliefs, such as Plato's rationalist view and Aristotle's 4th-century experimentalist. For instance, NCTM (1989, 2000) has supported the notion of mathematics as a dynamic process and structure rather than a product, since the 1980s. The discrepant views in history and philosophy on mathematics education between the United States and China reflect the divergent thinking about mathematics in different cultural contexts, and produce distinct belief systems.

Recently a number of studies have focused on the transition of mathematics teachers' beliefs and practices (Cooney and Shealy 1997; Fennema et al. 1996). These studies demonstrate that teaching practices embody teachers' beliefs, which are a reflection of their own values, experiences, and cultural background. Therefore, the beliefs of teaching act as filters to reflect teachers' views of teaching (Kagan 1992). However, there are no clear-cut answers to important questions such as: How do we cultivate the congruent relationship between teachers' beliefs and their teaching practice? How does belief play a role in making the transition in mathematics teaching? How do teachers internalize their beliefs? How and to what degree do cultural factors influence teachers' beliefs? What is the relationship between teachers' pedagogical content knowledge and beliefs? In order to address the above questions, it is necessary to study teachers' beliefs and their impact in depth and to compare the differences and impacts in different cultural perspectives.

FOUR ASPECTS OF TEACHERS' BELIEFS

Eight questions (see table 5.1) were designed to investigate teachers' beliefs about mathematics education as well as their understanding of the role of teachers' pedagogical content knowledge. Tables 5.2–5.5 display the percentages of two groups of teachers' responses according to the following four aspects.

In this study, teachers' beliefs consist of four main aspects: Goals of teaching, primary focus on teaching mathematics, importance of teachers' knowledge, and planning for instruction. These four aspects of teachers' beliefs relate to each other and play an important role in teachers' pedagogical content knowledge, which is vital for effective teaching. Table 5.1 shows the essential components of each aspect of teachers' beliefs corresponding to the eight questions about teachers' beliefs.

With a list of teaching goals in mind, teachers understand their primary focus in teaching, and they design and use various approaches in classrooms. To help all students learn mathematics successfully, teachers try to find an effective teaching method to meet individual students' needs. Furthermore, to teach effectively, teachers should enhance not

Table 5.1.   Categories for Describing Four Aspects of Teachers' Beliefs about Mathematics Teaching and Learning

Four Aspects of Teachers' Beliefs	Essential Components	Question Number
Goals of teaching	Goal of teaching in general	1
	Goal of teaching math	1
Primary focus on teaching mathematics	Primary focus	2
	Effective teaching methods	3
	Meet individual students' needs	4
Importance of teachers' knowledge	Know students' thinking	5
	Promote students' ability in thinking	5
	Knowledge of math content and math teaching	6
	Approaches to enhancing knowledge of math teaching	6
Grading students' homework and planning for instruction	Importance of assigning homework	7
	Approaches to grading homework	7
	Approaches to planning for math instruction	8
	Time spent on planning instruction	8

only content knowledge, but also pedagogical content knowledge, including knowledge of students' thinking.

Understanding students' thinking can be achieved through many approaches. One of the most important approaches is to grade students' homework. From grading homework, a teacher can fully assess students' weaknesses and strengths, which inform the teacher in planning for instruction according to students' needs.

THE GOALS OF TEACHING

> Math should be taught in a manner that shows math in real-life situations. If students do not see validity in learning, they have no connection.
>
> —Ms. Jenkins, U.S. teacher

> The goal of teaching is to have students learn mathematics knowledge and be able to apply this knowledge to analyze and solve the problems. Furthermore, teachers need to train students in the ability of logical thinking and the concept of spiral.
>
> —Ms. Zheng, Chinese teacher

QUESTION 1

What is the primary goal of teaching? What is the goal of mathematics teaching according to your point of view?

The Goal of Teaching in General

Table 5.2 shows that the U.S teachers provided various responses about the goal of teaching: 25 percent of the U.S. teachers believe that the primary goal of teaching is to teach students knowledge and skills; another 25 percent believe that the goal of teaching is to help students succeed in society; 15 percent reported that the goal of teaching is to cultivate students to be productive, responsible, and educated citizens; while 11 percent stated that the goal of education is to support students to become lifelong learners. These various responses reflect the diverse

Table 5.2.   Percentage of U.S. and Chinese Teachers for Each Component of Response of Question 1

Aspect of Teachers' Beliefs	Essential Components	Problem Number	U.S. %	China %
Goals of teaching	*Goal of teaching in general*			
	1. Increase confidence and self-esteem	1	28	0
	2. Be lifelong learners	1	11	6
	3. Be productive, responsible, disciplined, and educated citizens	1	15	28
	4. Teach general knowledge, methods, and skills	1	25	31
	5. Succeed in society or real world	1	25	34
	6. Provide equal opportunity to every child	1	11	0
	Goal of teaching math			
	1. Learn math with interest and fun	1	7	19
	2. Teach learning methods	1	0	28
	3. Teach math in real-life situations and connect math to concrete models	1	30	0
	4. Solve problems and apply math in the real world	1	22	63
	5. Gain math knowledge and skill	1	22	72
	6. Enhance students' critical thinking and logical reasoning ability	1	15	69
	7. Enhance the abilities of creativity, discovery, and exploration	1	4	6

Note: N = 28 for each type of response for the U.S. teachers. N = 33 for each type of response for the Chinese teachers. Each individual teacher response could be coded more than once, resulting in total percentages greater than 100 for each question.

belief systems in the United States. The significant difference is that 11 percent of the U.S. teachers claim that education should provide equal opportunities to all children and that every child can learn, compared to 0 percent of such responses from Chinese teachers, and 28 percent of the U.S. teachers believe that the goal of education is to increase confidence and self-esteem, compared to 0 percent of such responses from Chinese teachers.

These different answers reflect the degree of individualism in the two cultures. For example, seven U.S. teachers indicated that the primary goal of education is to teach students knowledge and skills. With such knowledge and skills, "they can survive in the real world" (Ms. Caldwell's words). Ms. Davis extended this point to students' needs, saying, "provide each student with as much knowledge as meets his ability." Ms. Wood realized the challenges that students will face in the future: "[Education] is to prepare young people for the challenges they will have, so they have the necessary skills that will enable them to meet things we don't even know about."

In order to help students solve problems in everyday life, Ms. Parker would like to teach students problem solving in order to

> teach people how to analyze every situation faced and to try to find the right solution by looking at the same problem from different views, and learning that you could have so many different ways to solve it. [Teachers should supply] every student with knowledge for everyday life.

Seven other U.S. teachers also emphasized the notion that education should "prepare students to be successful in life." Four teachers interpreted "to be successful in life" as "to be productive citizens." Ms. Ross believes the goal of education is "to produce productive, effective members of society," and Ms. William believes "the big picture goal is to produce or assist students to develop into responsible, educated citizens."

Three teachers believe that education is a lifelong learning process. "The primary goal of education is to prepare kids/adults to be lifelong learners. As long as you are learning, you are growing," said Ms. Hanks. She added, education should "provide everybody an equal opportunity to learn the material, to be able to use the material in their everyday life." In addition, Ms. Farris and Ms. Owen also believe, "Every child can learn when given a variety of methods and confidence." Six other U.S. teachers noted the importance of increasing confidence and self-esteem through education. Ms. Anderson explained:

> [The goal of education is] to increase the ability, confidence, self-esteem, and societal productivity of every student even if only by the slightest amount, to locate and fill in gaps in knowledge and lead the student to a higher level of knowledge.

In contrast, for the same question, Chinese teachers have limited dimensions in terms of goal of education. They focused on three areas: 28 percent of the responses from Chinese teachers indicated that the goal of education is to produce productive citizens; 34 percent stated that the goal of education is to help students to succeed in society; and

31 percent of Chinese teachers stated that the goal of education is to teach students knowledge and skills. For instance, Mr. Zhao said, "The original point of education practice is to produce a certain kind of person, so the goal of education should be the objective of cultivating people." Ms. Xui agreed that the goal of education is "to train qualified citizens."

Ten Chinese teachers argued the necessity of teaching students knowledge and skills to be productive citizens. Ms. Bao said, "Besides learning the principles of being a good citizen, students need to learn as much knowledge as they can in order to develop in all areas." Ms. Fang and Ms. Wang pointed out that "the goal of education is not only to teach students knowledge, but also to enhance their abilities to be socially independent and secure." Other teachers believe that the "learning method" is significant and the goal of education is not only to teach knowledge but more importantly also to teach them how to learn. Ms. Xui quoted the Chinese saying "teach how to fish rather than give a fish." This quote reflects an important view of teaching in China.

Eleven Chinese teachers believe that the goal of education is to help students succeed in society. For most teachers "succeed in society" means to become a productive human resource for the nation and to be able to enhance the quality of the whole nation. In order to achieve that, the goal of education is to help students fully develop in four areas: ideology, morality, schooling, and discipline. This addresses the Chinese goal of education as a whole: 教育. In Chinese 教 means teaching students and 育 means cultivating students' good mind habits and moral characters.

The Goal of Teaching Mathematics

In response to the question regarding the goal of mathematics education, the U.S. teachers had various responses. About 30 percent of the U.S. teachers agreed that mathematics should be taught in real-life situations and that mathematics should be connected to concrete models; 22 percent indicated that the goal of mathematics is to teach students how to solve problems in the real world; 22 percent considered the goal of education to be to help students gain mathematics knowledge and skills; and 15 percent thought that the goal of mathematics education should be to enhance students' critical thinking and logical reasoning ability.

Chinese teachers' responses, however, addressed their focuses on three areas: gain math knowledge and skills, enhance critical thinking and logical reasoning ability, and solve and apply math in the real world. Table 5.2 shows that 72 percent of responses indicated a belief that the goal of mathematics education is to help students gain math knowledge and skills; 69 percent of responses showed a belief that the goal of mathematics education should be the enhancement of students' critical thinking and logical reasoning ability, compared to only 15 percent of the U.S. teachers. Interestingly, 28 percent of Chinese responses indicated the importance of teaching "learning methods"; no U.S. teachers mentioned this goal. However, no Chinese teachers considered teaching math in real-life situations and connecting mathematics to concrete models as being important, as compared to 30 percent of the U.S. responses that did. These differences indicate that Chinese teachers know the importance of the learning method but ignore connections to concrete models, while U.S. teachers like to use concrete models but do not pay attention to learning methods. The following responses reflect the similarities and differences between the two groups of teachers.

For instance, Ms. Jenkins suggested, "Math should be taught in a manner that shows math in real-life situations. If students do not see validity in learning, they have no connection." Ms. Davis also claimed, "Mathematics education's goal is to provide a concrete way of problem solving." The reason to start with the concrete is that "Children understand the concept from the concrete to the abstract," said Ms. Flores. Ms. Wood further explained, "If you do mathematics in isolation, it becomes very boring and dry to the students. Making the connection makes mathematics easy."

Making mathematics interesting and fun to learn is also the focus of some U.S. teachers. To Ms. Waller, the goal of mathematics education is to help students learn and become interested in mathematics. The goal of mathematics to Ms. Larson is "to get students to learn math, enjoy it, and be motivated to learn it."

Some U.S. teachers thought that mathematics education should focus on strengthening problem-solving and thinking ability. Ms. Thomas's response indicated that mathematics education teaches thinking and problem-solving strategies that spread to all areas of life. Ms. Nelson believes, "The goal of math education is to teach students how to think logically, to discipline their minds, and to develop solution strategies involving mathematics." To Ms. Scott, helping students understand concepts and their applications is very important. Ms. Smith agreed with this point of view: "The goal of mathematics education is to reach understanding."

To Chinese teachers, gaining mathematics knowledge and skill is an essential part of the goal of mathematics education. About 23 percent of the teachers discussed this point in their responses. For example, Ms. Zheng remarked that the goal of mathematics education is "to have students learn mathematics knowledge and be able to apply this knowledge to analyze and solve the problems [and] . . . to train students in the abilities of logical thinking and the spatial concept." Ms. Dong agreed with Ms. Zhen: "The goal of mathematics education is that under teachers' direction in the classroom, students learn basic mathematics knowledge and computation methods, and they are able to apply what they have learned in the classroom to their daily life."

In recognizing the importance of gaining knowledge, 69 percent of Chinese teachers also stated that enhancing the ability of logical and critical thinking is a key component of mathematics education. For instance, Mr. Zhao would focus on increasing students' ability to think and the character of thinking. Ms. Jing interpreted students' thinking ability as "thinking things mathematically." Ms. Wu would like to train students in good learning attitudes, learning habits, and logical thinking. Ms. Yian would teach students learning methods instead of mathematics knowledge only. However, only 19 percent of Chinese teachers expressed the view that learning mathematics with interest and in a fun fashion is very important for students, and that it would increase students' abilities in observation, imagination, analysis, and summarization. Ms. Wang's views summarized the goal of Chinese mathematics education in general as "to have students understand knowledge of numbers and objects, to train in the abilities of computation, thinking, the spatial concept, observation, manipulation, and simple problem solving in the real world."

In conclusion, there are differences in the beliefs of the goals of education between U.S. and Chinese teachers. Most U.S. teachers believed that the goal of education is to teach students knowledge and increase students' confidence and self-esteem by providing an equal opportunity to all children, while the majority of Chinese teachers thought that the goal of education is not only to teach students knowledge but also to help students succeed in society, which means becoming a productive human resource for the country in order to enhance the quality of the whole nation.

U.S. teachers believe that mathematics should be taught in real-life situations and should be connected to concrete models so students can gain mathematical knowledge and apply it in the real world, while to Chinese teachers, the goal of mathematics education is to teach "learning methods," to help students gain mathematical knowledge, to enhance students' critical thinking and logical reasoning abilities, and to apply mathematics in the real world.

PRIMARY FOCUS ON TEACHING MATHEMATICS

> I always introduce things from a conceptual understanding. Then we go to skill development in terms of manipulating the numbers. I frequently have to go back to the concept.
>
> —Ms. Wood, U.S. teacher

> Only in the procedural development are students able to analyze, observe, discover, further reinforce knowledge, and apply knowledge to solve problems.
>
> —Ms. Wang, Chinese teacher

QUESTION 2

What is your primary focus in teaching mathematics: conceptual understanding or procedural development? Why?

Primary Focus

Table 5.3 shows that most U.S. teachers (41 percent) focus on both conceptual understanding and procedural development in mathematics teaching. However, some teachers (33 percent) emphasize conceptual understanding, and other teachers (22 percent) focus on pro-

Table 5.3. Percentage of U.S. and Chinese Teachers for Each Component of Response of Questions 2, 3, and 4

Aspect of Teachers' Beliefs	Essential Components	Question Number	U.S. %	China %
Primary focus on teaching mathematics	*Primary focus*			
	1. Conceptual understanding	2	33	31
	2. Procedural (skill) development	2	22	38
	3. Both conceptual understanding and procedural development	2	41	31
	Effective teaching methods			
	1. Teacher-centered lectures	3	15	3
	2. Student-centered inquiry	3	44	81
	3. Both methods	3	40	16
	Meet individual students' needs			
	1. Fewer than 35 students	4	93	3
	2. More than 50 students	4	0	97
	3. Give different assignments	4	19	75
	4. Motivate students	4	7	44
	5. Use different teaching methods	4	63	22
	6. Tutor students	4	15	9

Note: N = 28 for each type of response for the U.S. teachers. N = 33 for each type of response for the Chinese teachers. Each individual teacher response could be coded more than once, resulting in total percentages greater than 100 for each question.

cedural development. In contrast, Chinese teachers' responses seemed to distribute evenly among three areas: 38 percent of Chinese teachers focus on procedural development in mathematics teaching, 31 percent focus on conceptual understanding, and 31 percent use both ways to teach mathematics.

To explain the importance of conceptual understanding, the U.S. teachers considered a connection in conceptual understanding. "Students need to be able to make connections with something, it is important to see how things work." Ms. Davis explained her use of "why" for emphasizing conceptual understanding: "Conceptual understanding is my primary focus. A student needs to understand 'why' in order to apply the concepts learned to the next objectives." Ms. Griffin also concentrated on "how and why":

> I feel that if children know how and why a concept works, they can discover the procedure used to solve problems. I don't believe concepts are truly learned if they don't have personal meaning through conceptual un-

derstanding. When students have to solve the problems as adults, the procedure won't be given to them. They must understand the concept before the problem can effectively be solved.

Ms. Hanks admitted that she is more conceptual, but she recognized the importance of procedural development:

> The problem is you don't get to do as much of what you like because we have so much material to be covered in a short period of time. You have to also follow procedure or you're not going to get it right either. If you're not good at the basics then you can't apply what you know, and you can't use the materials because your basics are weak.

Six U.S. teachers believe that the primary focus in teaching mathematics is procedural development. Ms. Jenkins explained the reason for concentrating on procedural development is to help students build connections: "I believe that skills should be developed first and then connected with concepts in real-life, practical situations. Students must personally connect with learning to retain and find it useful." Ms. Goodwin uses procedural development: "because of the time limit and age of my students I introduce a conceptual approach but expect them to be proficient using procedure while understanding concepts." Ms. Madison emphasizes skills and drills for making students remember the knowledge they have learned. However, Ms. Smith does not focus on procedural development for all her students:

> In academic (regular class), I [use] procedure development because the students do not usually care about understanding. In pre-AP (honors classes) I use conceptual understanding because of the depth of teaching.

To Ms. Smith, not all students need to understand math concepts; only those in honors classes need to develop conceptual understanding. This misconception and low expectation lead her to teach only procedure in regular class.

Most U.S. teachers' responses focused on both conceptual understanding and procedural development. Ms. Nelson said, "My primary focus is teaching conceptual understanding without sacrificing skills. I emphasize connections between arithmetic and algebra." Ms. Larson explained why she focuses on both ways of teaching: "I combine conceptual and procedural learning. I believe that students learn from hands-on, but students must have drill and practice to reinforce the concepts learned and to be able to apply the information in other areas." Ms. Parker also teaches "procedure development and supplies it with conceptual understanding whenever possible."

Some teachers prefer to work on the procedure first and then go to concept. For example, Ms. Loving "often introduces basic skills with manipulatives. Once we get those skills then we can work with the concepts." However, Ms. Wood likes to start with concepts first: "I always introduce things from a conceptual understanding. Then we go to skill development in terms of manipulating the numbers. I frequently have to go back to the concept. Like what does this really mean?" Ms. Williams also starts on the concepts. She believes that

> they need to know the concept. They can't arrive at the concept at the same time, which is the difficult part. So you also have to do procedure. I continue to go back to conceptual understanding even if I taught procedure. I always start off on a conceptual level, never a procedural. Then after we develop the concept, then I'll go in to the skill. And we'll continue to go back and forth.

Teachers like Ms. Wood and Ms. Williams do not separate conceptual understanding and procedural development, and they knew the connections between these two important areas in learning mathematics.

It is interesting to note that to Chinese teachers, the concept of procedure is more than a series of steps followed in a regular definite order. To them, "procedure" is a "learning process" in which students engage in comparing, analyzing, applying, and synthesizing the learning process. Therefore, a number of Chinese teachers believe that in procedural development, conceptual understanding and thinking abilities can be fully developed. It seems that for U.S. teachers, to teach "procedure" is to teach steps only.

Twelve Chinese teachers believe that procedural development is the main part of teaching. Six teachers believe that procedural development could increase students' thinking ability. Ms. Chen explained her view about using procedural development:

Because I think that mathematics is the gymnastics of thinking; to teach mathematics is to train thinking. The training of procedure in problem solving displays the process of students' thinking. So procedure development helps the teacher know the students' thinking, and helps students form good character of thinking.

Ms. Wang believes in procedural development:

After students understand concepts, the structure of knowledge has changed, the ability of thinking has increased, and a basic skill has been mastered. But students cannot apply it yet; only in procedural development are students able to analyze, observe, discover, further reinforce knowledge, and apply knowledge to solve problems.

To Ms. Wang, procedural development is to analyze, observe, discover, and apply knowledge.

Ms. Gao agreed that the training of procedural development could promote students' thinking, but it also could strengthen deep understanding of concepts. She said:

The number of problems is not necessarily many, but they should be fine problems. Explaining well on the typical problem will help students gain a thorough understanding. It seems that students only solve one problem, but actually students master the method of one whole type of problems.

Ten Chinese teachers focus on conceptual understanding in their teaching. Most of them believe that conceptual understanding is the basis for learning. Ms. Xiu said that the concept is the origin; if one confuses concepts, success can only be achieved halfway, even with maximum effort.

Ms. Dong presented her opinion about conceptual understanding:

The concepts are foundations; all the difficult problems are constructed by basic concepts. From the small [concepts] we can see the large [concepts]; if more attention is paid to procedure without the understanding of concepts, it will be difficult to understand a problem and to solve it.

Ms. Pan agreed with Ms. Gao's view that only by understanding the concepts and knowing the deep meaning of concepts could one use unchanged knowledge to deal with changing knowledge. This view reflects Confucian philosophy: By understanding one concept you will understand three other concepts connected with the one you know (舉一反三). This is also the goal of learning for Chinese students: students are expected to use knowledge learned from teachers to reflect and extend to new knowledge.

Mr. Zhou believes that students' understanding the original concept and the trend of their knowledge will produce knowledge transformation in which skills will be formed and thinking ability and creativity will be increased.

Ms. Fang described the process of conceptual understanding from procedural development: "Conceptual understanding is abstracted from students' manipulative exercises, comparison, analysis, and summary. Then it involves simple deduction and induction. Concepts are the fundamental basis for students to understand and master mathematics."

Table 5.3 shows that 31 percent of Chinese teachers stress both conceptual understanding and procedural development in their mathematics teaching. Ms. Zheng uses both approaches: "I focus on the conceptual understanding first, then I give some problems to train in procedural development, so students can gain further understanding of concepts."

Mr. Zhao explained why he uses both ways of teaching. He said, "I pay attention to both conceptual understanding and procedural development in teaching mathematics. Concepts are the basis of knowledge, while the skill of problem solving and the procedure of problem solving are the capacities of mastering and applying knowledge."

However, Ms. Zheng suggested, "do not emphasize any one way; both of them complement the other." Ms. Jian agreed: "Because K–12 is the period of building foundations of knowledge, we need to attach importance to 'two basics' at the same time; we need to train students' thinking ability, so students will have the skill for creativity."

In summary, there are differences in the focus of teaching mathematics between the U.S. teachers and Chinese teachers. U.S. teachers focus on both conceptual understanding and procedural development in teaching mathematics, but they tend to separate conceptual understanding and procedural development into two disjoint dimensions;

Chinese teachers recognize the interplay between these two areas and believe that conceptual knowledge could be abstracted from procedural development, and that the main goal of conceptual understanding and procedural development is to develop students' thinking abilities.

QUESTION 3

What do you think is the more effective teaching method of teaching mathematics for your students: teacher-centered lectures and discussion or student-centered inquiry and working in groups? Why?

Effective Teaching Methods

Table 5.3 shows that 44 percent of the U.S. teachers believe that the more effective method of teaching mathematics is student-centered inquiry; only 15 percent prefer teacher-centered lectures; and 40 percent prefer both ways of teaching mathematics. Meanwhile, 81 percent of Chinese teachers believe that student-centered inquiry is the more effective method of teaching mathematics. However, in reality, few teachers use a student-centered way of teaching (see the next chapter).

A U.S. teacher, Ms. Griffin, explained the reason for using student-centered inquiry:

> Students are active participants in the learning process. I believe students learn best by doing; otherwise the brain will not often link to prior knowledge or experience. Student-centered inquiry also provides constant opportunities for thinking and problem solving—the two skills needed for solving problems in real-life situations.

Ms. Ridgway likes student-centered learning because "it promotes their thinking." Ms. Scott prefers student-centered learning because students gain understanding in it:

> I think student-centered inquiry is more effective for teaching students mathematics; they gain a deeper understanding of the concept through

this method. The students seem to be more interested and more attentive when this method is used.

Ms. Jenkins thinks that student-centered learning promotes a positive attitude: "Student-centered inquiry promotes self-esteem, assertiveness, confidence, cooperation, and students are able to solve higher level problems by bringing in a combination of learning styles and knowledge."

Ms. Parker, however, believes that it "depends on the kinds of students you have and the lesson you teach, but generally the student-centered inquiries are more effective." For Ms. Smith, the size of the class is a factor in deciding which teaching strategy is best to use: "Because our class is so large (30–35 students), teacher-centered lectures and discussion are the best." Ms. Madison expressed her view: "[I like] teacher-centered lectures. Not all students learn from discovery learning." Ms. Nelson also prefers the teacher-centered way: "My most effective method has been teacher-centered lecturing. I do a lot of group competition because most students enjoy time limitations and this prevents me from having discovery groups as much as I would like."

Some teachers would like to use both ways of teaching. Ms. Farris said, "Kids need variety," and Ms. Larson agreed, "Both are necessary because of different types of students and learners." "Kids need many ways to learn," Ms. Owen commented. Ms. Thomas also believes that all methods should be combined to keep students interested. Ms. Ross would use both ways, depending on the topic.

Table 5.3 shows that most Chinese teachers like student-centered teaching methods. They know that students are the main focus of learning, and the student-centered approach is the learning process by which students play a role and experience the learning. The reason for using student-centered learning, according to Ms. Shun, is the following:

Student-centered inquiry, exploration, and group discussion are more effective methods. Because students are the main body of learning, using student-centered approaches will encourage students to gain the initiative and to engage in learning actively. It also can increase students' abilities in multiple ways.

In addition, Ms. Yian noted the importance of students' own experience: "Since students experienced learning by themselves in the student-centered method, they appreciate the results of learning and of course they grasp the knowledge fully."

Furthermore, Ms. Xia realized that students could explore problem solving on their own in the student-centered activities, and this would give them the chance to discuss and solve problems.

Ms. Wang summarized the advantages of using a student-centered method: it stimulates active thinking, encourages inquiry and creativity, cultivates the spirit of cooperative learning, increases the capability of overcoming difficulty, and enhances the ability to learn.

Some teachers, however, have concerns about student-centered approaches in China. Ms. Dong said,

> According to the teaching situation in China now, teacher-centered learning is more suited to classroom teaching, because some students are lacking the ability for self-learning. Of course, student-centered methods are the direction of the future. It increases students' learning interests and helps students master learning methods.

Ms. Wang argued, "The goals of teaching are to accomplish the teaching of knowledge, enhance ability, and train thinking." According to her view, the teacher-centered method can only teach knowledge; it does not function too much in enhancing ability and in training thinking.

Some teachers prefer to use both ways of teaching. Ms. Fan's answer addressed this point:

> I like to use both ways in teaching. Student inquiry and exploration represent initiative learning from students. It is more focused and more suited to an individual student. Group discussion is easier to understand for students and will increase the ability to learn. However, the teacher's direction is very important; it always functions as a spark in the dark.

Ms. Zhou's view of the goals of teaching is the same: paying attention to the main body of learning, and at the same time bringing the teacher's role into full play to achieve the best results from teaching.

Ms. Qian would use both ways, but would choose the particular way

according to the content of the new knowledge. She said, "I would select the way by the character of the new knowledge; some knowledge
needs the teacher to explain and discuss it; another may require students to inquire, explore, and discuss in groups."

In summary, the U.S. and Chinese teachers are able to identify what
they consider to be the more effective methods of teaching mathematics. The U.S. teachers were split on which method they used most: One
group preferred student-centered instruction while the others liked to
use both student-centered and teacher-centered instruction. However,
most Chinese teachers acknowledged that the student-centered approach was more effective for them. Only a few Chinese teachers liked
both ways of teaching.

QUESTION 4

How many students are in each of your classes? How do you deal with
students' individual differences in your teaching?

Meet Individual Students' Needs

Table 5.3 shows that 93 percent of the U.S. teachers have fewer
than 35 students in their classes, while 97 percent of Chinese teachers have more than 50 students in their classes and only 3 percent of
Chinese teachers have fewer than 35 students in their classes. The difference in classroom size has produced different ways of dealing with
students' individual differences. Table 5.3 indicates that the U.S.
teachers deal with students' individual differences using a variety of
approaches: 63 percent use diverse teaching methods, 19 percent give
different assignments, 15 percent tutor students, and 7 percent use
motivation.

However, table 5.3 shows Chinese teachers deal with students' individual differences mainly in two ways: 75 percent give different assignments, while 44 percent use motivation. Only 22 percent of responses indicated that teachers deal with students' individual
differences by using different teaching methods, and 9 percent tutor
students.

Most U. S. teachers use different teaching methods to deal with individual differences. For instance, Ms. Larson "varies her teaching styles as much as possible." Ms. Caldwell also "varies her activities" to fit students' needs. Ms. Owen "shows different ways" in teaching. Ms. Parker varies her level of questions in teaching: "I teach on all levels of thinking by going deep in my inquiry questioning, and testing on the average level and adding difficult questions as a bonus."

Ms. Griffin described her ways of dealing with students' individual differences:

> My class sizes range from 15 to 33. I spend a lot of time interacting with the students during independent practice. [I do not give students work to complete] at home unless I have seen them solve at least half of the problems. This gives me a chance to remedy many individual problems. I also teach each concept using more than one strategy. I will verbally give an explanation, while also doing a tactile activity. Students all learn in a variety of ways, so concepts should be taught in a variety of ways.

Ms. Smith varies her teaching methods also: "I have 6 classes; the class size for each is 21, 23, 25, 19, 19, and 23. I try to use a variety of methods in teaching and I incorporate as many hands-on activities as possible. I always try to give students a 'visual.'"

Ms. Elliott also likes to connect visual models in everyday life:

> [I have] 20–25 students in each class. Special education students get study guides, special seating, modified tests, and extra time. Basic students have many points added to their work and in all of the above I tend to use everyday experiences in my lessons—rockets, cooking, and so on.

Ms. Nelson develops personal relationships with kids but does not vary her teaching style much. Ms. Ridgway "gets to know them, and vice versa." Ms. Davis explained how she interacts with students in order to help them:

> [My] regular class sizes are 26, 31, and 30; pre-algebra class sizes are 28 and 24. After lecture they sometimes work in small groups. The groups answer questions; I go around the room and help individual students and there's tutoring after school. We like note taking but do not insist on it.

Ms. Jenkins often has tutorials for her students, she said:

> [I have] 24–26 students in each class. [I do tutoring] on an individual basis, and after-school tutoring 3–4 times per week. I call it "study group" and "get those students ahead of the class." When a concept is taught, it is then reviewed for them. They come to this voluntarily, and each time I have about 20 students who attend. Most need the extra help; some just need the reassurance.

Ms. Anderson contacts the parents to discuss the students' needs:

> [I have] an average of 30 students in each classroom. Every problem question during class has a particular student's "name on it." I will sometimes give a couple of kids different (hard or easier) [problems]. Some students must come for tutoring. Some must be tutors. All parents are contacted to discuss individual needs.

Compared to the U.S. teachers, Chinese teachers have more than 50 students in each class and they like to deal with individual students' needs by designing different levels of practice problems and asking different types of questions during the class. For example, Ms. Bao teaches the examples to the whole class and give students practice at different levels. Ms. Qian believes that being patient and careful are the principal elements in treating individual differences; she designs these different levels of practice to have "low-level students eat well and high-level students eat fully." This means that high-level students are still challenged and low-level students can understand. Ms. Pan described her approach to the students' differences:

> There are 59 students in my class. In the teaching of mathematics, I pay attention to teach students in accordance with their aptitude. For example, in teaching, mainly I have basic problems and a few enrichment problems. I give basic problems to the students who have a difficulty in learning, and I praise them for answering questions and promoting their interests in learning. After class, I tutor students who need help. I also use different styles to praise or criticize students according to individual personality traits.

Ms. Chen also arranges different methods of teaching to meet individual students' needs:

> There are 51 students in the class. In order to motivate students, usually I let a weak student answer easy problems, and I have careless students answer the problems that are easily confused. For difficult problems, I have two to four students form a group to discuss these problems. Students will learn from each other in discussions and develop a sense of cooperation.

Ms. Wang uses group learning also:

> I group students to include low-, middle-, and high-level students, so students can help each other in discussions. When I ask various types and different levels of questions, I select different levels of students to answer them. I never discourage students when they try to answer questions; I always try to encourage different opinions.

In summary, both U.S. and Chinese teachers use many ways to approach individual differences. However, there are differences between the U.S. and Chinese teachers regarding their methods of dealing with students' needs. The U.S. teachers tend to vary teaching methods to fit the needs of individual students, while Chinese teachers tend to design different assignments and different levels of questions to meet the differences among students.

THE IMPORTANCE OF TEACHERS' KNOWLEDGE

> It is very important for a teacher to understand students' thinking so that she knows how to explain the concept in a way that the student is more likely to understand.
>
> —Ms. Scott, U.S. teacher

> With richer mathematics knowledge, teachers can instruct at a higher level, transfer a deeper knowledge in simple ways, and use the methods of mathematics thinking in their teaching.
>
> —Ms. Ren, Chinese teacher

QUESTION 5

How important is it that a teacher understands students' thinking in learning mathematics? How do you know about your students' thinking and understanding? How can you promote students' ability to think?

Know Students' Thinking

Table 5.4 shows that U.S. teachers know their students' thinking and understanding through many means: 56 percent of the responses referred to knowing students' thinking from students' explanations and discussion; 41 percent referred to knowing students' thinking by asking students questions. Although most Chinese teachers (72 percent) agreed about knowing students' thinking by explanations and discussion, 63 percent of the responses referred to knowing students' thinking by checking students' homework.

All U.S. teachers in this study believe that it is fundamentally important for a teacher to understand students' thinking and understanding. To Ms. Jenkins, "It is critical to the success of each student that the teacher understand the student's thinking." Ms. Caldwell believes "a teacher needs to understand the students' thinking to know where each student is at." "If you don't know how a student is thinking then it's difficult to help him," said Ms. Davis.

Three teachers pointed out that teachers' understanding students' thinking would help students correct their misconceptions. According to Ms. Griffin:

> I think it is vitally important that a teacher understand students' thinking; a teacher can't effectively remedy a conceptual misunderstanding without knowing what individual students are thinking. All students think and learn differently.

Ms. Elliott had the same view: "It is important to know what they are thinking so that you can teach them using their mistakes and explain why the problem is wrong." Ms. Scott believes "it is very important for a teacher to understand students' thinking so that she knows how to explain the concept in a way that the student is more likely to under-

Table 5.4. Percentage of U.S. and Chinese Teachers for Each Component of Response of Questions 5 and 6

Aspect of Teachers' Beliefs	Essential Components	Question Number	U.S. %	China %
Importance of teachers' knowledge	*Know students' thinking*			
	1. By asking questions	5	41	31
	2. By checking students' work	5	19	63
	3. From tests and quizzes	5	19	6
	4. From students' explanations and discussion	5	56	72
	5. From observation	5	22	9
	6. Through students' journals	5	7	0
	7. Through conversation	3	11	31
	Promote students' ability in thinking			
	1. By asking different questions	5	15	13
	2. By providing activity	5	11	28
	3. By engaging students in inquiry and creativity process	5	7	22
	4. Through cooperative learning	5	22	31
	5. From different levels of practice	5	7	44
	6. By problem solving	5	4	6
	7. By summary and review	5	7	25
	Knowledge of math content and math teaching			
	1. Teach effectively	6	41	84
	2. Understand curriculum and textbook	6	0	13
	3. Understand students' thinking	6	22	16
	Approaches to enhancing knowledge of math teaching			
	1. From in-school services and workshops	6	56	22
	2. From continuing education in college	6	11	44
	3. From independent study	6	33	88
	4. From sharing with colleagues and observing classes	6	11	28

Note: N = 28 for each type of response for the U.S. teachers. N = 33 for each type of response for the Chinese teachers. Each individual teacher response could be coded more than once, resulting in total percentages greater than 100 for each problem.

stand." Based on many years of teaching experience, Ms. Parker said, "You only can teach a student what he or she needs when you know their thinking and already existing knowledge."

Most U.S. teachers in this study would use various methods to know students' thinking. For example, Ms. Parker prefers "talking to them, working on activities with them, and testing them," while Ms. Reed likes to "have activities and summarize what they have learned." She also likes to "provide projects and have students give presentations." Ms. Griffin shared her ways of knowing students' thinking:

> We do mathematics journals in which students must write descriptions of problems or concepts. This explanation provides a lot of insight into the depth of students' understanding. I also ask a lot of why questions: Why does something work or not work?

Ms. Davis likes to ask questions too. "By questioning during the lecture, I've noticed that children solve problems in different ways and get the same answer." Ms. Thomas has her students explain their reasoning for their answers.

Ms. Scott noted the importance of listening: "If you listen to students explain how they got an answer, you can tell a lot about their thinking." In order to get a good response from a student, Ms. Smith suggested: "A development of trust and patience with the student will enable the student to be honest and willing to tell their thinking process."

All Chinese teachers in this study recognized the importance of knowing students' thinking and understanding. They were able to apply different methods to know students' thinking; however, they would also know students' thinking from checking their homework and their explanation of how they solved the problems.

Ms. Ren knows her students' thinking from "learning educational psychology, students' answering questions, and talking with students." Ms. Sheng measures students' thinking from the following: (1) observation during activities, (2) students' explanations, and (3) students' responses on homework.

Besides using the above ways to measure students' thinking, Ms. Li also uses subject review and tests to find out how her students think. Ms. Pan has group discussions and provides tutorials for students. Ms. Bao creates a democratic environment in the classroom, allows more time for student discussion, and offers encouragement and praise for active thinking.

Promote Students' Ability in Thinking

Table 5.4 also indicates that the U.S. teachers would promote students' ability to think in several ways: 22 percent of teachers would use cooperative learning, 15 percent would ask different questions, 11 percent would engage in various activities, 7 percent would use inquiry and creativity, 7 percent would use different levels of practice problems, and 4 percent would promote students' ability to think by problem solving. Although table 5.4 shows that Chinese teachers also would use a variety of approaches, 44 percent of the Chinese teachers' responses refer to promoting students' ability to think using different levels of practice, compared to 7 percent of the U.S. teachers' responses.

Some U.S. teachers would use questions to encourage students' thinking. For example, Ms. Caldwell would promote students' thinking by questions asked and activities given. Ms. Davis would prefer a different type of questions: "If you ask open-ended or leading questions, you encourage the students to think."

Several teachers realized the importance of cooperative learning. Ms. Elliott would challenge students with problem solving and cooperative learning, and Ms. Reed would provide peer tutoring. Ms. Elliott said, "I know what my students understand when they work, by how they work the problems. I can promote their thinking by letting them discuss problems together." Ms. Nelson would also aim to "provide good problems and encourage the students to share solutions." Ms. Thomas and Ms. Waller would have students work with a partner and present their ideas. Ms. Jenkins presented her strategy to promote students' thinking:

> I've found through cooperative learning activities, students are more inclined to take a chance. Once confidence is built through both successes and failures, students are comfortable with learning. I have high expectations for all of my students. Each child has a gift even if it's not math. It is my job to help them use their gift mathematically.

Furthermore, she listed examples of encouraging students' thinking:

> Using real-life experiences: Market—students create, sell, try products, keep a balanced checkbook; learn budgeting and supply/demand concepts. Using presentations (PowerPoint)—using varied strategies keeps students interested in everyday situations; as students see validity in math, they connect with it and synthesize it into their thinking skills. Us-

ing mental math—also a higher-level thinking skill. Using weekly re-view of basic skills.

Ms. Parker would give life-related situations and exciting topics to promote students' thinking.

Although Chinese teachers said they would use different ways to en-courage students' thinking, in the classroom most of them focused on practice problems. For example, Mr. Wang always designs different levels of problems to train students to think. Ms. Dong requires stu-dents to give more solutions to every problem, and asked students to consider different angles for solving the problem. Sometimes, to open wider points of view for students, she gives a simple clue to help stu-dents find a key point.

Ms. Zhen would encourage finding multiple ways to solve a prob-lem. She would evaluate students' work at every step of the procedure in each problem while encouraging positive strategies and explaining the reason for the mistakes. Ms. Pan would also encourage students to solve problems using multiple ways. Ms. Sheng would use the follow-ing ways to promote students' thinking:

1. Lead students to do all kinds of experiments. Have students find a problem and try to solve it in the experiments.
2. Direct students in classifying and summarizing their knowledge.
3. Guide students in independent study.
4. Guide students in organizing knowledge and understanding the re-lationships between different levels of knowledge.

The Chinese teachers would also use different approaches to en-courage students' thinking. For example, Ms. Wu would use the fol-lowing approaches:

1. Design problems at different levels, and train students' thinking ability.
2. Focus on the training of students' oral expression. Require stu-dents not only to know how to do a problem, but also know how to explain it.

3. Train students to do enrichment problems.
4. Have students do manipulative activities, and link math to the real world.

Ms. Li would also have students work on manipulatives. She said:

Have students be active in the classroom, using hands and brain, and use mathematics to encourage students' inquiry. Cultivate students to not simply believe the textbook, to not simply believe the teacher, but always to try to find questions, propose questions, and ask questions to enhance their ability to solve problems. And give more praise.

Ms. Qing designed a method of "five encouragements":

1. Encourage students to do hands-on activities.
2. Encourage students to observe.
3. Encourage students to create and explain the strategies of problem solving.
4. Encourage students to design and prove procedures.
5. Encourage students to imagine.

Ms. Jian would encourage students' thinking by creating a learning environment:

Stimulate students' interest in learning mathematics, encourage students to try, enhance students' confidence, have students discuss and share ideas, encourage students to become masters of learning, and promote students' ability in thinking and creativity.

In brief, there are differences between the two groups of teachers in their approaches to promoting students' thinking. The U.S. teachers would promote students' thinking by various approaches, such as co-operative learning; the majority of Chinese teachers would promote students' thinking by assigning various levels of practices.

There are also differences in the ways teachers gauge understanding in students. The U.S. teachers evaluate students' thinking by asking questions and from student explanations and discussion; Chinese teachers understand students' thinking not only from students' explanations and discussion, but also from checking students' work.

QUESTION 6

How important is it that a teacher has an in-depth understanding of the mathematics being taught? How do you develop and continue to enhance your mathematical knowledge?

Knowledge of Mathematics Content and Mathematics Teaching

Table 5.4 shows that 41 percent of the U.S. teachers' responses indicated that a teacher with an in-depth understanding of both mathematics content and teaching is critical for effective teaching, and 22 percent of the responses showed that a teacher with an in-depth understanding of mathematics content and mathematics teaching would know students' thinking and understanding. However, table 5.4 shows that 84 percent of the Chinese teachers' responses indicated that a teacher with an in-depth understanding of mathematics and teaching would know how to teach mathematics effectively; 16 percent indicated that a teacher with an in-depth understanding of mathematics content would help students' thinking and understanding, while 13 percent indicated that a teacher with an in-depth understanding of mathematics would better understand curriculum and textbooks.

The U.S. teachers recognized the importance of knowledge in mathematics and teaching. For example, Ms. Davis frankly explained: "It is most important that a math teacher have background knowledge in both content and teaching. Not every child will understand the first way you explain a concept, and you need a good math background to explain the same concept another way." In addition, Ms. Griffin was concerned that the lack of understanding of mathematics knowledge and teaching skills would cause a lack of thinking by students:

> The teachers must understand why a concept works or they will be unable to explain to students how the process works. I believe a lack of understanding by the teacher leads to a lack of thinking and thorough understanding by students. The teacher teaches the algorithm and students follow the example.

Ms. Scott said, "It is vital that a teacher have an in-depth understanding of the concepts to be taught." Ms. Ross also agreed: "You can't teach what you don't know effectively."

All Chinese teachers in this study believe that it is very important for a teacher to have an in-depth understanding of the mathematics being taught and mathematics teaching. Most Chinese teachers' beliefs about the pursuit of knowledge are influenced by Chinese culture. For example, to state the reason for continuing learning, 15 Chinese teachers quoted the Chinese saying "If you want to give the students one cup of water, you should have one bucket of water of your own." Ms. Ren said, "With richer mathematics knowledge, teachers can instruct at a higher level, transfer a deeper knowledge in simple ways, and use the methods of mathematics thinking in their teaching." Ms. Pan explained the needs for developing a deep and broad knowledge:

> When students gain knowledge in the classroom, they also actively receive other information and knowledge; their knowledge and the ability to think increase at the same time. Some students are not satisfied to learn knowledge in the classroom; they would like to go deeper and ask different kinds of questions. In order to help students learn more, teachers need to possess a deep and broad knowledge.

Ms. Qian related her mathematics knowledge to her understanding of curriculum, textbooks, and students' thinking. She said, "A teacher with a broad mathematics knowledge will have a deeper understanding of textbooks and will master key points of teaching; furthermore, such a teacher will know more about student thinking." Ms. Gao also had the same view:

> Only when the teacher has a deep understanding of the subject being taught can the teacher have a rich grasp of textbooks. And the teacher will know students better, select a proper way to evaluate, link the different subjects, and construct the whole system of knowledge.

Ms. Yian said, "A teacher does not only need to know how, but also needs to know why." This will enable the teacher to direct learning flexibly and be able to answer all questions. To Mr. Lu, the accuracy of answering questions is very important to a teacher. Only with a sound background of knowledge can the teacher succeed in teaching.

Approaches to Enhancing Knowledge of Mathematics Teaching

Table 5.4 shows that 56 percent of the U.S. teachers continue to enhance their mathematics and teaching knowledge through in-school services and workshops, 33 percent from independent study, 11 percent from college study, and 11 percent from sharing with colleagues and observing classes. In contrast, although table 5.4 shows that Chinese teachers use numerous approaches to develop mathematics knowledge, 88 percent of Chinese teachers' responses indicated that they enhance their mathematics knowledge from independent study, 44 percent from continuing education in college, and 28 percent by sharing with colleagues and observing each other's classes.

This data indicated the major different approaches in pursuing knowledge between the two groups of teachers: most U.S. teachers rely on in-school services and workshops; most Chinese teachers enhance their knowledge from self-study.

By attending professional development meetings, U.S. teachers are able to learn new ideas and techniques for their teaching. For instance, Ms. Davis learned new technology in the various workshops: "Attending workshops in our district keeps us aware of the latest techniques."

Ms. Griffin expressed her view on continuing learning: "Teachers must continue seeking opportunities to learn hands-on, conceptual processes, and be willing to ask for help or clarification from other math professionals." Ms. Scott agreed that sharing with colleagues is a good approach to enhance mathematical knowledge. She said, "I enhance my mathematics and teaching knowledge by doing professional readings, sharing with colleagues, and attending math in-services."

Ms. Elliott summarized her experience and said, "I have been successful because I take in several classes, and I am always open to new courses."

Some teachers enhance mathematics and teaching knowledge by independent study. Ms. Jenkins believes that a teacher should be a lifelong learner. She said,

A teacher must be a lifelong learner. I need to know what my students will need to know to be successful in life. I'm constantly reading and searching current events/staying up-to-date with the world today.

Besides reading teachers' newspapers, watching TV, and studying on the Internet, Ms. Waller strengthens her knowledge from "answering student questions." Ms. Nelson builds up her knowledge through directing students' activities: "My main enrichment during the past eight years has been as a Math Counts coach. This competitive curriculum has challenged me to grow as a math teacher."

In order to teach effectively, most Chinese teachers develop mathematics and teaching knowledge by independent study, in which teachers work on extensive problem solving. For example, Ms. Chen reads various books about mathematics, such as *Olympic Mathematics Reading: The Methods of Mathematics,* and often reads textbooks and reference books written for high school level. To recharge her knowledge and to broaden her views, Ms. Jian also reads many mathematics books and solve all kinds of problems to strengthen her ability in problem solving. Ms. Dong studies different textbooks and journal articles about mathematics teaching from experts to enhance knowledge theoretically. She often solves some high-level mathematics problems to improve her ability in problem solving. Ms. Yian said, "As junior teachers, we are required to do a set of practices every week in order to strengthen our mathematics knowledge. I also study more mathematics outside of school."

There are many ways to gain mathematics knowledge for Chinese teachers. Ms. Pan described how she pursues this knowledge: "I have taken B.A. mathematics courses in my spare time. I read a lot of mathematics magazines and did many Olympics mathematics problems for elementary school." Ms. Xia develops mathematical knowledge through several steps. She said, "First, I seriously participate in every staff development. Second, I am taking the exam by credit for teachers at the university level. I always learn from experienced colleagues inside and outside schools." Ms. Gao also likes to learn from others; she stated, "Always learn from teachers and students; share and discuss the questions with them to learn more knowledge."

In conclusion, both the U.S. and Chinese teachers know the importance of a teacher's having an in-depth understanding of mathematics; both the U.S. and Chinese teachers continue to enhance their mathematics knowledge using various approaches. There are some differences in ways of acquiring knowledge between two groups of teachers: most U.S. teachers enhance knowledge from in-school services and workshops, while the majority of Chinese teachers gain knowledge through independent study.

GRADING STUDENTS' HOMEWORK AND PLANNING FOR INSTRUCTION

> If you don't plan, then you miss out on opportunities to do things in a better way.
>
> —Ms. Williams, U.S. teacher

> Teach according to students' background and needs, and teach according to the textbook (因人施教，因材施教).
>
> —Chinese education philosophy

QUESTION 7

What is the purpose of assigning homework to your students? Do most of your students typically do their homework? How do you grade your students' homework? Do you grade each problem on each student's homework?

Importance of Assigning Homework

Table 5.5 shows that the U.S. teachers assigned homework for different purposes: 44 percent of the U.S. teachers believe that the purpose of assigning homework is to review and practice, 33 percent believe it reinforces knowledge, and 19 percent believe it helps to check for understanding. In addition, table 5.5 indicates that 74 percent of the U.S. teachers believe that most of their students typically do their homework, while 19 percent of the U.S. teachers believe that most of their students do not do their homework. In contrast, 94 percent of Chinese teachers believe that the purpose of assigning homework is to reinforce knowledge and understanding, 22 percent consider it is to check understanding, and 13 percent think it is to review and practice concepts. Table 5.5 also indicates that 94 percent of Chinese teachers believe that most of their students typically do their homework, while 6 percent of Chinese teachers believe that most of their students do not do their homework. This data indicates that 20 percent more Chinese teachers believe their students do homework compared to U.S. counterparts, and most Chinese teachers believe that knowledge and understanding can

Table 5.5.   Percentage of U.S. and Chinese Teachers for Each Component of Response of Questions 7 and 8

Aspect of Teachers' Beliefs	Essential Components	Question Number	U.S. %	China %
Grading students' homework and planning for instruction	*Importance of assigning homework*			
	1. Reinforce knowledge and understanding	7	33	94
	2. Review and practice	7	44	13
	3. Check for understanding	7	19	22
	4. Most students do their homework	7	74	94
	5. Most students do not do their homework	7	19	6
	Approaches to grading homework			
	1. By completion	7	25	0
	2. By effort	7	13	0
	3. Give answers to students	7	75	0
	4. Every problem	7	25	97
	5. Face-to-face	7	0	33
	Approaches to planning for math instruction			
	1. Plan for math instruction with team	8	48	3
	2. Plan for math instruction by textbooks	8	19	81
	3. Plan for math instruction by curriculum	8	11	34
	4. Plan for math instruction by students' needs	8	7	75
	Time spent on planning instruction			
	1. Less than 30 minutes daily	8	44	3
	2. About one hour daily	8	30	50
	3. About two hours daily	8	4	34
	4. More than two hours daily	8	0	3

Note: N = 28 for each type of response for the U.S. teachers. N = 33 for each type of response for the Chinese teachers. Each individual teacher response could be coded more than once, resulting in total percentages greater than 100 for each problem. Data on approach to grading homework on the U.S. side came from interviews with U.S. teachers.

be reinforced by doing homework, while most U.S. teachers believe that assigning homework is for students to practice and review knowledge. The following examples address some differences.

Some U.S. teachers give students homework for review and practice. Ms. Anderson explained why she has her students do homework:

> It is designed to practice what they are doing today, and to gradually evolve into challenging problems that make them think in order to earn a 100. We then have something exciting to go over the next day. Most students will always do their homework.

Ms. Scott also assigns homework for practice: "Homework can be practice and application of a concept that has already been taught. It can also be the beginning of an investigation. Most of my students typically do their homework." Ms. Jenkins said that "the purpose [of homework] is to develop study skills, to retain and to build skills. I give approximately five problems per night, four days a week."

Other teachers considered the purpose of assigning homework as reinforcing the recently taught topics or prior learning. According to Ms. Farris, "Homework reinforces what we do in class. My students have homework every night. All of my students usually have their work. Out of 140 maybe 5 won't have it." To Ms. Goodwin, assigning homework is "reinforcing skills learned in school as well as showing parents what the student is learning in school."

However, a few teachers, such as Ms. Griffin, Ms. Farris, Ms. Owen, and Ms. Reed, believe that the purpose of assigning homework is to check for understanding. For example, Ms. Griffin explained:

> The purpose of homework is to determine if students understand a concept that has been taught. It is an extension of class work—not just more similar problems. It is not to be given "just so students have work at home." I would estimate that 75 percent of my students regularly do their homework.

Ms. Reed called homework an "extension of thinking outside the classroom." Since some of her students do not do homework, she changed the word "homework" to "extra credit." Ms. Caldwell believes that the purpose of homework is to practice the objectives taught in class. However, she says, "Only above-level students do their homework." One of the reasons may be the school policy: "Our school has a policy that homework can only count [for] 10 percent of the student's grade," she said.

Most Chinese teachers believe that assigning homework reinforces knowledge and understanding, constructs basic skills, cultivates a good habit of mind, and increases the ability to think. For example, Ms. Wu said that homework will "reinforce the mastering of new knowledge, promote thinking, and train in two basics: concepts and skills." Ms. Ren would assign homework not only to reinforce learning so students' skills would be more efficient, but also to check students' understanding and the effect of teaching. Ms. Jian believes that homework would train students' ability to review and prestudy; it would also provide time and opportunity for students' independent thinking. Ms. Qian also agreed that homework helps students prestudy the knowledge for the next day and helps students know the relationship between prior and new concepts. Ms. Wang believes that homework gives opportunities for high-level students to further develop their abilities.

Ms. Qing gives different levels of problems in homework to address the different abilities of individual students. From the homework, Mr. Wang understands his students' thinking. Most of his students do homework, but few students do not do homework, because they lack good study habits. To encourage students to do homework, Ms. Sheng tries to cultivate good study habits for her students.

In summary, there are some similarities in the beliefs about purposes of checking homework between the U.S. and Chinese teachers. An almost equal number of teachers agree that the purpose of assigning homework is to check for understanding. Both groups of teachers think that most students do their homework. However, there are also differences in the beliefs about the purpose of assigning homework between the two groups of teachers. To most of the U.S. teachers, assigning homework is for review and practice, while most Chinese teachers assign homework to reinforce knowledge and understanding.

Approaches to Grading Homework

Since it is known that U.S. teachers do not usually grade each problem, questions like "How do you grade your students' homework? Do you grade each problem on every student's homework every day?" were not asked in the questionnaire; instead, more detailed questions were asked during the teacher interviews. Table 5.5 shows that U.S. teachers use various approaches to grade homework: 75 percent of teachers grade homework during class, 25 percent grade homework by completion, 13 percent grade homework by effort, and only 25 percent actually grade students' homework, although not every problem. However, 97 percent of Chinese teachers grade each problem for all homework.

Usually U.S. teachers grade homework in class. For example, Ms. Hanks described her approach:

> We all check them [homework] in class to make sure they understand. If they have questions, they can ask. We may do homework on it again another day. Then we'll take quizzes. We also have tutoring sessions, if they are not as sure, they can come back and ask for help. There are lots of opportunities to help them.

Ms. Loving said, "I have a hard time giving them something and not grading it or not counting it as a grade. I haven't got past that mentality yet. A lot of other teachers take completion grades but I grade everything." However, she admitted, "Actually the kids grade it and I take the grades in the grade book. I'll call [out] the answers and they'll grade the paper."

A number of U.S. teachers like Ms. Loving usually put the answers on an overhead projector or call out the answers to have students make correction by themselves. For example, Ms. Flores described her approach to grading homework:

> In class, the first thing we do is grade homework. I have the answers on the overhead as I walk around and monitor; they pass it up, I look at it. It all depends on the lesson. Sometimes I take grades on homework, sometimes I don't. I usually don't take a grade if it's a new concept; I usually let them have a night of practice. They raise their hand if they want a problem worked on the board.

Some teachers believe that grading each problem is just for accuracy, and it is not necessary to grade it for accuracy. Ms. Baker said,

"I don't grade it for accuracy, I just check to see if they have it; it's just practice for them. I grade it by completion." She described her way of grading: "We check it in class. Students check their own. At the beginning of class, we check, then they discuss and ask questions. If they have questions, I call it out. Sometimes it takes 15–20 minutes." To explain why she let students check their own homework, Ms. Baker said, "I let them grade their own because I want them to see their own mistakes. If I correct it the mistake will not be fresh in their mind."

Ms. Nelson also grades students' homework by completion for the following reasons: "I assign homework every day; it is a school policy. My homework does not count for accuracy. It counts for completion. They don't have mathematical support at home, so if you count them on accuracy, that's really going to shut them down. If they get in there and try, you've done more."

The following two teachers, however, seemed to understand the importance of grading homework and providing feedback to students. Ms. Wood said:

> I like to get feedback to the students. We go over it as a class, we pick out and do a few, we discuss it, and then I take it up. I still give them credit for trying. The grading depends on the assignment. We do some evaluation during class; I grade papers in my planning period. They know their mistake before they ever pick it up for evaluation. We'll talk about it. If many of my students don't get the concept then I have to go back and reteach it immediately; there is no reason to go on. Students are not penalized for their mistakes.

Ms. Williams recognized that "it is hard for the kids who come from an elementary class to come into a core class and have homework every day." However, she knew the importance of grading homework:

> If they are doing it incorrectly and you don't catch it, they will not realize what they are doing is incorrect. So the quicker and the faster we can catch their incorrect thinking, the better opportunity they have for mastering the materials.

Ms. Williams uses various ways to grade homework:

At the beginning of the year we take class time to analyze their errors. I would write sentences to tell them what they missed, until they start doing that themselves. If they miss something, then they'll go back and figure out what they missed. I don't give completion grades. I'm not really comfortable with that idea because I want kids to be real competent and I think the only way they can also be confident is by accuracy.

To model for students how to grade homework and find mistakes, in Ms. Williams's class, "students grade their homework every day when they come in."

Chinese teachers grade homework very differently than U.S. teachers: 97 percent of Chinese teachers grade each homework problem every day; besides grading on paper, 33 percent of Chinese teachers also grade "face to face." For example, Ms. Ren said:

> Everyday, I collect students' homework and grade them. I carefully evaluate every problem; if I find a serious mistake, I use a "face-to-face" grading approach to help the student; if it is a mistake among several students, I'll correct the misconception to the whole class.

Ms. Qin grades students' homework face-to-face after class or during the class, and she grades all the problems for each student. Ms. Wang not only points out students' mistakes, but also marks where and at what step students make a mistake. If she has time, she always does "face-to-face" grading. Ms. Xia also does "face-to-face" grading whenever she has time. Mr. Lu's approach is to divide students into two types. For students who have difficulty understanding he uses "face-to-face" grading; for average and above average students, he grades every problem.

Some Chinese teachers not only check for understanding, but also pay attention to attitude and neatness of writing on homework. For example, Mr. Zhou looks at the following aspects in grading homework: "Check homework to see if students do problem in correct way; find out if attitude of writing is positive; analyze if method of problem solving is creative."

Ms. Shun gives a "star" if a student writes well on the homework. Ms. Zhen likes to determine students' abilities in computation, problem solving, and writing, through grading homework.

In order to grade students' work effectively, "I usually do all the problems by myself before grading. I look very carefully at each student's responses, and I always write a comment if I find even a little error," said Mr. Zhang. Ms. Chen uses the following approach:

> First I grade two samples of homework, and then follow the samples to grade others so it speeds the grading. During the grading, I sort out the types of errors, and analyze the errors and find the reasons for misconceptions. I use red to highlight correct thinking and good methods of problem solving on students' homework. I also share these good strategies of problem solving with other students.

Ms. Dong likes to "look at an answer first, and then look at the student's thinking in the procedure of problem solving. Finally, point out errors and write comments on students' homework." Ms. Xu asks students to make corrections of errors after they receive the feedback. When she checks homework, she not only checks the current day's work, but also checks students' corrections on the previous day's errors, if any.

Ms. Jian believes that grading students' homework is a teacher's responsibility; the teachers should take it seriously and work hard on it. Ms. Nin is always conscientious in her grading because she believes that "students' homework is a product of my hard work."

In summary, there are differences in ways of grading homework between the two groups of teachers. The U.S. teachers usually do not grade every problem on students' homework; instead, they give answers to students, and have students check their own homework. Some of the teachers grade homework by completion or effort. In contrast, the Chinese teachers always grade students' homework problems one by one, analyze errors, and correct misconceptions.

QUESTION 8

How do you plan for mathematics instruction daily? How much time do you spend on planning instruction daily?

Approaches to Planning for Mathematics Instruction

Table 5.5 shows that the U.S. teachers use a variety of ways to plan for instruction: 48 percent of the U.S. teachers plan for mathematics instruction with a team, 19 percent plan for mathematics instruction using textbooks, 11 percent plan for instruction using the curriculum, and 7 percent plan for instruction according to the students' needs. However, table 5.5 shows that the Chinese teachers plan for mathematics instruction by focusing on the textbook and students' needs: 81 percent of the responses indicated that the Chinese teachers plan for mathematics instruction by using textbooks, 75 percent plan by gauging students' ability level, 34 percent plan according to the curriculum, and only 3 percent of the Chinese teachers plan in a team. Among the responses, 59 percent of the Chinese teachers would plan for instruction according to a combination of their students, textbooks, and curriculum.

Most U.S. teachers in this study plan for instruction weekly with a team. Ms. Baker said, "I like planning with the other math teachers and the department head and getting papers and materials ready. I spend about one to two hours doing this." Ms. Griffin described how she plans for instruction with a team:

On Monday, the sixth grade teachers plan for instruction for the following week. We make a rough draft lesson plan for the skill to be taught. On Wednesday, we create materials and share ideas for instruction. We create manipulatives or activities to be used. On Friday, we meet in vertical alignment with sixth, seventh, and eighth grade teachers to discuss methods used and the need for deep instruction. I spend approximately one hour on daily lesson preparation.

Ms. Williams believes that "if you don't plan, then you miss out on opportunities to do things in a better way, I think you need to plan. You have to have a long range as well as a short range plan." Furthermore she believes that team planning helps teachers learn from each other:

For four years, the sixth grade math teacher [have been getting] together, we plan at least a week for different preparations, and we share ideas. I believe when groups of people get together, it really improves the product. The more people we interact with, the more we learn.

Some U.S. teachers plan for a six-week period. For example, Ms. Flores's "planning is broken down into six weeks." Ms. Gibson said, "We have to turn in [a] lesson plan every week. But I basically look at what I'm going to teach every six weeks. I look at the big picture first. I do a week at a time, I know where I'm headed."

Most U.S. lesson plans are for a week or are outlines for several weeks. The teachers do not write details and examples on it. For example, Ms. Owen admitted,

> I don't include details and examples. For my personal lesson plans, I never have. Part of that was the fact that somewhere along the way the very first time I ever taught a topic, I probably did a lot of examples. I can't create [an example for] completing the square algebra equation so I would pull [one] out of the book.

In writing the lesson plan, Ms. Flores "had done both forms and outlines before." However, "since I have a lot of experience (26 years), I know what I'm going to do beforehand." Ms. Bakers's lesson plan is not really detailed. "I just write: okay on this day I'll do this and that. We don't have forms, we just have a lesson plan book, it's by days and you fill in your objectives, etc."

How do Chinese teachers plan for instruction? Table 5.5 shows that they focus on two key components in planning instruction: textbooks and students' needs or learning situations. Chinese teachers in this study frequently quote the famous Chinese education philosophy: Teach according to students' background and needs, and teach according to the textbook (因人施教，因材施教). An example of Ms. Pan's explanation illustrates this idea:

> Every day, I plan the lesson in two steps: first, I study the textbook in depth as well as the curriculum to understand the objectives, key points, and the difficult points. Then, I will consider the students' learning situation. Finally I combine both textbook and students' needs as the consideration to write the detailed lesson plan. I use more than one hour for preparation every day.

Chinese teachers' lesson plans are not a simple outline but a detailed teaching note that includes the objectives, materials, teaching methods, the types of questions asked, the examples given, alternative ways of problem solving, summary, and so on. Usually it takes at least two to five pages for one lesson. For example, Ms. Dong explained her way of planning:

Generally, I follow the order of the textbook. First, I will work on the outline of the lesson, then I will consider the details. I always focus on the students to prepare the lesson. Often I understand the materials and students; I design the questions according to the students' needs.

Some teachers also design their teaching method after they study the textbook and get to know their students' needs. "When it is necessary, we will discuss and share with colleagues," said Mr. Zhang. To plan by assessing students' needs, Ms. Fang does the following:

> First, summarize the effect of today's instruction. Second, analyze the misconceptions in the students' practice exercises, and design similar problems as the review for the next day; then constantly study the textbook and curriculum. I spend about two hours to prepare each lesson.

Like Ms. Fang, Ms. Qian considers the possible learning difficulties and tries to design strategies to help students understand the lesson; and she tries to "give students a systematic and accurate knowledge base." Ms. Lu also noted the importance of the review and the link between lessons:

> First, read the textbook carefully; find the role and position of this lesson in the whole textbook. Next, consider what new knowledge students should be taught and what the prerequisite knowledge is, then design the review for new lessons. Furthermore, consider key and difficult points in the new lesson. From the objectives, design the teaching procedure and method, and design problems for practice. This type of practice has latent knowledge for the following lessons.

Ms. Wu called these types of problems "layer practices." She designs different types of problems at various levels to make students think:

> After carefully studying the textbook, I integrate the real learning situation in class to plan the lesson. In the review part, I try to split key and difficult points. In the teaching part, I try to have students play the main role. For the practice, I try to do it with layers, and design divergence problems to promote students' thinking. I use about two hours to plan each lesson.

Ms. Wang explained how to follow students' needs:

> I use about two hours to plan the lesson. First I study the textbook and understand the key ideas of it. And then I plan the lesson according to students' needs. I try to understand the character of students' thinking and their background of prior knowledge. From there, I look for the best tangent point of students' learning. Before planning, I consider a choice of teaching methods and think about how students can play an active role. I also think about what materials we should use. After all this consideration, I start to write the lesson plan.

Besides planning lessons according to the textbook and student needs, most Chinese teachers also study the curriculum guild, sample lesson plans, and other reference books. Several teachers like Mr. Wang "plan a lesson from three angles: textbook, students, curriculum." Ms. Liu and Ms. Bao study the textbook first and then read the teachers' instructions and other references, and finally write the lesson plan.

Chinese teachers often observe each other's classroom teaching in their schools or other schools. Most school districts and cities in China have open classes for teachers to observe during the school year. Here "open lesson" means that a teacher from school A has an open lecture for all teachers in the district or city to observe on a selected date in another school B, and uses students from school B in teaching the particular lesson. Open lessons are evaluated and ranked by observers, and the best lessons are selected as models for all teachers. Every teacher can volunteer to teach an open lesson. These open lessons provide models for teachers and help them gain insights into teaching. Ms. Fang referred to this type of open lesson as a "research class." She said:

> Teachers often observe each other's classes and help each other with planning. The school requires every teacher to observe 20 classes in one semester, including observing each other's classes among colleagues, and observing "research classes." For research classes, each grade selects one teacher to give an open class for all the teachers in that particular grade. The school district also has open classes and meetings for teachers to help them plan for instruction. A teacher can select classes to observe during the semester.

To plan effective lessons, Ms. Gao reads educational journals and magazines, participates in open classes, and observes other classes.

Time Spent on Planning Instruction

Table 5.5 also shows that most U.S. teachers use 30 minutes to one hour for daily planning, while most Chinese teachers would use one to two hours for daily planning.

To answer how they plan instruction and how much time they spend daily, Ms. Anderson, a U.S. teacher, explained:

> There is no isolated amount of time. I am always, night and day, thinking about where each class is mathematically and what I'll need to do the next day. The actual writing and creating of problems and assignments occurs spontaneously in class depending on what will challenge them at that exact moment.

Some U.S. teachers like planning ahead weekly, by the six-week grading period, or yearly. For example, Ms. Waller plans "ahead weekly relating to previous years and scheduling, and using 30 minutes to one hour daily." Ms. Elliott explained her way of planning: "I keep a textbook by my bed and read the lessons constantly. I plan the entire six weeks at a time. I gather the manipulative that I will need weeks in advance."

Ms. Parker explained how she plans ahead: "I try to follow the road map given by the district in the beginning of the year. I add to it any other lessons that I think are good or needed. I spend an average of one hour planning." Ms. Reed mostly plans once overall for the year and she adjusts the plan monthly. She also spends 45 minutes daily on planning.

The U.S. teachers from different schools have various planning times with teams: Ms. Goodwin meets with the team for about 20 minutes for weekly planning, Ms. Madison has group planning by grade level one hour and a half per week, and Ms. Ridgway has grade-level meetings to plan weekly, and takes about 15 minutes to plan daily. Teachers from Ms. Ross's school "work as a team to plan for 30 minutes." And Ms. Thomas "works with other math teachers one hour every two weeks."

In addition, the U.S. teachers prepare their lessons using different strategies. For example, Ms. Scott tries applications in real life: "I plan during my conference period (but sometimes I get lots of ideas when watching TV, reading the paper, etc.). I try to plan for a real-life application to catch students' interest. Time spent on planning varies greatly—probably an average of one hour per day."

Ms. Larson uses the strategies of reviewing, revising, reflecting, and implementing in planning instruction, which usually takes 30–60 minutes daily. Ms. Smith uses the teacher's manual to plan daily instruction and draw on examples and warm-ups and notes, taking about 15–30 minutes to plan lessons. Ms. Jenkins prepares lessons based on where students are in their comprehension of a subject: "I plan about one hour daily, including preparation time. I must reevaluate where my students are on a daily basis."

Some U.S. teachers have a block schedule with a 90-minute planning period; they feel they do not have enough time to plan the lesson. "But some of that will be taken by meetings. I work a whole extra day a week," said Ms. Wood. Ms. Hanks agreed, "I don't have enough planning time at school. I always take stuff home."

Usually Chinese teachers have enough time to plan at school, and they always plan lessons ahead. Ms. Yian said, "I usually plan lessons a week ahead, and I use two or three reference books. Before the lesson, I'll look at it again, and recall details. I spend one to one and a half hours every day." While Ms. Lu plans the lesson two days prior, using one to two hours. Ms. Chen said, "Every day I spend one to two hours to design the lesson based on previous lessons and the requirements of the curriculum. If I did not have enough time, I would use the old lesson plan."

In summary, there are differences in the ways of planning for instruction. Most of the U.S. teachers plan for instruction with a team or in consultation with other teachers to keep the same pace as other teachers, to share teaching experiences, and to learn from each other. Although the Chinese teachers often discuss their lesson plans with colleagues, the majority of the Chinese teachers plan for instruction according to textbooks and students' needs. The Chinese teachers consider textbooks the basis of planning, and students' needs are the main source of planning. Furthermore, the Chinese teachers often observe colleagues' classes in their schools. The U.S. teachers do not write a detailed lesson plan but only a simplified outline for a lesson, while the Chinese teachers' lesson plans are detailed teaching notes that include the objectives, content, key points, difficult points, and procedure. In the Chinese teachers' lessons, sequential layered questions and problems are designed to enhance students' ability to master a method of thinking.

CHAPTER 6

What's Happening in the Classroom: Observations and Interviews

You have to do things that allow students to contribute. I prefer for students to do investigation to develop their own methods, even their own algorithms.

—Ms. Wood, U.S. teacher

Teaching mathematics is similar to teaching "thinking methods." At the primary and middle school levels, teaching thinking methods is more important than [teaching] content knowledge.

—Ms. Bao, Chinese teacher

Classroom observation is a very effective approach to record how teaching and learning take place in the classroom. Good classroom teaching models patterns of effective teaching and reflects the theory of instruction design. It can also provide a valuable insight for research on classroom teaching. Importantly, it addresses how a teacher's pedagogical content knowledge is applied in a classroom setting.

This chapter summarizes observations and interviews of ten teachers, five from each country. After each observation, the teacher was requested to provide his or her lesson plan, which was read by the author. However, not all U.S. teachers had lesson plans, while each Chinese teacher had a detailed lesson plan. These lesson plans were used to compare and confirm classroom observations for individual teachers. The goals of this chapter are to examine how teachers apply pedagogical content knowledge (PCK) in their classroom teaching, to explore how teachers' beliefs impact their pedagogical content knowledge, and to examine if there is a consistent relationship between teachers' beliefs and their classroom teaching.

This chapter examines U.S. teachers' pedagogical content knowledge in classrooms first, and then examines Chinese teachers' pedagogical content knowledge in classrooms. The examination of each teacher's pedagogical content knowledge includes three parts: the first part describes the classroom observation; the second part analyzes the application of pedagogical content knowledge in each classroom according to the framework developed in chapter 4; the third part reports the interview with the teacher and assesses consistency between beliefs and actual teaching practice.

THE U.S. TEACHERS' PCK IN CLASSROOMS

"Angle" and "Counting on You" Lessons: Ms. Wood's Classroom

Observation of Classroom Teaching

Ms. Wood had 27 years of teaching experience. This was her first year as a sixth grade teacher. She had taught first through eighth grades, and had been a math instructional specialist in an elementary school. She had 24 credit hours in math courses with some at the graduate level. Two class periods, 90 minutes each, were observed in Ms. Wood's classroom, one on the topic of classifying angles, and one with the "Counting on You" project.

In the class on classifying angles, Ms. Wood introduced the concept of angle first, and had students make notes about the angle. She drew two angles, explained that "B" and "F" are common end points, and showed three ways to name an angle:

Figure 6.1. *Two Angles*

For the first angle: 1. $\angle ABC$,   2. $\angle CBA$,   3. $\angle B$
And for the second angle: 1. $\angle EFD$,   2. $\angle DFE$,   3. $\angle F$

She asked if students agreed with these three ways. One student asked, "How about ∠*FED*?" By answering questions, she was able to correct misconceptions about angles. She then had students use three ways to name an angle on the worksheet. She had each student exchange papers with a peer to see if they did it right. She praised students who took good notes and then asked students to open their journal and to write down their own words about the angle. After students finished, she had students exchange journals and read each other's writing.

Next she gave definitions of acute, right, obtuse, and straight angles with graphs. She also asked questions on each example in order to understand students' thinking. To motivate students to express their ideas on classifying angles, she told them, "Instead of homework we will have an oral contest on the angle problems [between the] boys and girls." She called on one boy and one girl each time to stand up and answer the problem she read to the class. If a student answered correctly, she added to the tally on the board (see figure 6.2).

Boys   **Girls**

Figure 6.2.   *Sample of Tallies for Number of Boys and Girls*

The group who got the most markers was the winner. In the contest, students actively participated. Ms. Wood explained the problems for which students did not get correct answers and used questions to guide interpretation and reasoning. This activity lasted about a half hour.

In the last 15 minutes, she had students draw a clock in their journal and classify the angle made by the hands of a clock at each time: 3:00, 7:15, 2:45, 6:00, 1:00, and 10:00. Then she had students come up voluntarily to draw the clock with times and give answers on the board.

The second class was held immediately after the first. Ms. Wood first explained the previous day's homework on central angles and then two students picked up all homework. The main objective of this lesson was working on the project, Counting on You. Ms. Wood mentioned that last week they went over the directions for the project, so she had students read the directions again for about three to four minutes.

Naturalists in the park often make statements about the projected population of some species of animals in the future.

1. What factors do scientists consider when they predict the population of a given group of animals?
2. Biologists compile data on the death rate of animals and can make predictions about the size of a cohort of animals over a period of time. The survivorship of a cohort of animals can be modeled using probability.
3. Define cohort.
4. Complete the following experiments. Record the outcomes in a table. Use the data from the table to make a graph and write a summary of how the graph could be used to predict the population changes for a cohort of animals.

Ms. Wood explained the experiments for this project. First she asked students, "What kind of a table should you use to report the outcomes? Before we go outside the classroom, I would like you to design the appropriate table to record and report the outcomes." Students worked on designing the table for the activity to find mathematical models. She had students read the guidelines for the first experiment, then she showed the steps for experiment I and II with pictures on the board; she also showed how to write 50 percent as a fraction. Next she had the whole class go out of the building to do the experiments.

Outside of the classroom, students worked with partners on experiment I. They drew a big area first; then they shook a strong bag with 100 pennies inside and randomly scattered them across a designated area. The students counted how many "heads" were up, meaning the animal survives. If "tails" was up, it meant the animal died. Students recorded the results and placed all 100 coins back into the bag to repeat the experiment five times, representing five years. Students were required to write the probability that an animal would not survive for each year in one cell of the table.

For experiment II, students put a piece of paper on one section of the designated area. This paper represents an ecological disaster area. Every "animal" (coin) that lands on this paper will not survive. Students removed these coins from the cohort group and did not replace any coins that landed in the "death" zone. Repeating the experiment five times represents five years; students recorded results in a new table and calculated the probability that an animal would not survive in one cell of the table. By the end of the class, most students were able to finish experiments I and II, and some finished the chart with all probabilities. Ms. Wood asked students to create a graph of the results and compare the results in experiment II to the results in experiment I. Students were asked to write an explanation of the two experiments and answer the following questions:

> How did the "death" zone affect the probability that an animal would not survive?
> Is it higher or lower than the probabilities in experiment I?
> How would this set of experiments be useful for scientists in determining the future population size of a group of animals?
> What are the limitations to these mathematical experiments in predicting population changes?

Application of PCK in Ms. Wood's Classroom

The observation of classroom teaching indicated that Ms. Wood's PCK centered on engaging students in meaningful and inquiry learning processes in the following ways:

> Ms. Wood was able to build on students' math ideas and understanding about angles using definitions and examples with graphs of angles.
> Ms. Wood addressed students' misconceptions about the angle and made corrections on errors through explaining the problems during the oral competition and used this activity to reinforce understanding and skill development.
> To engage students in learning process, Ms. Wood used an oral contest on the angle problems between the boys and girls to motivate them to actively participate in learning and to practice their new knowledge.
> To support students' thinking on the angle concept, Ms, Wood provided an opportunity for students' reflecting their thinking by having students draw a clock in their journal and classify the angle made by the hands of a clock. This activity of connecting the concrete model of a clock makes the angle learning visual and meaningful.

The Counting on You activity in the second period introduced the concept of probability. and it also provides students ideas on how to do simulations and build mathematics models in the real world. Furthermore, the Counting on You experiments I–II involved students in a creativity and inquiry learning process and enhanced their abilities to predict and make decisions. This activity also gave students an opportunity to analyze, organize, and interpret data.

Interview with Ms. Wood

Ms. Wood explained that her goal of mathematics education varied according to students' backgrounds:

> It varies from person to person. My goal for some students is to be fundamentally proficient in daily mathematics, like being able to compare prices or organize a budget. For others, I want them to be able to use mathematics in higher-level problem solving. I don't think it should be the same for everyone.

In viewing other subjects, she believes, "If you do mathematics in isolation, it becomes very boring and dry to the students. I see things globally but I also see the steps individually; the connection makes math easy." She is able to connect mathematics with activities involving science, such as the Counting on You project she designed for her students. She thinks that most of her students enjoy mathematics:

> Because I try to make sure they are successful, and people always enjoy what they are successful with. There are some students that are never going to enjoy math. I think they must enjoy learning new things. I want my students to create their own knowledge.

During the angle lesson, students showed their enthusiasm and enjoyment in answering questions about the angle in the oral contest. In the Counting on You activity, students constructed their own knowledge about the survival rate and probability through experiments and data recording and analysis.

In teaching mathematics, Ms. Wood said that her primary focus is conceptual understanding. Observation of her class on the angle topic reflected her focus on conceptual understanding. In that lesson, she introduced definitions of angle, acute and right, obtuse, and straight angle; she asked questions that focused on conceptual understanding. She recognized that her teaching style is more teacher-centered because of the amount of material the class needs to cover. However, she said, "You have to do things that allow students to contribute. I prefer for students to do investigation to develop their own methods, even their own algorithms." She stated, "The traditional way is very isolated. If the student gets lost, the teacher may not know." So she would use "cooperative learning almost every period. It's something as simple as looking at your neighbor's paper. This is a team effort." In the Counting on You activity, she had students form groups by partners. She agreed that cooperative learning could greatly enhance students' learning. However, she noticed that many students do better by themselves. In the classroom, she used a lot of manipulative methods because "some students only can learn by touching [things], and moving them around and seeing the relationships." She further explained, "Everything has purpose. We're not just throwing pennies on the ground and counting them, we're looking at a relationship." Looking for the relationship is the key focus in her class activities. In the Counting on You activity, she asked students to use graphs to show the results of the survival rate. However, she thinks the manipulative method has some limits: "It's like you cannot teach division with manipulatives."

In responding to how to plan for instruction, Ms. Wood said, "I plan for the whole year. In terms of the pacing, of course I have to adjust it. I write a weekly or biweekly lesson plan." She realized that it is important to take time to develop a plan. However, she said, "I have a 90-minute planning time in my school day, but some of that will be taken with meetings with other teachers. I work a whole extra day a week."

Ms. Wood believes in the importance of homework: "Students also need the independent practice. There are a certain number of problems that we have to practice to show proficiency." She gives students homework every day: "They have to practice and discover how they do it." However, she would "rather them do 5 or 6 problems correctly than 20 incorrectly." She likes to provide feedback to the students; "We go over it as a class, we pick out and do a few, we discuss it and then I take it up. I still give them credit for trying."

Ms. Wood grades papers in her planning period. "I have 151 students so I spend an hour or two on overall schoolwork." On addressing students' misconceptions, she noted that

> they know their mistakes before they ever pick [the homework] up for evaluation. We will talk about it. If many of my students don't get the concept, then I have to go back and reteach it immediately, and there is no reason to go on. Students are not penalized for their mistakes.

In talking about how she knows her students' thinking and understanding, Ms. Wood explained:

> I see some of that in the papers they turn in. Much of it comes from having them present a problem to the class or explain something. A lot of it is oral communication and class participation. I like to know how they arrive at something so they can explain things. I always wanted to know what they are thinking. I ask them all the time. I say, "Show me." Sometimes I write down the wrong answer and let them correct it. Some of it comes from tests. I jump around the room and don't wait for volunteers. I would like the students to be fully engaged.

She also provided individual tutorials before school. She explained, "I pull out the students who could not master a concept and tutor them. I talk with them and discuss with them: 'Do you know why you are failing?' They know they can come in early and get help. Today maybe 30 students came up to got tutored on fractions."

Ms. Wood had an average of 25 students in each class. She recognized the diversity of the class: "I knew there were differences in culture but you have to make the culture connection. I relish all the differences. I noticed all the languages in this school. That is why I made posters." In her classroom, one side of the wall has the numerals 1–10 on posters in different languages, which represent the home languages of her students: Spanish, French, Tagalog, Swahili, Armenian, and Arabic. She will add Vietnamese and Chinese this year. As a child growing up in Washington, D.C., Ms. Wood had an advantage in seeing the differences in cultures, but she did not know the connection. The teaching experience helped her gain insight into the connection.

"Each one of those posters represents a child or a group of children in my heart." During the oral contest in her class, she called every student to answer questions. Students were seated around octagonal tables in her class, which showed her effort to make connections for multicultural students.

In responding to the importance of teachers' pedagogy in connection to multiculturalism, she explained:

> I think that any person who graduates from college is able to teach. So how you teach is more important to me than the content of knowledge. However, I would never want a teacher who was unsure about how to do something to try and teach it.

She believes that it is very important for a teacher to have a deep understanding of mathematics. She also believes that a teacher should have profound pedagogical knowledge, particularly in the United States, because "we are multicultural. We are not unicultural. If you know the culture of the students, you should know appropriate approaches."

"Scale Drawing" Lesson: Ms. Flores

Observation of Classroom Teaching

Ms. Flores had 26 years of teaching experience and a master's degree in curriculum and instruction. She was teaching sixth and seventh grades. One sixth grade class was observed. It was a 45-minute period.

In this class, students worked on a project—scale drawing—that used similarity and proportion to make original pictures larger. Students had been given the task the previous day to select favorite cartoons in books or newspapers, and to bring the cartoons to school for drawing.

First Ms. Flores gave instructions for drawing and mentioned the similarity and proportion concepts. Next she showed an example of pictures to students and answered some questions on how to draw the picture. Then she had students draw pictures. Students worked on drawing and coloring quietly by themselves.

Ms. Flores monitored students constantly; she went around the classroom to check drawings and answer questions.

By the end of class, most students had finished the outline; a few of them had finished coloring. She had students take their work home to continue as homework.

Application of PCK in Ms. Flores's Classroom

The observation of Ms. Flores's class revealed her PCK focused on using visuals and manipulatives to promote students' interest in learning:

- To build on students' ideas on similarity and proportion, Ms. Flores used the scale drawing activity.
- Ms. Flores corrected drawing errors by answering students' questions during the class.
- Students in Ms. Flores's class were able to engage in the learning process of scale drawing.

However, in this lesson, Ms. Flores did not make the connection between manipulatives and abstract concepts of similarity and proportion. Furthermore, she did not provide probing questions or tasks to promote students' thinking during the class.

Interview with Ms. Flores

Ms. Flores was interviewed in her classroom. Ms. Flores believes that the goal of mathematics education is to be sure that children understand a concept from the concrete to the abstract. She thinks that both conceptual understanding and procedural development are important, but students must start with the concrete and then build to the procedure. She said, "I balance between the two by starting with concrete materials, using manipulatives." She believes that hands-on activities help students understand the concept, and it's a lasting understanding. The observation in her class confirmed her teaching style focusing on manipulatives and hands-on activities. She explained further about using manipulatives:

> I use concrete manipulatives, draw pictures, diagrams, use problem solving for students; we have many different skills that we go through. Whether it's visualizing or drawing pictures, making a graph, making a

table, something they can see. Let them see it visually and then show them the mathematics part of it.

She suggested, "From a sixth grade standpoint, they need to learn the basic skills. They need to be able to solve higher-level thinking skill problems." However, observation of Ms. Flores's class did not confirm her beliefs about learning the basic skills, perhaps because the observation was done on the day before the students' holiday, so Ms. Flores focused on the activity to help students understand the concept of similarity and proportion.

In teaching mathematics, she used a combination of student-centered and teacher-centered methods: "I think I use a combination. You need to find the different abilities in students. You need to know what kind of learners they are. You need to teach in whatever way is best for that student." She believes that the student is dependent on the teacher. "So in the traditional way of teaching mathematics, students must have drill and practice to learn the concept and get it." Ms. Flores described how she plans for instruction:

> My planning is broken down into six weeks. Then I plan by chapters. I had done both form and outlines before. Since I have a lot of experience, I know what I'm going to do beforehand. Unless the children just don't understand; [then] I have to modify and adjust. You might have to move things back a day or two. I usually don't have any problems with that.

Talking about the time for planning, Ms. Flores explained, "We have two planning periods—a planning period and a conference period. I feel like I have plenty of time to plan." With 26 years' teaching experience, she does not need much time to prepare the lesson.

Ms. Flores realized the importance of having students do homework:

> It is very important that they do homework, because you can't learn a topic by just working on it just a few minutes in school. If children don't do homework, they come back the next day not knowing what we did. They need that extra practice. Somewhere between here and home, they forget what to do.

She assigned approximately 15 problems daily. Students started to work on homework in class so she could monitor and see if they understood it. Usually, students have 15 to 20 minutes to start homework in a class period. Ms. Flores described how she grades the homework: "When they come back the next day, the first thing we do is grade it. I have the answers on the overhead. As I walk around and monitor, they pass it up; I look at it. It all depends on the lesson." In answering whether she takes grades on homework, she said:

> Sometimes I take grades on homework. Sometimes I don't. I usually don't take a grade if it's a new concept; I usually let them have a night of practice. They raise their hand if they want a problem worked on the board. If they do not have it, I put their name down and put down the page numbers they owe me. And I have a tally of what they owe me. If they miss a few days in a row I call home.

In responding to how she knows about her students' thinking and how to promote students' thinking, she answered:

> As you know your students' ability, you know the ones who need extra help. Sometimes you can tell by the blank look on their faces. They might be weak in one skill. We do quizzes, class work, and tests. I try to test over only what we covered. I keep it to the basic. I try to give my Gift and Talent (GT) classes critical thinking problems to make them think. This is where I like to do a lot of the problem-solving skills. And making them draw pictures—I try to use charts and pictures to help them see what they are doing.

Ms. Flores recognized the differences among students. She noted, "We have special ed. students. We may have to modify their tests, homework. My GT students may be more aggressive in their ability to listen and to perform."

To determine the relationship between content and pedagogical knowledge, she believes:

> A teacher needs to have a deep understanding of math. I think it is very important that they know the content, and that they are able to disperse that knowledge among the students. However, you have to know the method you are teaching to be able to teach the content. Part of it is knowing what level the students are at, when they are ready to absorb the content. I think you have to start with the concrete.

"Flips and Line Symmetry" Lesson: Ms. Baker

Observation of Classroom Teaching

Ms. Baker had been teaching sixth, seventh, and eighth grade mathematics for four years. She was teaching sixth and seventh grade mathematics during this study. The observation in her class was the lesson on the flips and line symmetry section of the textbook.

First she defined the terms "congruent," "line symmetry," and "reflection" by showing each definition on a transparency, along with an explanation. She folded a paper into two equal parts to demonstrate the meaning of congruent, symmetry, and reflection to students.

Next she had her students read the definitions of the three terms in the book and had them write down the definitions on paper. While students read and wrote quietly, she passed out handouts to students for the next task.

She provided a set of problems with pictures to have students answer orally.

1. Congruent: She had students identify the congruent pictures from figure 6.3.

Figure 6.3.   Figures for Identifying Congruency

2. Line symmetry: she folded a paper rectangle along the diagonal and asked students if the diagonal showed line symmetry.
3. Reflection: on a paper she drew figure 6.4 to show reflection.

Figure 6.4.   Reflection on Paper

In the next activity, she used symmetry to create a name design. She showed the sample first and then explained it:

> You are going to create a mirror of your name. Because it creates different shapes, I called it "Alien." It depends on how you design your shapes; when you open it, you are going to see pictures, and you need to determine what picture you get.

She showed her name design and asked students what picture they see. Some students said a cow; some students said a horse. She told students that the beautiful pictures on the window and door in this classroom were the result of name designs from her other classes. She showed the steps to create a name design and pointed out how to avoid mistakes in their work.

She displayed two types of designs—horizontal symmetry, which she called "hot dog folder," and "vertical symmetry," which she called "hamburger folder." She allowed students to decide which type they liked and had students pick up some paper to work on their own designs.

Students folded the paper, designed their names, colored the names on the paper, and cut the names out. There was some discussion and help among students.

As the students worked, Ms. Baker sat at the back of the classroom and graded students' tessellation pictures from a previous lesson in order to return them that day; she was able to monitor students by answering questions and often walked around the classroom to help students who had difficulty. A special ed. teacher in her classroom also helped a few special ed. students. As students finished, they opened their papers and got different pictures. Students were excited to see what they got and interpreted the meaning of the pictures, relating to their experience and preference.

Application of PCK in Ms. Baker's Classroom

Using the framework of pedagogical content knowledge in this book to gauge Ms. Baker's class on flips and line symmetry, we found that Ms. Baker's pedagogical content knowledge was reflected in the following ways:

- Ms. Baker tried to build on students' mathematics ideas on flips and line symmetry through definitions, pictures, and concrete materials.
- During the class, she was able to make corrections to misconceptions by answering questions.
- To engage students in mathematics learning, she used manipulatives to have students design their own names using the concept of symmetry. This activity reinforced students' understanding of symmetry and involved students in "doing" mathematics.

However, during this observation, she did not explicitly ask questions or provide tasks to elicit and extend students' thinking.

Interview with Ms. Baker

Ms. Baker believes that the goal of education is "to make all kids feel successful." She wants to "make all the kids feel comfortable." Her goal in teaching mathematics is "to do activities that the kids can relate to, not just pen-and-paper work." The activity of the name design using symmetry in the lesson confirmed her appraoch to mathematics teaching. She expressed the reason for this approach: "Math is a subject kids don't really look forward to. I try not to intimidate them." She believes that most of her students do not like learning mathematics. "I really don't know why. It's a lot of computations. It is difficult for them if they are not on the level. They feel lost if they don't know what they are supposed to know." Therefore, comparing mathematics to other subjects, she thinks that mathematics is harder to teach, "Because you have different kids that are on different levels. Everybody's not at the sixth grade level." The fact that she has several special ed. students in her class may increase the difficulty in teaching.

According to Ms. Baker, her primary focus in teaching mathematics is for students "to understand how to complete something." However, she also wants students "to have an understanding of mathematics." She believes that conceptual understanding is more important. She pointed out, "I always try to give them vocabulary words so they can understand what the terms mean." She added:

I do it by giving them both [concept and procedure]. I would like them to know their basic facts and apply them. They need to know basic facts, and a lot of them don't. I [only] allow them to [look up numbers in] a multiplication table sometimes, because they should know it by sixth grade.

Usually she gives students notes, with a step-by-step procedure, and she has an activity that they enjoy doing. She prefers a student-centered method "because it gets them involved. You tend to lose a lot of attention with teacher-centered" lessons. When asked about collaborative work, she noted, "I do use groups every other class period; it depends on the activity." However, she had concerns about behavior: "Behavior is a major problem sometimes; you want to keep them on task. I don't use it as often as I [would] like." She explained her opinion of cooperative groups: "I think it could both enhance and prevent student learning. It enhances it because the students understand it better if it's coming from their peers. It prevents it because kids want to talk when they're with their friends."

Ms. Baker would like to learn integrating a manipulative for every type of activity because "the kids enjoy it better than instruction; it kind of relaxes them but they're still learning."

Ms. Baker believes that planning is very important "because I have to be organized or I can't present it successfully to the kids." Her colleagues meet as a team and plan what they are going to teach. She described the method of planning:

We just say what we're going to teach and we share ideas. We all do the same sometimes. My lesson plan is not really detailed. I just write: okay on this day I'll do this and that. We don't have forms, we just have a lesson plan book; it's by days and you fill in your objectives, etc. At school, I have about 45 minutes to an hour to plan. At home, I don't really plan, but I have books and I'll think of an activity to do; but I don't spend a lot of time at home.

Usually she follows the plan for instruction, but she said, "If I don't feel that they grasped the content, then I'll back up in my lesson plans." Ms. Baker realized the importance of having students do homework:

The homework is always related to the topic we did in class. I like them to get extra practice at home. The majority of the time, I give homework. I'll either give a worksheet or something similar from the book. It varies from 10 to 20 problems. It takes from about 15 to 20 minutes.

Ms. Baker believes that homework is just practice for students. She explained her approach to homework: "I don't grade it for accuracy, I just check to see if they have it; it's just practice for them. I grade by completion." However, she said,

> We check it in class. They check their own. At the beginning of class we check, then they discuss and ask questions. If they have questions sometimes it takes 15–20 minutes. I call it out. I let them grade their own because I want them to see their own mistakes. If I correct it, the mistake will not be fresh in their mind.

They do not have a time limit for the homework. She explained:

> I do allow them to turn it in as late work. We have something called a homework packet. It's turned in every two weeks; it's a collection of all the homework assignments they previously completed. If they didn't have it there the first time, they can turn it in with their homework packet.

Ms. Baker believes that it is very important for a teacher to know about students' thinking and understanding. Besides all the approaches noted by other teachers, she looked at students' body language: "I try to look at their facial expressions. You can always tell by looking at them if they understand or not. I try to watch their body language."

In response to the question of the importance of content knowledge and pedagogical knowledge, she believes both content and pedagogical knowledge are important. However, she said,

> I don't think you have to have a deep understanding but you have to be ready to answer questions that the kids may have. You should know what you're going to teach. I only have four years of teaching experience. I attend seminars just to keep increasing my knowledge. You have to use a variety of techniques. You have to keep gaining knowledge.

"Percent of Change" Lesson: Ms. Williams

Observation of Classroom Teaching

Ms. Williams had taught for 9 years at the junior high level, but she was an elementary school teacher for 12 years before coming to junior high.

The observation was conducted in her sixth grade class, 45 minutes a period. The topic of the class was percent of change.

The class began with students copying down the warm-up instructions from the overhead projector. The warm-up was to read the textbook for five minutes.

Next Ms. Williams had students in groups of three or five check their homework. Students discussed, compared, and corrected their mistakes. Then she asked students, "What did you learn from the discussion?" Two students answered and she explained some problems and corrected errors. She had students checkmark the missed problems and turn in homework to her.

Ms. Williams started the new lesson of percent of change with a transparency on which the topic and a set of problems were displayed. She had students read the introductory activity in the book again for about five minutes. Then she gave the students the following problems:

What is the percent of each section in figure 6.5(a)?
What is the percent of the shaded section in figure 6.5(b)?
What is the percent of each section in figure 6.5(c)?

Next she drew figure 6.6 and had students come up to show a 50 percent increase and a 50 percent decrease from the original figure. She taught the percent of change by showing problem 4 in the book:

Problem 4: Original: $85, new: $68

First she showed how to find the difference of the two amounts by using the original amount to subtract the new amount:

$$\$85 - \$68 = \$17$$

a.	b.	c.

Figure 6.5. Percent in Different Sections

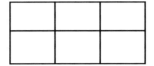

Figure 6.6. *Six Sections for 100 Percent*

Then she showed two ways to write the expression: one is a proportion expression and another is a percentage expression.

After she explained problem 4, she had students do problems 5–6:

Problem 5: Original: $456, new: $500
Problem 6: Original: 1.6, new: 0.95

Two students came up to the board to write their work:

Problem 5: $456 - 500 = -44$, $-44/456 = -.096$. It is a negative
number, but the student changed it to 9.6 percent.
Problem 6: $1.6 - 0.95 = 0.65$, $0.65/1.6 = .406 = 40.6$ percent

She asked questions to these two students and had them explain their work to the class. She praised them for doing good work.

However, one student had a concern and a question about problem 5: "Why does the percent increase in problem 5 have a negative sign?" Ms. Williams explained:

> You always take the original. Say we know it is an increase or a decrease when we study the numbers, but if we want to actually do the calculation using a calculator, you must find the amount of increase by comparing the increase amount to the original amount. If it looks like it is an increase, use the increase to subtract from the original. If it is a decrease, use the decrease to subtract from the original, but you end up with a negative number.

In this class, she allowed students to use calculators; that was why she mentioned calculators to help students understand the concept of percent change. She also mentioned that we could use mathematical reasoning to determine if it is a percent increase or decrease.

Application of PCK in Ms. Williams's Classroom

Using four components of PCK to examine Ms. Williams's teaching, the following indicated her PCK in classroom teaching:

- Although having students check their own homework helps students learn from each other, by not doing it herself she actually missed an opportunity to know students' thinking on prior knowledge firsthand before the new lesson.
- She did not explicitly and clearly address errors or make corrections for the students who worked on problems 5–6. To avoid the confusion on the signs in problem 5, she might indicate that to find the difference of two amounts in percent change, you could use the new amount to subtract the original amount instead of the opposite way. So the solution of problem 5 could be the following:

Problem 5: $500 - 456 = 44$, $44/456 = .096 = 9.6$ percent; since it is a positive sign, it is percent increase.

Using the same idea on problem 6:

$0.95 - 1.6 = -0.65$, $-0.65/1.6 = -.406 = -40.6$ percent; since it is a negative sign, it is percent decrease.

She did a great job in building students' mathematics concepts and engaging students in learning by using pictures to find changes in percents. However, if she could make a connection between picture understanding and abstract thinking by showing the mathematical expression related to changes in percents from figures, it would reduce confusion among students about the signs of results and the meanings of increasing and decreasing. She could do it the following way:

With figure 6.6, to show a 50 percent increase she could draw three more squares on the six squares. Now $9 - 6 = + 3$ is an increase, so percent of increase is to use the final amount 3 divided by the original amount 6 to get $3/6 = 1/2 = 50$ percent. With an understanding of this process, students would understand how to solve and interpret the results with different signs.

By asking "what" and "how" questions, she promoted students' thinking. However, she rarely asked "why" questions. With "why" questions, her students' thinking would be extended to a high level.

Interview with Ms. Williams

Ms. Williams was interviewed in her classroom. To her, the goal of mathematics education is "to have someone with confidence and a good sense of logical reasoning, and to enable students to make educated decisions, for example, on financial issues as they get older."

Ms. Williams believes that mathematics is more difficult to teach than other subjects:

> I think mathematics is more difficult. It's a more time-consuming job. It is also very detail oriented. Also, kids come to math prepared at a variety of levels. We have to get some kids caught up to the level. Perhaps they weren't ready to learn the topic, or maybe the way it was presented, they didn't quite grab hold of the idea. There is a lot more remediation, tutoring, and you have to use a variety of strategies and materials because kids seem to have a lot more difficulties in math than in other subjects. That is why it is a more challenging course to teach.

She further explained that most of her students like learning mathematics "because it appeals to a person's natural desire to figure things out. So I think that kids can enjoy math and like it."

The primary focus in teaching mathematics, to Ms. Williams, is to discover patterns and "to create confident and competent young people." She also would like to teach students independent study skills, which she called "life skills":

> I want them to understand how they can learn; I want them to understand some good study methods. They need to go back and analyze some errors that they specifically made, and that is very effective. They see that they used to use longer lengths of time unproductively. Only looking at the things that they don't know instead of looking of the things they already know, they spend that time much more effectively. And that is a life skill.

In the classroom observation, she had students check their own homework and discuss it with the group.

In contrast to the teacher-centered method, Ms. Williams would like to "use groups with summarizing, hands-on, and manipulative moveable things." She said:

> I think that there is value in the traditional way but I would want the students to discover and see the pattern rather than being told the pattern, because then they can have a greater sense of understanding. I use groups when they are analyzing or working out problems. Sometimes they work

independently and then get together to try to stimulate that knowledge a little bit better.

However, Ms. Williams noticed the need for balance between group learning and independent learning:

They have to be used in balance. I don't want my students to be dependent on someone else. That is why we might work in groups but also individually to develop each person's skill and then they come together. I have to make sure that everybody can do the skill independently. So there has to be a balance. If there was too much activity without individual accountability, you're losing out on the benefit of groups.

To explain why she uses manipulatives, she said:

I use them because my students can feel it, they can touch it, and they can see it. There is some movement in learning. I guess it stimulates the brain. There are more senses involved; all of these are involved in manipulative thinking. If I am doing the same thing every day, my students will not enjoy the class. But if I am doing something fun at least one day of the week and something new, they always come in and wonder: what are we doing today?

Ms. Williams believes in the importance of planning: "If you don't plan, then you miss out on opportunities to do things in a better way; I think you need to plan. You have to have a long-range plan as well as a short-range plan." She likes to plan instruction with a faculty team: "For four years the sixth grade math teachers have gotten together. We plan at least a week for different preparations, and we share ideas. I believe that when groups of people get together, it really improves the product. The more people we interact with, the more we learn." She wrote lesson plans weekly, which included an outline with a warm-up activity, practice activity, and homework.

Ms. Williams understood the challenge of homework on the part of students. "It is hard for the kids to come from an elementary class into a core class and have homework every day, and it is not always easy homework." She tried to give a reasonable amount of homework, between 12 and 15 problems, and she offered all kinds of tutorials and assistance "so students have very little reason not to get it done."

Ms. Williams believes that it is very important to grade homework. "If students are doing homework incorrectly and you don't catch it, they will not realize that what they are doing is incorrect. So the quicker and the faster we can catch their incorrect thinking, the better [the] opportunity they have for mastering the material." However, she did not realize that having students check their own homework made it difficult for her to understand her students' misconceptions. Ms. Williams would have students grade their homework every day when they come in. "It takes about 5–10 minutes checking homework every day," said Ms. Williams. To train students to grade their own homework, Ms. Williams pointed out, "At the beginning of the year we take class time to analyze their errors, and I write sentences to tell them what they missed, until they start doing those themselves. If they miss something, then they'll go back and figure out what they missed." To grade quizzes or tests, Ms. Williams added, "I circle the number and write the correct answer, so they can go back and redo it and see if they are right. I don't write any Xs, and I just put the grade on top of the paper."

Ms. Williams had different opinions on completion grades and late work from students:

> I don't give completion grades. I might maybe five times a school year. I'm not really comfortable with that idea, because I want kids to be real competent and I think the only way they can also be confident is by accuracy. I don't want them being confident and wrong. . . . Late work can really hinder a student's progress.

To know students' thinking is very important to Ms. Williams: "I need to know what they are thinking in order to know what the errors are. Maybe it was part of the lesson that I didn't stress for that particular group of students. So they don't understand what is going on in the lesson." In regard to promoting thinking, Ms. Williams suggested:

> You don't always give them the answers and you don't always tell them if they're right or wrong. In the end you do. I don't assume I am the source of all knowledge, I assume that they are capable of figuring things out on their own. So I try not to give answers too quickly. . . . I like to ask questions on how and why and comparing it to other things. The further into the year, I [more] like to see them compare it to other things. With the GT students, I want them to understand why things function the way they do.

Ms. Williams tried to help students be successful learners: "I tutor and do a lot of remediation. I do a lot of things. I say to my kids, everybody has the ability to learn sixth grade math. Some students either lack study skills or lack support at home. We just try to look at things that will make the child successful."

"Percent of Change" Lesson: Ms. Gibson

Observation of Classroom Teaching

Ms. Gibson had taught for 26 years, and 7 of those years had been at the junior high school. The observation was conducted on the percent of change section in a pre-AP (advanced placement) sixth grade class.

She started class with a five-minute warm-up that included two problems:

1. 57 is 60 percent of what number?
2. n/100 = 38/48, n = ?

She showed the procedures for solving the two problems on the board and used calculators to find the answers.

Next she checked the students' homework by calling out the answers for each problem. Students recorded the right answer and checkmarked the missed problems. Then Ms. Gibson called students one by one. As the students called out the grade they got on their homework, she recorded it in the grade book.

At the beginning of the lesson, Ms. Gibson showed the problems on a transparency:

1. Find the percent of change. Original: 35, new: 45.

She showed how to solve this problem in proportion format. Then she introduced the second problem:

2. Find the percent of change. Original: 60, new: 25.

She showed how to solve this problem by using the ratio of the difference to the original amount. Ms. Gibson asked questions for both problems but did not wait for students to provide answers. She used a calculator to find the answer for the students.

After modeling the first two problems, she had students work on the other two problems. After they finished, she had the students say the answers and explain how they got the answers.

Ms. Gibson had students do a quiz from the TAAS (Texas Assessment of Academic Skills) practice booklet for about 10 minutes. While students were working on the quiz, she walked around the classroom to monitor students and answer questions. She did not allow students to use calculators for the quiz because they are not allowed on the TAAS.

After students finished the quiz, Ms. Gibson called out the answers for the quiz; students marked the missed problems and calculated their grade by themselves. Ms. Gibson then called the students' names one by one; the students told her their grades, and she recorded the grades in the grade book.

Application of PCK in Ms. Gibson's Classroom

The observation of Ms. Gibson's teaching indicated that her focus on this lesson is procedural development.

- To build on students' ideas of percent of change, she was able to provide warm-up problems to help students build a connection to new knowledge. However, she did not use any visual materials or pictures; instead she introduced procedure only.
- By calling out their answers to homework and quizzes to the class, students take responsibility for grading; Ms. Gibson only recorded the grades. It seemed to save time for Ms. Gibson, but it did not provide any information to her on students' thinking and their misconceptions.
- By providing no waiting time for students' thinking, Ms. Gibson failed to allow and promote students' thinking.

Interview with Ms. Gibson

Ms. Gibson was interviewed in her classroom. First she talked about her primary focus on teaching mathematics:

My primary focus is to relate it to reality. Why learn it if they can't apply it to reality? I try to teach with that in mind. Everything that I do in class, students know there is a place they can use it in the real world. I always try to give them a purpose. I try to always introduce my lesson with a manipulative, whether or not it is hands on. So they have something to fall back on if they don't understand it. When we do percent, we use base ten blocks, so that they have a visual picture. It is hard to bridge a manipulative to the abstract. You can learn better by seeing or doing than by just hearing. I believe in learning by doing and then we learn by using a manipulative, and then we do. We go back to a manipulative if they are in trouble; then we do practice.

However, during the observation of her class, Ms. Gibson did not use any manipulatives to help students' understanding.

Asked whether most of her students liked learning mathematics, she answered, "At the beginning of the year I gave them a survey to see if they like it or not. The results vary depending on the class. Half of them didn't like mathematics. A lot of students have a fear of mathematics. You have to make them think they can do it." She added, "I think a lot of times the students don't even see the manipulative as work. A lot of times they are not aware of that they are learning by doing. It really helps to break down that fear barrier."

She believes that mathematics is a hard to teach because it is more reality based and you must have the skill to get along with people. However, she noted, "I think it is the hands-on stuff and getting the kids involved in the teaching. I always read books on that to get better. Trying to reach every student is hard every year. Learning styles really interest me."

Ms. Gibson believes in a student-centered method of teaching mathematics: "My method is more student-centered. I always ask them how they solve a problem. I ask why and get them to explain it. I ask questions to see if they really understand it. I try to get them to do more of the talking. We do quite a bit with partners." To compare the student-centered with the teacher-centered method, she explained:

I have students who can do the math but can't apply it. That's why I try to use the manipulative. I think drill is good but they can remember the hands-on more than the drills. I don't think you can use the traditional way in the world today. When we were kids, that's what we did. But now, they'll ask you where you can use it. When I was in school, we were never told why we did anything.

In talking about how to plan for instruction, she said, "We have to turn in lesson plans every week. But I basically look at what I'm going to teach every six weeks. I look at the big picture first. I do a week at a time, and I know where I'm headed."

She had students grade their own homework. To answer why she graded students' homework in this way, she said that at her school students check their own papers. "The principal thinks that it is good for the good students to see their own mistakes, and it is also rewarding for all students," she added. However, to know students' understanding, "they have to show me all their work. I let them use calculators now because I know they know multiplication and division. My policy is no [work shown], no credit. I take up every kid's paper every day. I look over it, and I can tell if they know it or not. They have to write it all out." She further explained how she was able to know students' thinking and understanding: "I'm always listening to them; I test them every other week so that I can see how they are doing. I do quizzes, tests, and daily work, and I pay a lot of attention to . . . their work. I walk around and listen to what they say." To promote student thinking, she "does activities that get them to think. And give[s] them a lot of real-life problems."

Ms. Gibson also pointed out the importance of responding to individual differences. She said, "I have almost 140 students. I have some students that zip through stuff; I have students that are very sensitive. You can give the general assignment to everyone. I help the ones who are struggling. It's very important in the beginning to figure out what they need."

In responding to the question about content knowledge or pedagogical knowledge, she said, "I think you really need to understand math. You need to know from where you need to go with this concept. Students need someone who knows it thoroughly." However, she added:

> You might have all the math knowledge in the world, but if you do not have the presentation skills or you're not a people person, or if you intimidate the student or if you don't have any discipline, you can't reach

the students. You need to be compassionate and not judgmental. I want them to enjoy math. My goal is to get the students to a point where they're comfortable with it. You have to teach it at different levels.

These remarks showed that Ms. Gibson recognized the importance of pedagogical knowledge in teaching.

THE CHINESE TEACHERS' PCK IN CLASSROOMS

"Comparison of Volume and Surface Area of Rectangular Prisms": Ms. Ren

Observation of Classroom Teaching

Ms. Ren was a fifth grade teacher with 14 years' teaching experience. One class period of 45 minutes was observed. The topic of the class was comparison of volume and surface area of rectangular prisms.

First Ms. Ren stated that since they had already learned how to find the surface area and volume, today they were going to compare the volume and the surface area of rectangular prisms. She put three questions on the blackboard:

1. What is the meaning of the surface area of the rectangular prism? What about the volume of the rectangular prism?
2. What are the basic units of the surface area and volume for the rectangular prism?
3. To calculate the surface area of the rectangular prism, what sides do we need to measure? What about for volume?

She had a student read the problems to the class first, and grouped the students by four to observe the rectangular prisms they made using paper; they then discussed these three questions.

Ms. Ren asked two students to report the results of the group discussion, and she summarized the students' key points: the differences between the surface area and the volume of a rectangular prism are in meaning, basic units, and method of calculation; to find the surface area and volume of rectangular prisms, one needs to measure the length, width, and height. She asked further questions: What are the basic units of measurement for area and for volume? What are the relationships between two consecutive basic units of measurement, and how do you transfer from one to the other? Students gave examples of square meters and square centimeters for area, and cubic meters and cubic centimeters for volume. In addition, they figured out the rate of conversion for two consecutive basic units for area and volume.

To help students progress in their understanding, Ms. Ren had them work with partners to measure the rectangular prism they had on their desks and find the surface area and the volume. After students finished, she had them report the result of their measurements and the procedures for calculations. She asked questions: What is the difference between the volume and the surface area? What is the difference between the two basic units for surface area and volume? What is the difference between the calculation of surface area and of volume? Each time students answered, she repeated the answer to reinforce understanding. Then she summarized the key points again: because there are differences in meaning, basic units, and the method of calculation between the surface area and volume, we need to read the problems carefully, pay attention to what the problems ask for, and then select a proper way to solve them.

To reinforce students' knowledge, Ms. Ren gave the following problems:

1. A cube has a side measuring 6 centimeters; find its surface area and volume.
2. A rectangular prism has a length of 5 centimeters, a width of 6 centimeters, and a height of 9 centimeters; find its surface area and volume.

After five minutes, she had two students give the answers and explain their procedure. The two students used different procedures to solve the first one:

Problem 1: Student 1: $(6 \times 6 + 6 \times 6 + 6 \times 6) \times 2 = 216$ square centimeters
$6 \times 6 \times 6 = 216$ cubic meters
Student 2: $(6 \times 6) \times 6 = 216$ square centimeters
$6 \times 6 \times 6 = 216$ cubic meters

Problem 2: Both students: $(9 \times 6 + 9 \times 5 + 6 \times 5) \times 2 = 245$
square centimeters
$9 \times 5 \times 6 = 2700$ cubic centimeters

Since problem 1 has the same results for surface area and volume, she had students compare the results in problem 1 and asked, "Are there any differences between the two? Do they have the same meaning?" Students analyzed the differences: "The units of measurement are different, and the meanings are different." For problem 2, Ms. Ren had students discuss it again. Students found that there is a difference between calculations for area and for volume besides the different units of measurement and meanings. Ms. Ren summarized students' responses and repeated the differences between area and volumes in terms of units of measurement, meanings, and calculations. She asked the students who got the right answers to raise their hands; all students raised their hands. So she went on to the next activity.

To introduce the new task, she explained, "Since you all understand the difference between the surface area and the volume, we can now use this knowledge to solve real-world problems." She gave students nine problems at five levels to practice, and she had students explain each problem using probing questions, "What is your thinking on this? And why?"

Finally she ended the lesson by asking the students, "What did you learn today?" and she repeated the students' summary to the class.

Application of PCK in Ms. Ren's Classroom

In examining Ms. Ren's PCK in teaching the lesson about comparison of volume and surface area of rectangular prisms, we found that she focused on conceptual understanding by providing probing questions and problem-solving strategies:

- To build on students' mathematics ideas, Ms. Ren posed three questions at the beginning of the lesson to determine students' thinking on prior knowledge; to construct students' concrete understanding, she had them observe and measure the rectangular prism they had made on the previous day to find the surface area and the volume. By asking further questions to compare the results, Ms. Ren developed students' abstract thinking.

- By asking probing questions, Ms. Ren identified students' misconceptions. By repeating and summarizing student responses each time, Ms. Ren reinforced correct thinking in the whole class.
- Ms. Ren provided problems to engage students in the learning process of comparing and contrasting the results, methods, and meanings.
- By having students work on five levels of nine problems, Ms. Ren promoted and extended student thinking at a high level.

Interview with Ms. Ren

Ms. Ren considers mathematics teaching easier than other subjects "because it teaches thinking methods." She believes that most of her students like mathematics. She noticed the differences among students at that age: "In the lower grades, there is no burden for students; every student likes mathematics. However, in the fifth grade, mathematics becomes difficult." Ms. Ren believes when she teaching mathematics, she is teaching thinking methods and skills.

She likes using a student-centered method because it allows students to play the main role and enhances their creativity. She believes that the traditional way of teaching has more disadvantages: "The teacher talks more, and does not know the students' thinking." Although the observation of her class showed that she had a teacher-centered way of teaching, she was able to know students' thinking through carefully designed layered questions.

In responding to the question about what other teaching methods she would like to learn or try, she admitted, "There is no way to go beyond the textbook. We have to follow the requirement and do not have too much latitude. In addition, with so many students in the class, it is difficult for students to freely function in their role." She hoped that all students in her class would be able to communicate with the teacher freely.

According to Ms. Ren, she used more manipulatives in the lower grades; however, in the fifth grade she focused more on abstract thinking and used manipulatives more in the geometry lessons. She thought that cooperative learning was very difficult in her class with 62 students. In cases such as these, she suggested, the teacher should arrange groups carefully and try to put the same level of kids together. Otherwise, cooperative learning is superficial and some students do not actively participate. In the observation of her class, she grouped students by four for discussion, and she also had students work with partners.

Ms. Ren believes that planning is very important. She said, "To be able to teach 62 students in 45 minutes, you have to plan instruction thoroughly." Usually she spends one and a half hours on planning every day.

In addition, she believes that doing homework reinforces learning. She assigned homework every day, especially to fifth and sixth graders. She also required students to memorize some basic facts of mathematics in order to help them solve problems. She graded every problem on each student's homework. A student who made a mistake was called to her office and made corrections until she or he understood. Chinese teachers call this "face-to-face grading." She taught only two class periods in the morning, so she had time to grade and help students. Usually she spent two periods of class time on grading the students' work.

Besides using homework to get to know her students, Ms. Ren also used observation, students' explanations, and tests to learn how the students think. Ms. Ren believes that understanding students' thinking directly affects her ability to teach and her ability to distinguish differences in students' needs." She realizes "a responsible teacher has to work very hard." She spent lot of time during lunch and after school on helping students who were struggling. However, she felt sorry for the higher-level students because they sometimes did not receive the attention they deserved.

She believes that pedagogical knowledge is important for a teacher. She has been trying to gain more teaching knowledge by taking continuing education courses.

"Finding Simple Ways to Add or Subtract Fractions": Ms. Bao

Observation of Classroom Teaching

Ms. Bao was a fifth grade mathematics teacher with eight years' teaching experience. One class period of 45 minutes was observed. The topic of the lesson was finding a simple way to add or subtract fractions.

At the beginning of the class, Ms. Bao gave eight problems to students and called on students to answer problems orally:

$$\frac{5}{9} + \frac{8}{9}, \qquad \frac{3}{4} + \frac{1}{2}, \qquad \frac{7}{8} + \frac{1}{4}, \qquad 1\frac{7}{10} + \frac{8}{10},$$

$$\frac{2}{3} + \frac{1}{6}, \qquad \frac{3}{4} + \frac{1}{6}, \qquad \frac{5}{12} + \frac{3}{8}, \qquad 1\frac{3}{4} + \frac{3}{5}.$$

In two minutes, students answered the questions one by one, and all students got the right answers.

After assessing students' prior knowledge, Ms. Bao had students complete a problem mentally from the book; whoever finished stood up until the entire group (row) of students finished. She then told the groups to sit down and asked students in each group to explain how they got the answer. She selected the group that answered all questions correctly for a first-place ranking. This activity took about five minutes.

Next she gave two problems for all students to complete independently in five minutes. These two problems are:

$$2\frac{1}{2} - \frac{3}{4} + 1\frac{7}{8} \qquad\qquad 5\frac{2}{9} - 3\frac{2}{9} + 1\frac{1}{2}.$$

She then asked the students who had finished the problem to raise their hands. Students had to explain how they arrived at their answers orally. She selected the work of two students, which she showed on the projector.

To introduce the new lesson, Ms. Bao connected prior knowledge to it by asking, "What properties have we learned for addition?" Students all answered simultaneously, "Commutative property and associative property."

She wrote:

$$a + b = b + a \qquad\qquad \text{Commutative property}$$
$$(a + b) + c = a + (b + c) \qquad \text{Associative property}$$

"Can these properties be used in fraction addition?" she further asked. Some students answered, "Yes."

She had students observe two groups of problems and find the relationship between the two expressions in each problem:

$$\frac{3}{7} + \frac{2}{5} \; ? \; \frac{2}{5} + \frac{3}{7} \qquad\qquad \frac{3}{8} + \frac{1}{2} \; ? \; \frac{1}{2} + \frac{3}{8}$$

$$\left(\frac{2}{3}+\frac{1}{4}\right)+\frac{3}{4}\;?\;\frac{2}{3}+\left(\frac{1}{4}+\frac{3}{4}\right)\qquad \left(\frac{1}{3}+\frac{1}{2}\right)+\frac{1}{4}\;?\;\frac{1}{3}+\left(\frac{1}{2}+\frac{1}{4}\right)$$

The students found that both sides of the four expressions are equal because of commutative and associative properties.

Ms. Bao had the students read page 141 in the textbook, about how to use these two properties in the addition of mixed numbers, for five minutes.

Next she had students find a simpler way to solve a problem on adding mixed numbers:

$$2\frac{2}{7}+3\frac{3}{4}+4\frac{1}{7}+5\frac{1}{4}$$

One student said that the easy way to do it would be to add the whole numbers first. Ms. Bao asked, "Is there any other way?" After two minutes, a student shared her work:

$$\left(2\frac{2}{7}+4\frac{1}{7}\right)+\left(3\frac{3}{4}+5\frac{1}{4}\right)=6\frac{3}{7}+9=15\frac{3}{7}$$

Ms. Bao asked, "Why did you do in it this way?" The student explained, "Grouping common denominators is easier, and it is by the associative property also."

Students started to practice with two problems in the book independently. She asked the students if they felt it was easier and faster using the simple way. All the students answered, "Yes." After the students finished, she called on a student to give the answer and asked those who agreed to raise their hands. She then had two students with different opinions come up to write their procedures on the board. These two students explained their thinking on these two problems:

Problem 1 (student 1):

$$2\frac{1}{2}-\frac{3}{4}+1\frac{7}{8}$$
$$=2\frac{4}{8}-\frac{6}{8}+1\frac{7}{8}$$
$$=2\frac{4}{8}+1\frac{7}{8}-\frac{6}{8}$$
$$=3\frac{11}{8}-\frac{6}{8}$$
$$=3\frac{5}{8}$$

Problem 2 (student 2):

$$5\frac{2}{9}-\left(3\frac{2}{9}-1\frac{1}{2}\right)$$
$$=5\frac{2}{9}-3\frac{2}{9}+1\frac{1}{2}$$
$$=2+1\frac{1}{2}$$
$$=3\frac{1}{2}$$

Ms. Bao asked, "Why did you change positions of the two fractions in step 2 in problem 1?" The student explained, "In this way I could avoid borrowing." Ms. Bao asked another student who had problem 2, "Why did you remove the parentheses in problem 2?" The student answered, "It is easier to add to numbers with common denominators." Ms. Bao instructed the class to discuss and evaluate two students' work on the blackboard. She also directed students to find the right and easier way to do the problem. She asked students' their feelings about using the simple way. All students said, "It is convenient and easier to solve problems using the simple way."

In order to check students' understanding, she gave six additional problems and asked students to answer orally. Students only needed to explain what they thought about the problem first and then students selected any two problems to work on their own using the simple way. Ms. Bao reminded students to pay attention to changing the signs when parentheses are removed. After a few minutes, she called on students who selected problem 1 to answer first, and then went over every problem.

Finally, she gave eight problems for students to answer orally to see who could answer them most accurately and fastest. Most students raised their hands to answer questions after they looked at the problems. For problem 3,

$$6\frac{2}{7} - 3\frac{4}{5} + 9\frac{5}{7} - 2\frac{1}{5}$$

One student said that he added $6^2/_7 + 9^5/_7 = 16$ first, then calculated $-3^4/_5 - 2^1/_5 = -6$, and last subtracted $16 - 6 = 10$. Ms. Bao repeated the student's explanation and finished the class by asking review questions and summarizing the lesson.

Application of PCK in Ms. Bao's Classroom

Evaluating Ms. Bao's class, we could see that Ms. Bao focused on cultivating understanding and proficiency through intensive practice.

- To build on students' math ideas, Ms. Bao designed 10 problems related to prior knowledge of adding or subtracting fractions and properties of addition for whole numbers. This made a smooth transition for students to learn the new lesson.

Ms. Bao was able to identify students' misconceptions by asking layered questions and listening to students' explanations.

- To engage students in learning, Ms. Bao designed 14 problems to have students explore and find simple ways to solve them. Through analysis and comparison of different strategies, students actively participated in discussing and answering questions.
- To promote and extend students' thinking, Ms. Bao had students find strategies to solve complex problems. By using oral practice, Ms. Bao enhanced students' abilities in mental computation.

Interview with Ms. Bao

Ms. Bao thinks that mathematics is more difficult to teach compared to language arts because "it is boring compared to language, and some students do not have an interest in it."

However, she believes that most of her students like mathematics: "When students can solve problems that involve critical thinking, they feel successful; some students give problems to each other and try to beat each other." The observation of her class confirmed this belief. The problems that Ms. Bao provided to students were not one-step problems; students had to think to find a simple way to solve these problems.

Ms. Bao believes that "teaching mathematics is similar to teaching 'thinking methods': Students should learn methods (skills) and enhance their thinking ability." In order to increase these thinking skills, students should "learn basic knowledge and skills."

She would like using a student-centered teaching method because "students are more relaxed and have more freedom and are free to express their opinion." The observation of her class showed all students actively participated in the learning process of discussion, sharing, and communication under Ms. Bao's direction, though it appeared to be a more teacher-centered way. She did not like teacher-centered teaching because "only the teacher talks; students are not interested and are not engaged. The teacher and students do not have a close relationship. The students do not have an opportunity to use manipulatives." However, she acknowledged that traditional teaching provided students a strong basis in knowledge and skills and more training in problem solving.

Ms. Bao's class reflected the combination of both ways of teaching, focusing on eliciting students' thinking and building proficiency.

To answer how she deals with the individual differences among 53 students in one class, she said, "I design class work and homework by layers, and require all students to do basic problems. In the class work, I grade "face-to-face" for 10 minutes. Whoever finishes class work comes to the front and shows me their work; I grade it, and they return to their seats to continue to the next-level problems." In addition, to communicate with students, she encourages them to write her a small note expressing their ideas or identifying the problems they had difficulty solving. Students put their notes in her drawer, so Ms. Bao knows what her students are thinking and how their understanding is proceeding. This approach helps build a strong communication relationship between the teacher and students. Ms. Bao believes that the relaxed classroom environment makes students close to a teacher, which in turn makes it easier for the teacher to understand and promote students' thinking.

Ms. Bao knew that manipulatives make learning interesting, but she would use manipulatives only with graph problems. She does use oral competition activities every day. During morning independent study time, students have 15–20 minutes to practice orally. In mathematics class, before starting a new lesson, she always gives a set of problems for students to do orally. For example, in the observed class, she had students answer eight problems orally before the new lesson. During the new lesson, she usually has an oral competition. Students who got the right answer stood up until the whole group was standing up. This activity increased the students' interest in problem solving, and also gave students a chance to stretch.

Ms. Bao believes that planning is very important; she focuses on the students' needs in planning, and she usually spends two hours preparing a lesson. She spends at least two periods of class time daily on grading students' homework. The students are required to write clearly and neatly with detailed procedures for their homework.

The teachers are also required to write neatly and clearly on the blackboard. In the observation of Ms. Bao's class, all teaching notes were organized logically on the blackboard from the beginning to the end of the class period; some notes were prepared before class on small boards. This structure of writing in teaching provides students a full picture of the lesson and helps students reflect on their learning during the class.

Ms. Bao believes that "at the primary and middle school levels, teaching 'thinking methods' is more important than [teaching] content knowledge." To improve her teaching methods, she often observes other teachers' classes and explores new knowledge.

"Change Fractions into Decimals" Lesson: Ms. Jing

Observation of Classroom Teaching

Ms. Jing had been teaching for four years. One class period of 45 minutes was observed. The topic of the class was changing fractions into decimals.

The first introductory activity was to have students change the following fractions to decimals, solving these five problems mentally and answering them orally:

$$\frac{3}{10}, \frac{7}{100}, \frac{9}{100}, \frac{35}{100}, \frac{125}{1000}$$

After students answered the questions, Ms. Jing said that fractions with denominators like 10, 100, and 1000 can be changed to decimals directly. "But if fractions do not have denominators like 10, 100, 1000 . . . how can we change these fractions to decimals?" she asked. "Let's make some changes on the first set of problems." She showed a second set of problems with different denominators to students:

$$\frac{3}{4}, \frac{7}{25}, \frac{9}{40}, \frac{3}{14}, \frac{7}{9}$$

All students did the above problems and explained how to change the fractions to decimals in two different ways: use division, or for some problems, change the denominators to 100.

Ms. Jing wrote the above problems again using division:

$$3 \div 4, 7 \div 25, 9 \div 40, 3 \div 14, 7 \div 9$$

and asked, "Why do you solve problems in this way? What is the relationship between a fraction and division?" A student answered the questions: $a \div b = {}^a/_b, (b \neq 0)$.

Ms. Jing said to the class, "Today we are going to use the relationship between fraction and division to change fractions to decimals." Ms. Jing started the new lesson by putting two groups of fractions on the board:

<table>
<tr><td>Group 1</td><td>Group 2</td></tr>
</table>

$$\frac{3}{4}, \frac{7}{25}, \frac{9}{20}, \frac{11}{50} \qquad \frac{3}{14}, \frac{7}{9}, \frac{11}{15}$$

Two minutes later, the answers the students got were terminating decimals in the first group and nonterminating decimals in the second group. The teacher asked students to observe the above results, to explain how they got the answers, and to address the differences between the two groups of problems. Students summarized the differences and showed the two methods of solution: (1) denominators in group 1 could be changed to 100; (2) problems in group 2 could be solved using division. Ms. Jing selected one problem from each group to continue addressing how to change fractions to terminating and nonterminating decimals:

$$\frac{11}{50} \qquad \frac{11}{15} \qquad .$$

Two students came up to write their solutions on the blackboard:

Problem 1: $\dfrac{11}{50} = \dfrac{22}{100} = 0.22, \dfrac{11}{15} = 11 \div 15 \approx 0.733 \ldots$

Problem 2: $\dfrac{11}{50} = 11 \div 50 = 0.22, \dfrac{11}{15} = 11 \div 15 \approx 0.733 \ldots$

Teacher: Why did you use division for 11/50?
Student 2: Based on the relationships between fraction and division.
Teacher: Which way is easier to solve problem 1?
Whole class: Changing the denominator to 100 is easier for problem 1.
   Ms. Jing wrote the words "terminating" and "nonterminating" in two columns, and posed the following questions: How can we determine if a fraction is terminating or nonterminating? What factor affects the result? The teacher had the students observe the above problems again and give new examples of these two types of problems. For nonterminating, students gave examples of 6/7, 8/9, and 8/15.

One student explained, "The key is the denominator." The teacher asked, "Why?" The student answered, "If the denominator of a fraction can be changed to 10, 100, or 1000, then this fraction can be changed to a terminating decimal." However, another student argued that it couldn't be used for all cases, such as 3/9. He explained that the key is looking at the denominators because the above problems such as 7/25 and 7/9 have the same numerator but different denominators. Some students also gave arguments using 8/15.

To clear up students' confusion and direct them to find a way to determine if a fraction can change to a terminating or nonterminating decimal, Ms. Jing had students do prime factorization on the denominators and find out what prime numbers are in each denominator. Students did the following prime factorizations:

Group 1: $25 = 5 \times 5, 4 = 2 \times 2, 20 = 2 \times 2 \times 5, 50 = 2 \times 5 \times 5$
Group 2: $14 = 2 \times 7, 9 = 3 \times 3, 15 = 3 \times 5$

Students observed that in group 1, there are only factors of 2 and 5, while in group 2, there are other factors besides 2 and 5. To find the way to determine the terminating decimal, students summarized: If the fraction has a denominator with prime factors of only 2 and/or 5, then the fraction can be changed to a terminating decimal.

To continue building on the students' concepts and skills, Ms. Jing then gave the students the following oral practice from a preprepared small blackboard:

$$4/5, 5/6, 9/10, 8/11, 7/16, 19/25, 12/30.$$

Students had an argument about 12/30. Because it could be $^{12}/_{2 \times 3 \times 5}$, some students said it could be changed to a terminating decimal. But some students said that there is a factor 3 besides 2 and 5, so it could not be changed to a terminating decimal. Ms. Jing guided students to reduce it first and then look at the prime factors. So it becomes $^{6}/_{15} = ^{2}/_{5}$, and students realized that it could be changed to a terminating decimal. From discussing this problem, students understood that two steps are involved in changing a fraction to a terminating decimal: First, reduce the fraction. Second, look at the prime factors. Ms. Jing summarized these two steps again by putting the written rule on the blackboard.

Ms. Jing had students read their textbooks to check their understanding. All students seemed to understand, since they said they had no questions. Ms. Jing had students do two problems from the textbook:

$$\text{Problem 1: } 3\frac{8}{21}$$

$$\text{Problem 2: } \frac{11}{15}$$

Ms. Jing evaluated the two problems from students. There were two solutions on problem 2, and Ms. Jing had students decide which way was a simpler way:

$$3\frac{8}{21} = 71 \div 21 = 3.381 \quad 3\frac{8}{21} = 3 + (8 \div 21) = 3 + 0.381 = 3.381$$

Students all agreed that the second way was a simpler way.

To reinforce students' understanding, Ms. Jing had students change the following 10 fractions to decimals in 3 minutes:

$$1/2, \ 1/4, \ 3/4, \ 1/5, \ 2/5, \ 3/5, \ 4/5, \ 1/8, \ 1/20, \text{ and } 1/25.$$

She had a student give answers to the class and required all students to try to memorize them in one minute. Then she asked students to give the answers again one by one. All students answered simultaneously.

Finally, she ended class with a set of problems. She asked the students to determine which fractions can be changed to a terminating decimal:

$$3\frac{3}{4} - 0.67, \qquad \frac{7}{8} - \frac{1}{2}, \qquad 4.5 + 3\frac{5}{6}, \qquad 2\frac{2}{5} + \frac{14}{15}.$$

Students answered orally and simultaneously. She summarized the key points of the lesson.

Application of PCK in Ms. Jing's Classroom

An important feature of Ms. Jing's lesson was the fast pace and close sequential order from easy to difficult levels with extensive layered practice, which elicited students' thinking, reinforced understanding, and built proficiency in mathematics.

- To build on students' idea of changing fractions to decimals, Ms. Jing used two sets of 10 problems to connect students' prior knowledge and develop abstract thinking on changing fractions to decimals.

- To clear up confusion and misconceptions on the prime factors that determine terminating decimals, Ms. Jing provided problems for students to compare and contrast, and had students summarize their own findings on the rules.

- Ms. Jing was able to engage students in the learning process by using examples and different representations for changing fractions to decimals, and had students provide their own examples to classify two different methods. By providing more than 30 problems during the lesson, Ms. Jing had students, "discover, rather than instilling knowledge into the students," which enhanced conceptual understanding and built a solid procedural development for students.

- By comparing different ways of solving problems and finding a simpler and easier way, students' thinking was elicited and extended. Ms. Jing also had students summarize the rules and strategies, which provided students a chance to abstract and generalize their thinking at a high-order level.

Interview with Ms. Jing

Ms. Jing said she liked teaching mathematics because learning mathematics helps students develop their thinking ability, which they can use in all areas of life. She said, "If students are interested in mathematics, then it is easier to teach." Some of her students like learning mathematics, while some students learn mathematics because of the pressure of exams.

Ms. Jing believes that both conceptual understanding and procedural development are important:

Skills cannot be separated from concepts. Depending on the lesson to be taught, I decide to focus on the concepts or procedure. In today's lesson, I focused on skill development; I had students discover, rather than instilling knowledge into the students. Usually proficiency relates to skills, and the mastery method relates to concepts.

Ms. Jing would like her students to master basic skills and learn thinking methods. In order to develop thinking methods and skills, Ms. Jing would require students to have clear concepts and do intensive practice sometimes. However, she would not emphasize the results, but the thinking process. She suggested selecting practice problems that concentrate on the thinking method: "Sixth graders should learn to think through solving problems in order to be able to apply methods."

Ms. Jing believes in the student-centered teaching method. "The teacher can guide the students in the right direction in order to avoid them taking the long way to obtain knowledge." Her view of the student-centered way is to guide students to learn. In teacher-centered teaching, she said:

> If the teacher talks too much, the students will be too tired to listen. At least at fifth and sixth grade levels, the teacher-centered method is not very effective. Teaching should attract students. Students are learning, not the teacher. Let the students say what they want to say, even if they say something wrong.

About cooperative learning, Ms. Jing expressed her concern that there was not enough time for such discussion. However, she noted that the results of discussion were very good, so she tried to use it. She realized the importance of organization in cooperative learning. She gave different levels of questions for group discussion so that every student had a chance to speak in the group discussion.

Ms. Jing described how she plans for instruction: "The school requires teachers to write lesson plans during summer vacation; the teacher also plans ahead during the semester. However, before giving the instruction, the teacher should go over it and adjust it." She thought such lengthy planning was unnecessary; she would like to plan ahead only by one day. During the planning of instruction, she would also consider the students' thinking. Usually she knows how students think from experience and students' exercises.

To promote students' thinking, Ms. Jing would motivate students to engage in learning. She explained, "Mathematics is abstract; if students engage in learning, students will think. Understanding how students think is very important to the teacher."

To deal with the differences among students, she paid attention to the majority of students, and used "increase high, remedy low" at both ends, referring to the high-level and low-level students.

She believes that knowledge is very important to a teacher, but knowledge should be connected to context. For example, the concept of limit in calculus exists in the circle section in the sixth grade. She said, "I hope my students do not say 'new' for every day's lesson, meaning students should be able to connect their prior knowledge to the new knowledge."

"The Mixed Operation of Fractions and Decimals" Lesson: Ms. Fang

Observation of Classroom Teaching

Ms. Fang had been teaching mathematics for six years. One 45-minute class period was observed with Ms. Fang's fifth grade mathematics class. The topic of the lesson was the mixed operation of fractions and decimals.

At the beginning of the class, Ms. Fang provided three groups of problems for students. One group was to change fractions to decimals:

$$\frac{1}{2}, 1\frac{1}{4}, \frac{3}{4}, 4\frac{1}{5}, 10\frac{2}{5}, \frac{3}{5}, 2\frac{4}{5}, \frac{1}{8}, \frac{3}{8}, \frac{5}{8}, \frac{7}{8}, \frac{9}{10}, \frac{1}{20}, \frac{1}{25}, \frac{1}{50}, \frac{1}{100}.$$

The second group was to determine which fractions can be changed to terminating decimals:

$$\frac{2}{6}, \frac{3}{11}, \frac{3}{8}, \frac{5}{14}, \frac{4}{15}, \frac{9}{20}, \frac{3}{16}, \frac{7}{12}.$$

The third group was to calculate the problems by fractions and then by decimals:

$$3.6 + 2\frac{4}{5} \qquad 3\frac{1}{2} - 1.75$$

She called students one by one to answer problems in the first group orally. Next she gave students a few minutes to do the second and third groups of problems; then she had students answer and explain their reasoning.

The new lesson was about mixed operations of fractions and decimals. Ms. Fang told the students, "When a problem contains fractions and decimals, we can change fractions to decimals, or change decimals to fractions, according to the problem." She gave an example on the preprepared small blackboard:

$$3\frac{3}{4} - 0.63 + 1\frac{2}{5}$$

She asked, "If there are fractions and a decimal in a problem, how do you solve it?"

Students answered, "You can use two ways to solve the problem." She then had students do this problem both ways quietly by themselves. After a few minutes, she had two students come up to write their procedures in two ways on the blackboard:

$$3\frac{3}{4} - \frac{63}{100} + 1\frac{2}{5} = 3\frac{75}{100} - \frac{63}{100} + \frac{140}{100} = 4\frac{52}{100} = 4\frac{13}{25}$$

$$3.75 - 0.63 + 1.4 = 3.12 + 1.4 = 4.52$$

Then Ms. Fang asked, "Which way is easier? Why?" Most students answered that they liked the second way because in the first way, they have to reduce the fractions and change the mixed numbers to fractions. Ms. Fang summarized students' responses: "If fractions can be changed to terminating decimals, then mixed operation problems can be solved by changing the fraction to a decimal. It is a simpler way."

Ms. Fang gave two problems in order for students to practice using the easier way.

$$6\frac{4}{25} - 0.13 + 1\frac{5}{8} \qquad 24.56 - 2\frac{1}{8} - 0.08$$

After students finished these two problems, she asked, "Can the fractions be changed to terminating decimals? If the fraction cannot be changed to a terminating decimal, how can you get an accurate result?" Ms. Fang provided example 5:

$$3\frac{5}{6} - 4.5 + 1\frac{3}{4}$$

Every student tried this problem. Ms. Fang had two students come up and show their procedures for changing decimals to fractions:

$$3\frac{5}{6} - 4.5 + 1\frac{3}{4}$$

$$= 3\frac{5}{6} + 4\frac{1}{2} - 1\frac{3}{4}$$

$$= 3\frac{10}{12} + 4\frac{6}{12} - 1\frac{9}{12}$$

$$= 6\frac{7}{12}$$

Ms. Fang asked students to compare examples 4 and 5. Students found that $3\frac{5}{6}$ could not be changed into terminating decimal; to get an accurate result, using fractions is a good way to solve this example.

However, Ms. Fang told students, "If the problem allows you to approximate the result, you may change a fraction to a decimal, and then round the result." She gave students two problems to practice in order to get approximate results:

$$15\frac{1}{3} - 2.75 + 5\frac{1}{8} \qquad 2.25 + 3\frac{5}{6} - 2\frac{7}{9}$$

Ms. Fang told the class, "When you are allowed to get approximate results, you can round it to two places after the decimal point." She had students do one problem for rounding:

$$3\frac{5}{6} + 4.5 - 1\frac{3}{4}$$

$$\approx 3.83 + 4.5 - 1.75$$

$$= 6.58$$

Then Ms. Fang summarized the rules of the mixed operation of fractions and decimals again by putting them on the blackboard:

1. In the mixed operation of fractions and decimals, if a fraction can be changed to a terminating decimal, using decimals is a simpler and easier way.

2. If a fraction cannot be changed to a terminating decimal, changing the decimal to a fraction is an easier way.

3. If you are allowed to get approximate results, change fractions to decimals and round them also.

Finally, to reinforce students' learning, Ms. Fang had them work on three levels of 14 problems before finishing class. The first level of problems was oral practice. The second level of problems involved deciding which solution was right, which was not right, and which did not use the easier way, and finally to make the correction. In the third level of problems, students actually calculated the problems.

Application of PCK in Ms. Fang's Classroom

The observation of Ms. Fang's lesson on the mixed operation of fractions and decimals indicated her emphasis in this lesson is problem solving with intensive practice to develop skills in procedure and proficiency.

- To build students' ideas on the mixed operation of fractions and decimals, Ms. Fang provided students with 26 problems at three levels. These 26 problems not only helped students review prior knowledge of changing fractions to decimals, but also paved a road to the new knowledge of the mixed operation of fractions and decimals.
- From students' answering questions and working on problems, Ms. Fang was able to identify their misconceptions and make a correction to the whole class.
- To engage students in learning, Ms. Fang posed questions first from a small preprepared blackboard, and then provided problems for students to explore the proper and easier way to solve different types of problems. Oral practice in this lesson reinforced students' thinking at the proficiency level.
- To promote and extend students' thinking, Ms. Fang provided probing questions and layered practice to encourage students to think and ponder at a sequential and logical level.

Interview with Ms. Fang

To Ms. Fang, mathematics is relatively easy to teach compared to Chinese language because every day the new lesson is only taught for about 5–6 minutes; the rest of class time is spent on review of the prior lesson. Ms. Fang believes that most of her students like mathematics.

Ms. Fang's primary focus on teaching mathematics is the development of conceptual understanding. She said, "Only if students have conceptual understanding can they answer questions; by answering questions, they develop skills." About procedural development, Ms. Fang believes "computation development is using the knowledge learned in class, so students can do it on their own at a later time." Usually she would help students develop skills though practice of all kinds of problems. The observation of her teaching showed this strategy.

She believes that the student-centered method is better than the teacher-centered method. However, she said, "Currently, I still use the teacher-centered method. In the traditional way of teaching, the teacher gives the lecture and the students follow the teacher, so learning will be fast and of higher quality." The observation of her teaching indicated this fast pace and high quality. She realized that some good students seemed not to like to listen to basics they have already mastered, and this made it difficult for the teacher to identify problems in learning among the students.

Often she would use various approaches in her teaching such as multimedia, computer, and projector. According to Ms. Fang, using cooperative groups depends on what lesson will be taught; sometimes she would use it in her teaching, such as for dividing a circle into congruent parts and finding how many ways to fold a rectangle into 1/4. She believes that promoting students' interest in mathematics is very important. "Usually the low-level students do not have an interest in learning mathematics." While drills can be repetitive, she agreed, "Learning occurs by doing." She also believes that "too many practice problems produce repetition and reduce students' interest in learning." To avoid this problem, she would assign only 10–20 minutes of homework every day. To meet the needs of all students, Ms. Fang said, "My practice exercises have layers. The practice problems in the first layer are basics, and all students are required to master this level of problem; the problems in the second level are high-level thinking problems, and good students are required to master these problems."

To promote students' thinking, Ms. Fang used practice and questions. She designed practice problems with layers, from easy to difficult. By working on the problems and orally answering questions, students would engage in the thinking process and communicate their opinions. "This training of thinking, using both written and oral practice, will improve students' abilities to think for themselves and extend their thinking to a higher level." To know the character of thinking of the individual student, Ms. Fang would like to "ask for several ways of solving one problem and try to find a unique approach from students' problem solving."

Ms. Fang believes that it is very important to know students' thinking in mathematics. She was able to enhance her knowledge of students' thinking through students' practice and explanations in class. She believes that knowing students' thinking helps her develop clear and systematic goals to teach students. To better understand students' thinking, Ms. Fang grades every homework problem for every student. If a student made a mistake on the homework, she would call the student in and grade the problem "face-to-face" in order to help the student understand how to solve it. If a student made a careless error, she would comment on it and have the student read it and make a correction. She usually allocates one period of class time to grade homework. She said that usually all her students do homework. A student who missed a homework assignment would stay after school to make it up. If a student did a good job on homework, she would praise the student. She believes that all students in her class "like to submit homework because they want to get praise."

Ms. Fang plans for instruction every day. For each lesson, she uses two periods of class time to prepare. If there is not enough time in school, she prepares the lesson in her spare time. Besides teaching two math classes in the morning, she also teaches some elective courses, such as music and natural science, during the week. According to Ms. Fang, the school administrator checks teachers' lesson plans once per semester. The school administrators often observe classes according to the teachers' lesson plan. Teachers often observe each other's classes and help each other with planning. The school requires every teacher to observe at least 20 classes a semester and observe one research class per semester. (School policy includes selecting a lesson from each grade level as a model lesson for all the teachers at that particular grade, and having teachers observe the lesson and analyze it. This class is called a research class.) The school district also has an open class and meetings to help teachers plan instruction. By observing other teachers' classes, Ms. Fang was able to compare the differences and adjust her lesson plan by adding some good strategies, activities, and examples.

Ms. Fang believes that pedagogical knowledge is more important for elementary and middle school teachers than at higher levels. Because mathematics is simple at these levels, the key is getting students to understand. In order to enhance her pedagogical knowledge, she observed classes, read various references and resource books, and participated in workshops. Through continuing education at the university, she was able to enhance her knowledge in both mathematics content and teaching areas.

"Introduction to the Circle" Lesson: Mr. Xiao

Observation of Classroom Teaching

Mr. Xiao had been teaching for six years. He taught a sixth grade class, and the topic of the lesson observed was an introduction to the circle. In this lesson, he integrated multimedia with animation features to teach basic concepts about the circle.

Mr. Xiao started his introduction by asking, "What geometry figures have we learned?" He showed the rectangle, parallelogram, triangle, and trapezoid on the screen from a computer. "What common features do these figures have?" he asked. The students answered that they are all formed by line segments. He told the students that today they are going to learn a new figure—the circle.

First he showed an animated picture. There were two points on the screen; a red point moved around a blue point, and the distance between the two points always remained the same. He asked, "Is a circle formed by line segments? From the screen, we can see the circle is formed by a curve." He drew a circle on the blackboard and asked, "What are some circle figures in real life?" Students provided examples: VCD, clock, coin, cakes, and so on. At the same time, Mr. Xiao showed figures of such objects on the computer and then hid the objects, leaving a circle outline over each figure. He told students, "The surface areas of these objects are circles."

Mr. Xiao showed how to use a circular object to draw a circle on the screen and had the students draw it and cut it from paper. Mr. Xiao had students fold it through its center several times in different positions. He asked students to observe their circles: "How many times did you fold the circle? How many lines did you get? What did you find?" Students responded, "All the lines go through a center point." He informed students that this point is the "center" of the circle, and had them label it "O." Then he asked, "What is the center of a circle?" He gave a definition of the circle.

He demonstrated radius by picking a point on the circle and connecting it to the center. He asked students to do theirs in the same way on their paper, and asked, "What did you get? How did you get this segment?" He told students, "We call this a radius." He wrote the word "radius" and its definition on the board. He asked further questions: "Since the radius is a segment, where are the two end points? Can you draw one more radius? In a circle, how many radii can you get?" He had students measure several radii and find their measurements. A student answered that his radii were all equal to 6 centimeters. "Is your radius equal to the radius of the student sitting next to you? In what situation do all radii have the same length?" Mr. Xiao also showed the comparison using animation on the screen. Students found that only in the same circle do the radii have the same length.

To check student understanding, Mr. Xiao gave them a set of problems to practice.

1. Fill in the blank: Radius is a ____ connecting ____ and _____.
2. True or False:
   a. There are many radii in a circle.
   b. All the radii have the same length.
3. Are the segments in the following figures radii? Why?

Figure 6.7.   *The Radius of a Circle*

Next Mr. Xiao had students play a game in groups of four: in a paper circle, draw a segment; each student can only draw once; whoever gets the longest segment is the winner. After all students finished, he expected students to observe the segments to see what features the longest segment had. He showed an animation picture on the screen. Students found: "The longest segment goes through the center; its two end points are on the circle." He added the conjunction word "and" and gave the definition of a diameter: "The segment goes through the center, and its two end points are on the circle. This segment is called the diameter of the circle." He wrote a definition of diameter on the board and asked again, "What important feature does it have? Can you draw a segment which is longer than the diameter? What does this mean?" He had students draw the diameter again and measure it using a ruler. After students answered the questions, he showed the animated diameter on the screen again and gave a group of problems for students to answer orally.

1. Fill in the blank: Diameter is a _____ connecting _____ and _____.

2. True or False:
   a. There are many diameters in a circle.
   b. All the diameters have the same length.
   c. The diameter is the longest segment connecting two points on a circle and passing through the center.

3. Are the segments in the following figures diameters? Why?

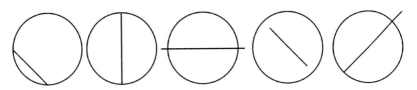

Figure 6.8. The Diameter of a Circle

To teach the relationship between radius and diameter, he organized students in groups of four to do an experiment: three students measured the radius and the diameter in their circles separately, and one student recorded the data of the other three students. He expected students to observe the data and find a pattern for the data. After working with a group, students came to the correct conclusion: in the same circle, the radius is half of the diameter. He continued, "How can you represent the relationship between the radius and diameter by letters?" He wrote on the board: In the same circle, d = 2r, r = 1/2 d.

Finally, he had the students read their textbooks on how to use a compass to draw a circle, and asked the students how many steps it took to draw a circle. Students identified the following key steps:

1. Fixed segment → Radius → Length
2. Fixed point → Center → Location
3. Rotation

He showed students how to draw a circle on the screen using the above three steps, and he also showed how to draw a circle with a 3-centimeter radius using compass on blackboard. He explained the meaning of the distance between two branches of a compass and the meaning of the fixed point. He asked students to draw the same circle on a paper and observe the result. To reinforce students' understanding, he asked questions again: "What is the distance between two branches of a compass? What is the fixed point on the compass? And what is the relationship between the size of circle and the center? What is the relationship between the size of circle and the radius?"

At the end, he had students summarize what they had learned and had them answer a set of eight "divergent" questions, including "Why does the wheel consist of a circle? Where should you put the axis?"

On the blackboard, he arranged the lecture notes in a structured way gradually from the beginning to the end of the lesson:

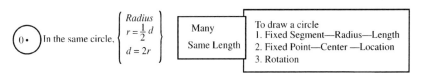

Figure 6.9. *Lecture Structure Displayed on the Blackboard*

Application of PCK in Mr. Xiao's Classroom

The observation of Mr. Xiao's teaching on the circle showed that his primary focus of this lesson was building conceptual understanding.

- To build students' ideas on the concept of circle, Mr. Xiao used the figures of rectangle, parallelogram, triangle, and trapezoid to help students connect the concept of line segment to the radius and diameter of the circle. He used technology to design an animation of the circle, which provided visual and meaningful understanding. He also connected the circle to the figures in students' real lives by having students list examples of circles.
- He designed conceptual problems to address students' misconceptions, and made corrections with the help of students' explanations of problems.
- From doing the game and group activity and drawing radii and diameters, students were able to engage in the inquiry learning process for radius and diameter and to understand the relationship between these two concepts.
- Mr. Xiao provided sequential and layered questions to promote and extend students' thinking about circles and the relationship between radius and diameter.

Interview with Mr. Xiao

Mr. Xiao started teaching mathematics in 1994. During his six years of teaching, he taught physical education for about one year. Mr. Xiao believes that mathematics is not easy to teach compared to other subjects. However, since he considers himself a friend to his students outside of class and cares about them, all his students enjoy learning mathematics. He believes that a teacher should cultivate creativity, but mathematics sometimes is abstract. "Not all the concepts of mathematics can be represented concretely and with hands-on examples; in this case, a teacher needs to teach students knowledge because the truth is there."

In responding to questions about conceptual understanding and procedural development, he quoted a Chinese saying: " 'The purpose of learning is to apply,' but the Chinese do not do well on this because they focus on problem solving too much. There are too many methods for solving mathematics problems. What are the benefits of these? How many of my students will become mathematicians?" He believes that students should learn something that will help them in their lives; he calls this "ability." Mathematics should train students in good habits such as thinking and analyzing. This thinking includes many aspects, including expression of language. He said that in the classroom, a teacher's language expression is very important; students should be able to understand what the teacher says. Students should be able to imitate the teacher and to express themselves. One of the strategies he likes to use is: "I do not pay too much attention if a student did the problem or not; I listen to see if the student can explain it or not." He said, "If the student can explain it, the student understands it. I also require the parents to help their kids stay on track."

Mr. Xiao believes that a teacher should combine both teacher-centered and student-centered ways of teaching. However, he apparently does not believe that it is possible for kids to do some research projects in school. In comparing the traditional and modern way of teaching, he compared the education of China and the United States; he believes that the Chinese are advanced in K-12 education, but in higher education, the Chinese are behind. "China is running ahead at the beginning of education from K through 12th, but it falls behind later. . . . Although Chinese students get a lot of awards in international competitions, Chinese students put more effort into the competitions than students from other countries. Because students spend so much time on test preparation and drills, they lack creativity and hands-on ability." He summarized his view:

> The advantage of Chinese education is that students can get a solid foundation in knowledge. The disadvantage is that the ability of students to develop is limited. The teacher has too much authority, and students are not allowed to speak freely in class. Because of limited class time, the teacher has to finish certain objectives, so students only can follow the teacher in learning.

In his teaching, he believes that if a teacher shows one method, students should not be limited to this method; they can have their own way to solve the problem. "Children often have their own unique way to solve a problem; even a teacher could not come up with that way sometimes."

He described his method of teaching as a combination of both teacher-centered and student-centered ways. In his teaching, he often uses cooperative learning. "The development of our future society depends on the spirit of cooperation; China should focus more on cooperative training." For cooperative learning, he believes that the management of teachers' and students' interests is very important. When he talked about manipulatives, he said, "Students will be too tired to sit and listen. Manipulatives used properly are relaxing for students; like adults who play with a pen in meetings, it helps to reduce stress." However, he believes that learning by doing and learning by practice are equally important for students learning mathematics.

He thinks that planning is very important for teachers, and teachers should plan not only according to the textbook and curriculum, but also according to students, which means to observe and know students' thinking and to use easy language to explain abstract mathematical concepts and terms. Usually he needs to spend one evening preparing the next day's lesson. To compare the differences between teachers in China and the United States, he said that U.S. teachers considered the textbook a reference, but the Chinese considered the textbook the base. He plans instruction every day; he even spends time in the evenings and on weekends. Answering why he works so hard, he said:

> Teachers are different in China than in the United States. In the U.S., a teacher considers teaching a job, while in China, a teacher treats teaching as a great cause. Teachers in China are willing to devote themselves to education. Society recognizes the teacher's work. One of China's popular songs reflects this view: "When I pass the window of the teacher at night, the lights are always bright."

However, he complained, "The actual value is the opposite of the recognition of the teaching profession in China; people give teachers a high reputation. For example, they may say teaching is the brightest career under the sun; a teacher is the engineer of the human soul. However, teachers do not get the pay that matches such a reputation. Also, in China, it is difficult for a teacher to change to another job. In the United States, teachers may do so anytime they wish."

To know students' thinking, he grades each problem on their homework. He has two classes every day; in each class he spends about 40 minutes grading homework. He requires the students to correct mistakes. Sometimes he would design a trap and have students explore it. He would also design different questions to ask students and demand a thorough answer from them. Usually students use half an hour to do homework every day, finishing 80 percent of their homework. He explains the 20 percent of difficult and key problems in class the next day. He believes that if 20 percent of students do not understand the lesson, it would be a big problem for teaching. Usually most of his students understand his lessons.

In conclusion, the observation of teachers' lessons for both groups indicated huge differences in teaching between U.S. teachers and Chinese teachers. These differences were reflected in their pedagogical content knowledge during actual classroom teaching.

All U.S. teachers believe in the importance of conceptual understanding and procedural development. However, in their actual teaching, they seemed to lack the skills to teach effectively. The U.S. teachers focused on manipulatives and hands-on activities to develop conceptual understanding, but they ignored building the connections between concrete understanding and abstract thinking, and ignored proficiency development. In contrast, all Chinese teachers focused on both conceptual understanding and procedural development in teaching by providing practice problems that connect to prior knowledge, asking probing questions in sequential and logical order to elicit students' thinking, giving layered and intensive problems to reinforce understanding, and having students answer problems orally (mentally) to enhance thinking and achieve proficiency. Furthermore, the organization of U.S. teachers' lessons looked very loose and unstructured, while Chinese teachers' lessons displayed high structure in logical and sequential order, from easy to difficult levels, at a fast pace.

CHAPTER 7

Approaches to Enhancing Teachers' Pedagogical Content Knowledge

The effective way of study should integrate "review" in the learning process (学而时习之).

—Confucius

In reviewing prior knowledge, one can always find new knowledge (温故而 知新).

—Confucius

This comparative study was conducted in public schools in the United States and China during the regular academic school year. Previous chapters in this book described the differences in mathematics teachers' pedagogical content knowledge in the United States and China. These differences were revealed by comparison of teachers' responses on mathematics teaching problems, examination of their beliefs, and observation of their actual teaching in the classrooms.

This study cannot necessarily be generalized to all mathematics teachers in the United States and China because the samples included are only from one city in each country, with 23 schools from China and 12 schools from the United States. The results of this study addressed the importance and the components of pedagogical content knowledge and promoted further understanding of effective mathematics teaching from an international perspective. This study of teachers' pedagogical content knowledge has supplied the missing piece in the base of teachers' knowledge system as a whole system. It has also reshaped teachers' knowledge base into an interactive network with powerful and meaningful pedagogical content knowledge as a core and leading component in the system of teachers' knowledge. Furthermore, the results of this study revealed some loopholes in mathematics teaching in both the United States and China, although the results reported in this book showed that both U.S. and Chinese teachers in this study had some degree of pedagogical content knowledge and were able to apply various methods to help students learn mathematics. There were differences between U.S. and Chinese teachers in building on students' mathematics ideas, correcting students' misconceptions, engaging students in learning, and promoting student thinking. These differences had a deep impact on actual classroom teaching. They were derived from the disparities in teachers' beliefs about the goal of math teaching, teaching methods, planning instruction, and students' thinking.

This chapter identifies eight missing components in teachers' knowledge base. These missing components are pertinent to pedagogical content knowledge and play an important role in effective teaching. The analysis of missing components of teachers' knowledge leads to a discussion of reshaping teachers' knowledge and recommendations for enhancing their pedagogical content knowledge.

WHAT IS MISSING IN TEACHERS' KNOWLEDGE BASE?

The missing components in teachers' knowledge base in one or both of the groups of teachers are clearly revealed in the examination of teachers' pedagogical content knowledge on mathematics teaching problems in chapter 4, the analysis of the beliefs on education in chapter 5, and the observations of actual classroom teaching and interviews with teachers in chapter 6. Eight missing parts are identified in a framework of four aspects of pedagogical content knowledge: (1) building on students' mathematics ideas and understanding: *missing component 1—* the bridge from manipulatives to mathematical ideas, and *missing component 2—*the knowledge of a pyramid of understanding; (2) addressing and correcting students' misconceptions: *missing component 3—*approach to students' misconceptions by using probing questions, and *missing component 4—*knowing students' thinking by grading homework; (3) engaging students in mathematics learning: *missing* *component 5*—engaging students in study question–study review process of inquiry, and *missing component 6*—proficiency in procedural development; and (4) promoting and supporting student thinking about mathematics: *missing component 7*—aim at "thinking methods" rather than content, and *missing component 8*—the whole picture and structure in the knowledge network.

Missing Component 1: The Bridge from Manipulatives to Mathematical Ideas

Results in this study show that U.S. teachers tended to build on students' ideas about adding fractions by focusing on concrete models and manipulatives. In observed U.S. teachers' classrooms, a component that could bridge between manipulatives and mathematical ideas was missing.

Concrete models help students visualize and explore mathematics ideas and connect learning to students' experience. This learning is meaningful and makes sense to students if it is used properly. This is supported by Fennema and Romberg (1999), who indicate that mathematics should serve the students' needs to make sense of experience arising outside of mathematics instruction. However, if a teacher only has students engage in manipulatives and concrete models, but she or he does not know how to build or ignores building a connection between manipulatives and mathematical ideas, the teaching is incomplete. In this teaching, students achieve learning only superficially, only knowing "what" but not knowing "how" and "why." Knowing "what," students have only factual and separate pieces of knowledge; this type of knowledge cannot be internalized.

To make the connection between manipulatives and mathematical ideas, a teacher interprets the meaning of mathematical ideas behind manipulatives using definitions and examples, and translates the real meaning of manipulatives into a mathematical idea and a mathematical sentence. Through building and solving mathematical models, students internalize their learning and abstract their thinking.

In contrast, Chinese teachers build on students' ideas about adding fractions with the unit fraction concept, emphasizing procedures and rules. This model would be ideal if Chinese teachers could use more concrete materials to introduce the fraction concept.

Chinese teachers consider concepts and procedures to be important for students. They view the unit fraction as a critical concept. This concept is easily understood by children, and it will build a solid base for learning fractions later. Using the concept of unit fraction in teaching makes the concept of fractions more meaningful than the part–whole relationship. It also shows a consistent relationship between ordering fractions, operations of fractions, and problem solving involving fractions, and it indicates a connection between fractions and whole numbers. This connection will help students perceive fractions as numbers. However, by emphasizing this rigorous and abstract concept, Chinese teachers may use too few concrete models to build understanding. Consequently, students will view mathematics only as abstract numbers and sometimes even lose their interest in learning.

Missing Component 2: The Knowledge of a Pyramid of Understanding

From the differences among responses about understanding fractions, two aspects of understanding in building students' mathematics ideas are observed: concrete understanding and abstract understanding. U.S. teachers usually emphasize concrete understanding by using concrete models and hands-on activities in teaching mathematics, while Chinese teachers focus on abstract understanding. Concrete and abstract understandings are related and build on each other; any focus on one that ignores the other will not build a deep conceptual understanding and will lead to superficial understanding or misunderstanding in learning.

Understanding has a pyramid structure (see figure 7.1): Concrete understanding is the base for abstract understanding. By applying concrete materials and hands-on activities, teachers make mathematics visual and meaningful to students. In order to arrive at abstract understanding, teachers need to help students transfer their concrete understanding to mathematics ideas, symbols, definitions, and algorithms. On a base of abstract understanding, students will identify the relationships between mathematical ideas, definitions, and rules, recognize the connection between prior and new knowledge, make generalizations based on the rules and relationships, apply knowledge to solve problems, and arrive at a conceptual understanding level. However, to help students achieve suc-

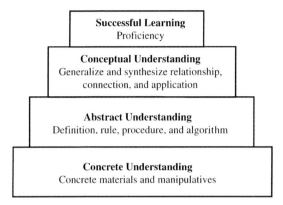

Figure 7.1. The Pyramid Structure of Understanding

cessful learning in mathematics, teachers cannot let learning stay on the conceptual understanding level; they should design various levels of questions and problems to have students practice on paper and orally (or mentally) to enhance students' proficiency in both conceptual understanding and procedural development.

Both U.S. teachers and Chinese teachers concentrated only on one part of understanding. Using concrete models and hands-on activities, U.S. teachers ignored building a transition between concrete and abstract understanding. As the result, students only know mathematical facts and do not have proficiency in procedural development. Applying definitions and rules, Chinese teachers ignore building students' understanding on a concrete base. Although students have proficiency in computation, their ability to connect and apply in the real world remains superficial. To help students achieve a conceptual understanding and procedural development, teachers need to pay attention to both stages of concrete and abstract understanding and build one on each other with connections.

Missing Component 3: Approach to Students' Misconceptions by Using Probing Questions

Asking questions is an effective way to elicit students' thinking and learning. Providing probing questions for students about their misconceptions will guide them to identify errors by themselves and to develop a deep conceptual understanding. Carroll (1999) confirmed that questions involving errors would engage students in the reasoning process. In addition, questions assess learning, promote discussion, and provide direction for teachers in planning.

U.S. teachers in this study demonstrated very little knowledge about asking probing questions to help students correct misconceptions in comparing fractions. They used a variety of concrete models to support students on correcting misconceptions, but often stopped at this level. The use of concrete models helps students build ideas about mathematical concepts if a teacher can guide student thinking toward the connection. This approach is supported by NCTM (2000), which states that concrete models provide students with concrete representations of abstract ideas and support students in using representations meaningfully. In contrast, Chinese teachers dealt with misconceptions with a variety of activities and focused on developing the explicit connection between the various models and abstract thinking by probing into carefully and intellectually designed sequential questions.

Posing questions in mathematics teaching is a feature of Chinese education, which is a reflection of *Arithmetic in Nine Chapters*. The book is organized through a sequence of questions, answers, and principles. One of the emphases in Chinese mathematics instruction is on designing questions while planning instruction, and asking questions while teaching the lesson. To help students learn, teachers pose questions to promote and support students' thinking. In this study, the questioning strategies were displayed extensively in Chinese teachers' responses on mathematics teaching problems, interviews with teachers, and observations of classroom teaching. Chinese teachers not only asked layered questions to address misconceptions but also used questions to elicit student thinking, and applied examples and activities to support and extend students' thinking toward a higher level.

Missing Component 4: Knowing Students' Thinking by Grading Homework

It is very important for mathematics teachers to understand how their students think. U.S. teachers evaluate students' thinking by asking questions, observing students, testing, talking to students, and reading students' journals. Through all these approaches, teachers learn about their students' weaknesses and strengths in mathematics; therefore, teachers can help their students with various approaches and meet the needs of all their students. However, all of above approaches can only help teachers know their students' thinking at a superficial and external level. Some of the U.S. teachers in this study realized that a teacher couldn't effectively remedy misconceptions without knowing what an individual student is thinking.

How does a teacher know students' thinking at an internal and sophisticated level? One effective way is to check daily homework. In this study, Chinese teachers know students' thinking not only from explanations and discussion, but also from checking their daily homework. Homework is powerful evidence, where teachers can examine students' understanding and thinking. Each step of students' work mirrors how and why they think in a particular way. Grading homework is a great opportunity for teachers to know students' thinking at a deep level on a routine daily basis. Unlike Chinese teachers, U.S. teachers in this study barely checked every homework problem; most of the U.S. teachers only gave students completion grades, in order to encourage them. Checking homework by providing answer sheets or calling out answers leads to low student expectations. More importantly, it deprives teachers of an important opportunity to know how their students understand and think at an internal and sophisticated level.

Missing Component 5: Engaging Students in a Study Question–Study Review Process of Inquiry

According to Confucius, the effective way of study should integrate "review" in the learning process (学而时习之). The Chinese word for "learn" (学习), is constructed by two verbs: learn (学) and review (习), which means that one must consistently review the knowledge that has been learned in order to learn well. This learning is formed by two phases: learning new knowledge and reviewing learned knowledge. Confucianism also teaches that in reviewing prior knowledge, one can always find new knowledge (温故而之新). Furthermore the word "knowledge" (学问) in Chinese is formed by two verbs: "learn" (学) and "question" (问). This addresses another important approach of learning: to learn well, one must ask questions.

In the study question–study review model, learning becomes a cycle in the inquiry process. This inquiry process provides a model for effective teaching and learning. To help students gain knowledge, teachers pose questions to promote thinking in which students review prior knowledge and acquire new knowledge. To reinforce new knowledge, teachers guide students in review and toward gaining new insight from the review. Mathematics education in China has followed this idea for classroom teaching and learning for centuries.

In the introduction of new concepts, using prior knowledge not only helps students to review and reinforce the knowledge being taught, but also helps students picture mathematics as an integrated whole rather than as separate pieces of knowledge. Connecting the new and prior knowledge in context will also help students know why and how to learn the new topic and grasp new knowledge with better understanding. NCTM (1989) supported this connection: "Connection among topics will instill in students an expectation that the ideas they learn are useful in solving other problems and exploring other mathematical concepts" (84). Furthermore, NCTM (2000) pointed out, "Because students learn by connecting new ideas to prior knowledge, teachers must understand what their students already know" (18).

The observations of classrooms in this study showed that Chinese teachers spent at least one-third of the time on reviewing prior knowledge at the beginning of or during class. One of the Chinese teachers said that she spent only five or six minutes teaching a new lesson; the rest of the time was reviewing and reinforcing prior knowledge.

The observations of teaching in this study also indicated that there were differences in the way U.S. and Chinese teachers engaged students in mathematics learning. Most U.S. teachers motivate and engage their students in learning the procedure of multiplication with concrete models and manipulatives, while Chinese teachers motivate and engage their students in learning with examples of prior knowledge and stories. By applying manipulatives, such as cutting a paper circle, singing a fraction song, playing with money, using base-ten blocks, or drawing and coloring areas, the U.S. teachers sparked students' interest in fraction multiplication and engaged students in a meaningful and concrete learning process. This "learning by doing" approach should enhance students' inquiry and creative ability if a teacher knows how to connect it to prior knowledge in the review process and how to use questions to connect the "doing" activities to mathematical abstract thinking. Chinese teachers were able to build on this connection by focusing on the importance of determining and reinforcing students' prior knowledge. However, very few U.S. teachers gave examples connecting students' prior knowledge to help students learn fraction multiplication. To teach effectively, U.S. teachers should consistently engage students in the inquiry learning cycle process of study question–study review.

Missing Component 6: Proficiency in Procedural Development

In this study teachers from two groups have different perspectives about procedural development. In China, procedural development is developing more than skills from drill; it is also the process of organizing thinking and reinforcing conceptual understanding. Alternatively, U.S. teachers usually see "drills as kills"; they would rather create new ways to help students that do not include procedure and skills development. The result of this misconception leads U.S. teachers to deemphasize procedural development and focus on using manipulatives, concrete models, and hands-on activities to reach understanding. Few U.S. teachers in this study believe that using procedures and rules is effective in building on fraction concepts. In contrast, Chinese teachers focused on procedures and rules to build on student ideas of fractions. In observations of classroom teaching, all Chinese teachers provided different levels of problems to build proficiency in procedural development. This result is not surprising. Throughout history, Chinese teachers have focused on developing procedures and skills as an integral part of learning. The history of mathematics development in China has had a great impact on mathematics teaching in China. Under the influence of the classic work *Arithmetic in Nine Chapters,* the Chinese mathematics develops and practices accurate and efficient means of computation and applies these in real life. In addition, under the influence of the Chinese examination system, in order to help most students pass the rigorous exams, teachers pay attention to proficiency in computation and problem solving, as well as students' conceptual understanding. Chinese teachers believe that developing proficiency in procedural skills helps students reinforce what they have already learned and allows them to transfer skills and understanding easily to new knowledge. Most importantly, it aids student confidence.

What is an efficient approach to help students develop proficiency in procedural development? This study identifies oral practice as one effective way used in Chinese mathematics teaching. Oral practice helps students build a solid base for mathematics. It also helps students solve a problem quickly, and it enhances their thinking ability. Further examination of the connection between the theory and effects of oral training in mathematics teaching is needed in future studies.

Chinese teachers emphasize oral practice. This oral practice is not simply an oral reading of the problem or the explanation of it; it involves doing the problem mentally, expressing the problem orally, and solving the problem quickly. Usually at the beginning of lessons, Chinese teachers use a few minutes to give a set of problems and require students to answer them quickly and accurately, calling on students one by one; sometimes teachers have students answer problems orally and simultaneously. In order to do oral problems quickly and accurately, students are required to memorize many facts, concepts, definitions, and formulas that form the base of their conceptual understanding. Usually students use independent study time in the morning to read their textbooks and try to memorize these basic facts. Sometimes teachers have students read definitions aloud simultaneously during class. Intensive oral practice challenges students and builds a solid foundation for their further learning. It is like learning English—even though you know the words, you have to learn spelling. Without good spelling skills, you cannot write quickly and accurately. Without familiar basic facts, students' learning and thinking will be slow, leading to difficulty in problem solving. For example, Chinese teachers require students to memorize the squares of 1–20. By remembering these facts students will be able to easily and quickly solve problems involving area, simplifying square roots, and simplifying fractions such as 169/13. Most importantly, this kind of learning also enhances thinking skills. During the learning process, if students remember the basic facts, the thinking goes smoothly; otherwise, the thinking will be blocked.

Intensive oral practice is neglected in U.S. mathematics classrooms. The lack of oral practice deprives students of the basic skills they will need to learn subjects such as algebra. U.S. teachers from high schools often complain that some of their students do not even remember the times table. High school teachers must spend a lot of time on reviewing what students should have learned in middle school; consequently, there is not enough time for learning algebra. This may be one of the main reasons why Chinese students are more proficient in basic skills than U.S. students.

**Missing Component 7: Aim at "Thinking Methods"
Rather Than Content**

According to Confucius, without thinking in the process of learning one will be deceived (学而不思则罔). To most Chinese teachers, the goal of mathematics teaching is to teach "thinking methods." This idea can be found in the observations and interviews with Chinese teachers in this study. Teachers elicit students' thinking with probing questions and making connections, support students' thinking with examples and activities, and extend students' thinking by layered practices. As a result, students' abilities in abstract thinking and problem solving are enhanced, and reflection occurs as students expand their thinking abilities. However, with the focus on teaching content, a teacher will aim at teaching facts. This fragmenting method does not promote students' thinking. In this study, classroom observation showed that U.S. teachers tended to use concrete models, charts, and pictures to promote students' thinking, but learning was often disconnected. One characteristic of Chinese teaching is to engage students in an intensive and sequential order of thinking. Furthermore, Chinese teachers tend to encourage students' thinking by developing reflection.

Chinese teachers encourage their students to think about their problem solving and to substitute their answers back into the original equations, to check to see if they make sense. Reflection occurs when students check and analyze their work with critical thinking. Reflection helps students reorganize relationships, reinforce knowledge, and find their errors by themselves. Importantly, reflection develops a deep understanding and fosters good learning habits. Reflection has been viewed as a critical learning strategy constantly taught in mathematics classrooms in China. The importance of reflection was noted by

Fennema and Romberg (1999), who state that reflection plays an important role in solving problems, and a critical factor of reflection is that teachers recognize and value reflection. In this study, Chinese teachers such as Ms. Wang and Ms. Lu encourage students to be a "mathematics doctor," which means to reflect on and examine errors in problem solving. They also value reflection by praising students who do well on checking procedures and answers.

To extend students' thinking to a higher level, Chinese teachers in this study also guide students to discover alternative methods of problem solving and use concepts and definitions to support students' thinking.

Furthermore, Chinese teachers support students' thinking by assigning various levels of practice problems. Designing layers of problems for students is a main focus in mathematics teaching in China. This provides the ladder for students to arrive at a higher level of thinking. Through different levels of practice, teachers expect students to learn the thinking method—the way of thinking—rather than simply solve problems. Most teachers encourage students to use multiple paths to solve problems. Through inquiry and exploring different ways of solving problems, students are able to think globally and connect separate topics in context.

Missing Component 8: The Whole Picture and Structure in the Knowledge Network

An old Chinese saying states that knowledge building is accumulated from "few to many" and then from "many to few." This view about two ways of learning addresses an important idea in teaching: it is not enough that a teacher has a deep knowledge of content; he or she must be able to get out of the rich content area and be able to abstract and synthesize the knowledge, to see clearly through the relationships between different levels of knowledge, and to have insight into the key points in the knowledge network. The ability to go from "many to few" distinguishes the completeness of teachers in mastering knowledge. A teacher who is able to go from "many to few" stands on a higher level to view the knowledge in a systemic network and see the connections among different bits of knowledge; in contrast, a teacher who lacks this ability often perceives knowledge as a collection of separate and fragmented pieces and cannot see the linkages between the components of knowledge. This is true for students' learning also. The principle from "many to few" is reflected on knowledge of a pyramid in missing component 2.

In this study, Chinese teachers were able to build students' mathematics ideas by connecting prior knowledge of whole number addition to fraction addition using the "unit" concept: numbers with like units can be added. No matter what kind of numbers (such as whole numbers, decimals, and fractions) are being used, as long as the numbers have the same unit, they can be added together. Observations in Chinese classrooms showed that all Chinese teachers were able to design a series of problems at the beginning of each lesson. These problems were carefully chosen and designed in layers, not only connecting students to prior knowledge but also bridging student understanding from prior knowledge to new knowledge. In contrast, some U.S. teachers provided warm-up problems, often from textbooks; some were for review of a previous lesson and were not related to the new lesson. Connecting the knowledge in different stages coherently provides a close link between the components of knowledge and makes learning easier. This is supported by NCTM (2000): "The study of rational numbers in the middle grades should build on students' prior knowledge of whole-number concepts and skills and their encounters with fractions, decimals, and percents in lower grades and in everyday life" (215).

However, developing understanding also involves the construction of a rich and integrated knowledge structure (Carpenter and Lehrer, 1999): "When knowledge is highly structured new knowledge can be related to and incorporated into existing networks of knowledge. . . . This structuring of knowledge is one of the features that makes learning with understanding generative" (21). To help students develop structured knowledge that supports their thinking, Chinese teachers in this study were able to spend time to fully design the lessons, to present the lessons in a logical and sequential order, and to display lecture notes in a highly structured and organized layout. The observations of Chinese teachers' lessons showed this characteristic of teaching. An example of this could be found in Mr. Xiao's written structure displayed on the blackboard in figure 6.9, which provided students structured knowledge and a whole picture of relationships involved in the concept of circle. In contract, the U.S. teachers did not show this structured knowledge in observed classes.

Furthermore, Carpenter and Lehrer (1999) indicated that when knowledge is highly structured, it is less susceptible to forgetting and there are multiple paths to retrieving it. Chinese students' quick thinking and proficiency in oral practice in the observed classes confirmed the advantage of such structured knowledge.

THE IMPACT OF TEACHERS' BELIEFS

The results of this study suggest that teachers' beliefs have an impact on constructing their pedagogical content knowledge and classroom teaching. In turn, the differences in pedagogical content knowledge shape various teachers' beliefs in mathematics. Generally speaking, there is a positive correlation between teachers' beliefs and their pedagogical content knowledge. However, some cases in this study indicate an inconsistent relationship between a teacher's beliefs and pedagogical content knowledge. This inconsistency may be due to external factors such as the pressure of the testing system or too many students in a class. Internal factors, such as the habit of teaching or teachers' knowledge, may hinder a teacher from implementing new ways to teach. Overall, the differences in teachers' beliefs are reflected in the pedagogical content knowledge and in actual classroom teaching. A discussion of the disparities and differences according to the framework of teacher's beliefs presented in chapter 5 follows.

The Goals of Teaching

The U.S. and Chinese teachers differ in their goals for teaching. Most U.S. teachers believe that the primary goals of teaching are to develop students' knowledge, increase students' confidence and self-esteem, and cultivate students to be productive citizens by providing equal opportunity to all children. The majority of Chinese teachers believe that the goal of teaching includes not only developing students' knowledge but also helping students succeed in society. In China, social success means students will become productive human resources for the country and enhance the quality of the whole nation.

U.S. teachers believe that every child can learn, and thus it is not surprising that they attempt to raise confidence and self-esteem by providing equal opportunity to all children. Teachers' beliefs are influenced by the democratic society and democratic educational system in the United States. In turn, these beliefs impact the teachers' pedagogical content knowledge. This study found that teachers in the United States tried very hard to explore numerous teaching approaches to reach out to all children. Teachers tried to connect learning to concrete models and students' daily life. Although there was no single focus on specific teaching approaches, teachers respected the differences among students and provided equal opportunity to all children. This is supported by the NCTM (2000), which states that "excellence in mathematics education requires equity, high expectations, and strong support for all students" (12).

Although both groups of teachers believe the goals of teaching are to give students knowledge and help students become productive citizens, the majority of Chinese teachers believe that the goals of teaching are to help students gain knowledge and succeed in society. In order to cultivate students to become productive human resources, Chinese education aims to develop students fully in four areas: ideology, morality, school, and discipline. The main characteristic of centrally controlled education in China is to advocate loyalty and devotion to the nation; students are nurtured to become productive human resources to the nation. Under this nationalistic education, the purpose of learning is to be useful and contribute to the country rather than to pursue personal interests. Consequently, students' personalities and individual values are neglected. The rigorous examination system is another feature of centralized education. In order to enter high schools and universities, students must pass entrance examinations. Students are sorted according to their grades so that they may enter schools at different levels. As a result, many students are sent out of high school every year and their only choice is to go to vocational schools, which means low-paying jobs in the future. Under the influence of the Chinese educational system, teachers believe that the goal of teaching is to teach students knowledge and skills, and to help students to be successful in society. This belief directs teachers' pedagogical content knowledge in the direction of focusing on proficiency in skills. Teachers work very hard to fully prepare students in basic concepts and skills in order to meet the needs of examinations. Spring (1998) observed that the examination system determined students' chances in life and placed tremendous pressure on students and teachers. Additionally, teachers were forced to teach to the test. He also indicated that the examination system reproduced social class. However, in recent years, China has been trying to decentralize education by allowing the publication of different versions of textbooks, by abolishing the entrance examination at the middle school level, and by drawing on the educational experiences of other countries, particularly the United States. Ironically, U.S. education is trying to strengthen its testing system by implementing testing at different levels.

There are different goals of mathematics teaching between the two groups of teachers. U.S. teachers believe that mathematics should be taught in real-life situations and should be connected to concrete models so students can gain mathematical knowledge. Chinese teachers believe that mathematics should be taught to help students gain mathematical knowledge, enhance students' critical thinking and logical reasoning ability, and apply in the real world.

Teaching mathematics in real-life situations and connecting it to concrete models are important approaches in mathematics teaching. According to Boaler (2000), knowledge is socially constructed, and cultural processes have an important impact on learning. Placing students' learning in real-life situations will make learning meaningful, visible, and applicable. This type of learning usually takes root more easily in students' minds.

Unlike U.S. teachers, Chinese teachers believe that the goals of mathematics teaching are to help students gain mathematical knowledge that can be applied in the real world and to enhance students' critical thinking and logical reasoning ability. Chinese teachers' beliefs may be due to the influence of educational history. In Chinese, the word "teacher" means "old master" who has deep knowledge. So in school, students always learn from the old master. In addition, traditional mathematics during the early development period was listed as one of six important skills for scholars in China. Teaching mathematics means to teach one of these skills.

Chinese teachers realize that logical and critical thinking capability is the key component of mathematics teaching. This belief has a great impact on teachers' pedagogical content knowledge. The interviews with Chinese teachers revealed their belief that teaching thinking methods should be a main focus. Classroom observers noted that teachers posed different levels of questions not only to promote students' thinking but also to give instruction on how to think. In their lesson plans, teachers designed layered questions and problems to enhance students' ability to master thinking methods, which is an important way of improving middle school students' mathematics learning. Fifth to eighth grades form a critical transition stage in mathematics learning. Students should be further trained to think logically and critically so that they can adjust easily and succeed in learning algebra. NCTM (1989) supported the idea that middle school students must progress from reasoning to making conjectures and that they must apply both inductive and deductive reasoning.

Primary Focus in Teaching Mathematics

Conceptual Understanding and Procedural Development

In this study, U.S. teachers tended to focus on concrete understanding by using various concrete models that ignore procedural development, while Chinese teachers paid more attention to procedural development in teaching mathematics on a base of conceptual understanding.

Concrete understanding is the fundamental base for conceptual understanding of learning mathematics. After developing a deep conceptual understanding, students need to develop a proficiency in skills in order to reinforce the concepts. Both conceptual understanding and procedural development are the base for using logical and critical thinking to solve problems. Most U.S. teachers realize the importance of both conceptual understanding and procedural development, but they do not know how to balance or apply them in their classroom teaching. As a result, they ignore procedural development.

To Chinese teachers, procedural development is not simply skill training; it involves the "thinking method." Chinese teachers believe that training in procedural development can promote students' thinking and strengthen their understanding of concepts. The observation of Chinese classes confirmed this view. Most teachers designed layered practices for students from lower-level problems to higher-order thinking problems in the classroom. Unlike U.S. teachers, who usually give classwork on the same type of problems at a very basic level and have students do them at once after instruction, Chinese teachers have students do two to four problems each time. After intensive practice, Chinese teachers make sure that students understand the problems, and then they go on to the next level. This style of teaching is a repetition of the process of "explanation and practice" with progress toward a higher level each time. By the end of class, students usually understand the concepts well and master skills proficiently through such extensive training.

Effective Teaching Methods

Both groups of teachers were able to identify what they considered to be the more effective methods of teaching mathematics. U.S. teachers were split on methods. One group preferred student-centered instruction, while another liked to use a combination of student-centered and teacher-centered instruction. However, most Chinese teachers acknowledged that the student-centered approach was more effective.

Classroom observations showed that most U.S. teachers were able to apply student-centered or a combination of student-centered and teacher-centered methods. They did activities such as name design, "Counting on You," and scale drawing. During these activities, students were relaxed and free to speak to one another. These student-centered activities, according to the teachers in this study, promote self-esteem, confidence, and cooperation, and provide opportunities for students to think and solve problems. This type of teaching is supported by NCTM (2000): "In effective teaching, worthwhile mathematical tasks are used to introduce important mathematical ideas and to engage and challenge students intellectually" (18).

Most Chinese teachers acknowledged that the student-centered approach was more effective. They believe that students are the main part of learning and the student-centered method encourages inquiry and creativity and enhances students' ability to think and learn. However, not all Chinese teachers in this study applied the student-centered method. The majority of them still use the teacher-centered method. In China, teacher-centered instruction is considered to be a heuristic method, in which a teacher inspires students to think deeply and to learn actively.

Some Chinese teachers feel that the heuristic method, which is rigorous and solid, can build a strong foundation in basic knowledge, computation, and systematic analysis through a step-by-step process of training. In applying this method, teachers pose different levels of questions, encouraging students to think, inquire, question, discuss, and reflect.

Chinese teachers, however, realized that teacher-centered instruction often ignores students' thinking, neglects character development of the individual, ignores the cultivation of creative ability, disconnects learning from real-life experience, and overlooks the interchangeable relationship between teacher and students. The observation of Chinese classroom teaching in this study showed that some Chinese teachers tried to use the student-centered method. They often grouped students in fours and had them discuss a question or problem for a few minutes. Although all students engaged in activities attentively, they were not relaxed; every student tried to express ideas and speak aloud simultaneously. With more than 50 students in one classroom, it was difficult for a teacher to use the student-centered teaching method, and it was also difficult for students to interact with and learn from one another. Chinese teachers need to have a high level of organization and direct activities in order to use a student-centered method in teaching mathematics.

Large class size seems to be the main factor influencing Chinese teachers to use the teacher-centered method. Even U.S. teachers in this study admitted that class size is a factor in deciding which teaching method is the best to use. In fact, there is no best way to teach; no matter which method is used, the only purpose of teaching should be to help students succeed in learning. Multiple ways should be explored; NCTM (2000) suggested that teachers use different ways to help students learn mathematics. There is no "right" way to teach; teachers must make decisions on the most effective way to create a rich setting for learning. So teachers should explore multiple ways to reach out to all the students.

Addressing Individual Differences

Both U.S. and Chinese teachers used various ways to approach students' differences. However, there are differences between U.S. and Chinese teachers regarding the methods of dealing with students' needs. U.S. teachers tend to vary teaching methods, while Chinese teachers like to design different levels of assignments. The U.S. teachers pay much more attention to individual differences using different teaching styles and activities and interacting with students, such as connecting through visual models, offering after-school tutoring, and contacting parents. This may be due to cultural factors because the United States is a multicultural society, and recognizing individual differences is critical for U.S. teachers. They realized that to teach effectively, a teacher must connect these cultural differences to provide equal opportunities to all students and motivate them to be successful.

To deal with individual student differences, Chinese teachers tend to design different levels of practice. Usually teachers give at least two types of problems: basic and enrichment problems. Basic problems are for all students, and enrichment problems are only for certain students. In the classroom, a teacher asks different levels of questions to different levels of students in order to encourage their learning. Chinese teachers use the strategy: "Focus on two ends, develop the middle" to deal with individual student differences. This strategy focuses on low- and high-ability students. However, this strategy often ignores middle-level students. Learning how to fully treat the individual differences among students and provide equal opportunity for all students is still a challenge to Chinese teachers.

Structure of the Lesson

The structure of the lesson is very important for successful learning. A clear and organized lesson structure makes learning easy and understandable. When teaching is logical and follows a sequential order, thinking will be promoted gradually. The observation of classroom teaching in this study found that U.S. teachers' lessons seemed loose and unstructured, while Chinese teachers' classes displayed organized structure in logical and sequential order, from easy to difficult levels at a fast pace. This is reflected in the way teachers deliver the lesson. U.S. teachers usually use transparencies on an overhead projector. After the teacher's explanation is finished the transparency is removed. In contrast, Chinese teachers pay much attention to writing structure on the blackboard; they view this skill as a part of effective teaching. They usually write definitions and formulas on a preprepared small blackboard and hang it on the large classroom blackboard. Throughout the lesson, they use different strategies (tree diagrams, concept mapping, etc.) to display key points on the blackboard, and these writings are displayed from beginning to the end of the lesson. This structure provides students an overview of the lesson and encourages them to reflect on knowledge back and forth at any time. Importantly, it allows students to see the connections and relationships among the parts of knowledge and supports students' thinking during the lesson. In China, this skill of delivering the lesson is considered an art of teaching. Teachers are provided special training and requirements on how to address and display their lesson clearly, neatly, and structurally in a logical and sequential order.

Importance of Teachers' Knowledge

Content and Pedagogical Knowledge

Although the U.S. teachers recognized the importance of an in-depth understanding of mathematics, almost twice as many Chinese teachers as U.S. teachers believe that a teacher with an in-depth understanding of mathematics is critical for effective teaching. The majority of Chinese teachers believe a popular Chinese saying, "If you want to give the students one cup of water, you should have a bucket of water of your own." Chinese teachers believe that teachers with deep mathematical knowledge are able to teach mathematics at a higher level and explain mathematics in simpler ways. In addition, they understand textbooks and grasp key points better. Importantly, with deep mathematics knowledge, teachers are able to enhance their abilities in connecting other subjects with mathematics teaching.

Both groups of teachers interviewed in the study agreed that it is important for a teacher to thoroughly understand mathematics, while realizing that pedagogical content knowledge is critical for teaching at the elementary and middle school levels. Teachers know a variety of methods, have presentation skills, understand students' thinking, know how to teach students at different levels, and are able to teach content effectively. Since the United States has a diverse and multicultural education system, possessing pedagogical content knowledge is especially important to U.S. teachers. It helps them know individual students' thinking and understand how students learn mathematics. Teachers' decisions and actions in the classroom should be based on pedagogical knowledge (NCTM 2000); mathematics instruction uses context and pedagogy that allows students to use their own cultural preferences (Malloy 1999).

Promoting Student Thinking

There are also differences between the two groups of teachers in their approaches to promote students' thinking skills: most U.S. teachers in this study would promote students' thinking by cooperative learning; the majority of Chinese teachers would promote students' thinking by assigning various levels of practice.

U.S. teachers believe that cooperative learning is one important way to promote students' thinking. In cooperative learning, students explain their ideas and share their thinking. This peer communication provides insights for further understanding and deeper thinking.

However, Chinese teachers promote students' thinking by assigning various levels of practice problems. Designing layers of problems for students is one of the main aspects of mathematics teaching in China. It provides the ladder for students to arrive at a higher level of thinking. Through different levels of practice, teachers expect students to learn the thinking method—the way of thinking—rather than just solve problems. Most Chinese teachers encourage students to use multiple ways to solve problems. In this way, students learn to think critically and logically and to connect separate topics in context.

Planning for Instruction

Approaches to Planning for Math Instruction

This study found that there are differences in teachers' planning for instruction. Most U.S. teachers plan instruction with a team, and the majority of Chinese teachers plan instruction according to textbooks and students' needs.

Planning with a team is an important way for teachers to keep at the same pace, to share teaching experiences, and to learn from one another. Planning with a team also enhances reflection on how and what teachers have been doing and promotes collaboration with colleagues. Some teachers meet in vertical alignment with upper-grade teachers to discuss the needs for in-depth instruction, which provides teachers opportunities to make connections for their mathematical knowledge. These connections inform teachers about the knowledge that students already have and the knowledge that students need to learn in order to succeed at the next level. NCTM (2000) indicated that reflection and analysis could be greatly enhanced by teaming with colleagues. Collaboration with colleagues is not only a powerful approach to reform in the United States, and but also saves some time for teachers (Stigler and Hiebert 1999). This study noted that U.S. teachers do not write a detailed lesson plan; they write only an outline for a lesson. This may be due to the limited time in school for U.S. teachers to plan and may also be due to lack of requirements for detailed plans by the schools.

In contrast, Chinese teachers' lesson plans are detailed teaching notes, which include the objectives, content, key points, difficult points, and procedures. The teaching procedure is the main body of the lesson plan, which includes review and introduction, the new lesson, the types of questions to be asked, examples given, problems for practice, and a summary. Usually, it takes at least two to five pages to write a plan for one lesson.

The majority of Chinese teachers plan for instruction according to the content of the textbook and students' needs. Chinese teachers consider textbooks to be the basis for planning, while students are the main focus of planning. Teachers study textbooks carefully and try to understand the key and difficult points, and design various questions and layered practice exercises and problems. Chinese teachers also plan for instruction according to students' needs. They analyze the weaknesses and strengths of their students and develop teaching strategies to help students learn mathematics. This type of planning places students' needs in the planning phase. It has a clear purpose, which is to help students understand and learn mathematics. As NCTM (2000) stated, "Effective teachers must know how to ask questions and plan lessons that reveal student prior knowledge; they can then design experiences and lessons that respond to, and build on, this knowledge" (12).

Chinese teachers often observe their colleagues' teaching. Some school districts require all teachers to observe classes. Teachers can choose which classes to observe. Some schools also provide a "re-search class," a model class for development of teaching methods, by selecting one teacher from each grade. Observing other classes helps teachers broaden their views of teaching and to learn new teaching methods. Most school districts and cities have open classes for teachers once a month. They are taught by experienced teachers from different schools. All teachers can apply to teach open classes as long as they have new ideas and new ways to teach mathematics effectively. After attending an open class, teachers who observed submit their comments on the class and nominate lessons for awards. These open classes provide models for teachers and help them gain insights into teaching. By teaching outside of their own schools, teachers who give open classes are challenged and fairly judged.

In the United States, by contrast, most school districts spend a lot of money and time on workshops provided by people from outside the classroom. This kind of workshop often looks good, but most classroom teachers have difficulty applying what they learned from workshops in their own classrooms. Most of them do not even apply to the regular classroom setting.

Planning Time

In this study, most Chinese teachers spent more than one hour daily in planning mathematics instruction, while less than half of the U.S. teachers spent more than one hour daily in planning math instruction, and most of them use less than 30 minutes per day. This difference may be due to the educational system. In China, most mathematics teachers only teach two periods of 45 minutes per period each day in the morning; the rest of the day is used for lesson planning and grading. Sufficient time in school enables teachers to understand the subjects and their requirements fully, so they can prepare instruction thoroughly.

In the United States, teachers in this study teach five periods of 45 minutes daily, or three periods of 90 minutes daily. Every day after teaching, most teachers are exhausted in both mind and body. This was observed during the interviews and observations with U.S. teachers. During the conference period, most teachers have to do administrative paperwork required by the school, make phone calls to parents, or attend meetings. Work environments for teachers in the United States are more stressful than those in China. Although U.S. teachers have many more resource books and teaching materials, they do not have sufficient time to study and to plan in schools. As the economy and technology become more highly developed, everything moves at a faster pace, including education. Schools keep teachers and students busy at all times: teachers teach one class following the next class, and students move from one class to the next class in just 5 minutes (Chinese student have 10 minutes' break time between classes). Schools try to produce learning outcomes quickly and efficiently; consequently, many students fail to learn. Some people call this phenomenon the McDonald'sization of education. However, the nature of education is totally different from the business of education. An old Chinese saying is "The teacher is the engineer of the human soul." This reflects the idea that a teacher should take time and prepare to nurture students' learning. Another popular Chinese saying is "The teacher is a gardener of a garden." This also reflects the view that the teacher should take time to prepare and cultivate students' learning. In China, most teachers consider teaching a great cause; they devote a lot of energy and time to teaching. In the United States, under such difficult work conditions, many new teachers leave the profession within a few years.

Checking Homework

There are some similarities between U.S. and Chinese teachers in their beliefs about the purpose of checking homework. For example, an almost equal percentage of teachers in both countries agreed that assigning homework is to check for understanding. Both groups of teachers stated that most students do their homework. However, there are differences in the views on the purpose of assigning homework in the two groups of teachers. To most U.S. teachers, assigning homework is simply for review and practice, while to most Chinese teachers, assigning homework is to reinforce understanding.

Beliefs about homework as review and practice are reflected in U.S. teaching methods. In this study, U.S. teachers spend less time emphasizing prior knowledge and most of them spend no time grading homework, because they believe the students had reviewed and practiced this knowledge sufficiently as homework. On the other hand, Chinese teachers believe homework reinforces understanding of knowledge and firmly roots the ideas and procedures in students' learning. Reflecting this belief, Chinese teachers spend more than one-third of their time on reviewing prior knowledge and connecting it to new knowledge in class, and design different levels of problems in homework to reinforce understanding of the knowledge step by step. It is important to note that every Chinese teacher not only grades each problem on a student's homework but also corrects mistakes "face to face," which means to correct student's work in front of the student, to talk with the student, and help the student understand mathematics in the correct way. Chinese teachers try to nip the "blind point" in the bud. Students can avoid making mistakes if the teacher can help them realize and eliminate errors at an early stage.

When grading student work, Chinese teachers always point out the mistakes in the problems and praise what is done well. They then record and analyze the mistakes in student work, thereby establishing the patterns of errors. By analyzing the errors in class, teachers provide feedback to students immediately and help students learn from their mistakes. Students are required to make corrections on their mistakes after they receive the teacher's feedback. According to Ashlock (1994), "Errors are a positive thing in the process of learning—or at least they should be. In many cultures, errors are regarded as an opportunity to reflect and learn" (1). Chinese culture promotes learning from errors. The famous Chinese saying "Failure is the mother of success" reflects the Chinese teachers' attitude toward students' mistakes. However, if students are not required to correct their mistakes, this "failure" never has a chance to be "success," and students' learning will be hampered and teaching will fail.

In observing U.S. teachers' classes, we found that most teachers grade students' homework during the class by calling the answers out to students in a few minutes. Students record the answers and correct the wrong answers. If students have questions, the teacher will explain. But only the better students ask questions; the majority of students just change the incorrect to correct answers. This way of checking homework seems to save the teachers time but wastes instructional time. Consequently teachers will have to spend more time to mend a big "hole" later. This practice does not help students progress in learning nor does it help the teacher know students' thinking.

WHICH WAY SHALL WE GO?

Reshaping Teachers' Knowledge Base

Four Aspects of Analysis of Pedagogical Content Knowledge

Comparative study can increase our understanding of how to produce educational effectiveness and enhance our understanding of our own education and society (Kaiser 1999). However, it is difficult to conduct a valid comparative study between different cultures without setting essential components as a norm in the analysis of data. This study included comparisons and contrasts of teachers' pedagogical content knowledge between the United States and China by using four aspects of pedagogical content knowledge of teaching: building on students' mathematics ideas and understanding, addressing and correcting students' misconceptions, engaging students in mathematics learning, and promoting and supporting student thinking about mathematics. Each of these aspects consists of several essential components (see table 4.2). Through analyzing essential components, this study provides a sample and insight in how to set up dimensions and scope for further cross-cultural comparative studies in teachers' knowledge. Although the four aspects in this study only partly covers pedagogical content knowledge, this study focuses on a critical way to assess teachers' knowledge of student thinking.

Pedagogical Content Knowledge as a Leading Component

Teacher knowledge of mathematics is not isolated from its effects on teaching in the classroom and student learning (Fennema and Franke 1992). Teachers' pedagogical content knowledge combines knowledge of content, teaching, and curriculum, focusing on the knowledge of student thinking. It is closely connected with content knowledge, connected both with the transformation of content knowledge in the learning process, and with the way of knowing students' thinking. It balances teachers' focus on conceptual understanding and procedural development. This study indicates that deep and broad pedagogical content knowledge is important and necessary for effective teaching and plays a leading role in teachers' knowledge base. With deep pedagogical content knowledge, a teacher is able to teach for understanding in a convergent process in which teachers build students' mathematics ideas by connecting prior knowledge and concrete models to new knowledge, and by focusing on conceptual understanding and procedural development. In addition, deep pedagogical content knowledge enables a teacher to identify students' misconceptions and to correct misconceptions with probing questions and various tasks; it also advances teachers' strategies for engaging students in learning by providing examples, representations, and manipulatives. Finally, it enhances teachers' ability to promote and support students' thinking with a variety of focusing questions and activities.

The results of this study support the idea that a balance is needed between conceptual understanding and procedural development. Although conceptual understanding can be achieved through developing a concrete understanding of mathematics, procedural development is an essential learning process for reinforcing understanding and achieving mathematical proficiency. Procedural development is a necessary step for applying the strategies in problem solving. Without developing a firm understanding and proficient skill in procedures, students will not be able to solve problems efficiently and confidently. Last and most importantly, attention to learners' cognition is a key component in teachers' pedagogical content knowledge. Knowledge of students' mathematical thinking helps teachers enhance their own knowledge of content and curriculum, prepare lessons thoroughly, and teach mathematics effectively. Without knowledge of students' thinking, teaching cannot produce successful learning.

Deepening Pedagogical Content Knowledge

The findings in this study show that there are differences between the pedagogical content knowledge of middle school mathematics teachers in the United States and China. These differences are revealed in teacher beliefs, planning, teaching methods, and knowledge of student cognition. These differences also address the importance and impact of pedagogical content knowledge in effective teaching. How do teachers deepen their pedagogical content knowledge? What approaches enhance pedagogical content knowledge for teachers? Discussions and suggestions are provided in the following sections to answer these questions.

Knowing Student Thinking by Grading Homework

Pedagogical content knowledge not only addresses how to teach mathematics content successfully but also focuses on how to understand students' cognition. There are many ways to know students' thinking; however, the importance of grading homework has been ignored in the United States. In order to do homework, students not only need to recall, review, and understand the concepts and skills learned from the classroom, but they also need to apply them to solve problems. The recalling, reviewing, understanding, and applying are the parts of a process of internalizing knowledge and are skills learned in class. This internalization enables students to transfer the knowledge of others into their own knowledge base. Such critical transformation also provides a lens for teachers through which they can view students' thinking at a deep internal level and provide feedback immediately to correct misconceptions. Furthermore, through analyzing patterns of misconception from homework, teachers are able to adjust instruction according to students' needs, develop students' understanding, and enhance the effectiveness of their teaching.

Unfortunately, the importance of grading homework has been ignored by teachers and research in mathematics education in the United States. *Adding It Up: Helping Children Learn Mathematics* (National Research Council 2001) asserts: "The limited research on homework in mathematics has been confined to investigations of the relation between the quantity of homework assigned and students' achievement on test scores. Neither the quality nor the function of homework has been studied" (426). The pivotal role of grading homework and the relationship between grading homework and knowing students' thinking have been overlooked in most studies of mathematics education. This study strongly recommends that U.S. mathematics teachers take time to grade students' homework, although they do not have enough time to do so in school. Furthermore, the findings in this study show that Chinese teachers grade each problem in students' homework, while U.S. teachers call out the answers on homework and have students check their own homework. Further comparative study is needed to examine how well teachers understand students' thinking by giving answers to students, as compared to grading homework problems.

Planning According to Student Needs

Planning is a vital factor in successful teaching. It is not enough for teachers to plan instruction according to standards and textbooks. An effective teacher also considers the students' understanding level and individual needs as the basis of planning. During the planning, an effective teacher needs to write a detailed lesson plan to analyze students' thinking and needs, rather than a simple outline of the lesson. A teacher who writes a detailed lesson plan reflects and synthesizes pedagogical content knowledge, analyzes students' understanding, and evaluates textbook and curriculum. With this preparation, a teacher will have more confidence and will be more effective. However, most U.S. mathematics textbooks provide a lesson plan as an outline for each lesson. Although this seems convenient for teachers, it eliminates the opportunity for teachers to design and analyze and evaluate the lesson. It also limits teachers' thinking and cultivates the habit of using the thinking of others instead of their own creativity in teaching. Although U.S. teachers do not have enough time to plan for instruction when compared to Chinese teachers, who have adequate time at school, with rich teaching resources, technology, and small class sizes, U.S. teachers might teach more effectively if they could spend more time on planning according to students' needs and planning by creating a detailed lesson plan.

Observing Classes and Analyzing Model Lessons

Results of this study indicate that U.S. teachers enhance pedagogical content knowledge by attending workshops and continuing education after college, while most Chinese teachers develop pedagogical content knowledge by observing the classes of experienced teachers. Teachers who observe other classes gain insight on teaching. They are encouraged to compare and contrast lessons, and observation provides a different angle and perspective on the same lesson. Observing other classes builds confidence in new teachers. In China, open classes are an effective way to promote excellent teaching and provide models of teaching for teachers at the school district level. Since open classes are model lessons, they engage teachers in analyzing model lessons that relate to their own lessons, and provide practical ideas for teachers to adapt and use immediately following the observation. This study suggests that the U.S. educational system should deemphasize workshops, which are not generally useful or practical, and instead emphasize open classes and classroom observation during the semester, followed by reflection and analysis. This will lay a solid foundation for U.S. teachers to master effective teaching strategies and deepen their pedagogical content knowledge substantially. A further recommendation for U.S. mathematics education research is to thoroughly examine the connection between the development of pedagogical content knowledge and the observation of other classes.

CONCLUSION

The findings in this study show that there are many differences between the pedagogical content knowledge of middle school mathematics teachers in the United States and China. These differences are reflected in teachers' beliefs, planning, teaching methods, and knowledge of learners' cognition. U.S. teachers are able to create various teaching approaches to reach out to all students, such as concrete models, cooperative learning, projects and journals, and manipulatives. These activities encourage students to practice inquiry and creativity. On the other hand, Chinese teachers focus on two basic approaches—conceptual understanding and procedural development—by emphasizing thinking methods and intensive layered practice.

Currently education in China realizes its disadvantages in teaching and is attempting to relieve pressure on students. Chinese teachers would like to learn how to apply activities to develop inquiry and creativity through approaches such as manipulatives and cooperative learning from U.S. teachers. On the other hand, U.S. educators would like to learn how to strengthen their testing system and achieve proficiency in mathematics as compared to Asian countries. Both educational systems are trying to learn from each other. However, caution should be exercised in learning from each other, since cultural factors make a difference in learning. For example, China is trying to reform the examination system by abolishing the middle school entrance examination. In addition, teachers are not allowed to assign homework to lower grades in elementary school. China also made a new version of the K–12 curriculum by studying the curricula of other countries, especially the United States. This reform action could bring a new perspective to education in China; meanwhile, China may lose its advantage of having a strong base in K–12.

The "math war" in the United States involves enhancing the testing system. This could place much pressure on students and teachers. Teachers would not have as much time to provide concrete models and meaningful activities to students. The United States could lose the advantage of inquiry and creativity in learning. Furthermore, under the pressure of testing, teachers will tend to teach mathematics for tests, which might result in students' learning fragment, separated, and unstructured knowledge. Consequently, proficiency in mathematics will have be difficult to achieve.

Therefore, both countries should consider the characteristics of their educational system and their cultural factors in mathematics education reform. In addition, both countries should learn from the other's successful experience and be aware of failed experiences in mathematics education reform.

The results of this study show that mathematics teachers from different cultures and countries have their own beliefs; therefore, they should develop their unique teaching approaches, which may be viewed as backward by others. This notion is supported by Paul Ernest (1989), who indicates that cultural and social contexts affect teachers' belief systems. The results of this study support the idea that teachers' beliefs in mathematics and teaching play a significant role in shaping their instruction (Thompson 1992). This study provides powerful evidence that teachers' beliefs have a deep impact on pedagogical content knowledge. In turn, pedagogical content knowledge plays an important role in determining the effectiveness of mathematics teaching. To deepen pedagogical content knowledge, teachers should gain knowledge of students' thinking from grading homework and plan for instruction according to textbooks, but also consider student needs and observe classes to learn from other teachers.

This comparison study of pedagogical content knowledge of middle school mathematics teachers lends itself to the studies of beliefs, planning, teaching methods, and knowledge of learners' cognition. This study paves the road for the further systematic inquiry of pedagogical content knowledge and its relationship to beliefs, planning, teaching methods, and knowledge of learners' cognition at different grade levels and in different areas of mathematics.

References

American Association for the Advancement of Science (AAAS). 1989. *Science for all Americans*. Washington, D.C.: AAAS.

———. 2000. *Project 2061: Curriculum materials evaluation*. Washington, D.C.: AAAS.

An, S. 2000. Globalization of education in China. *International Journal of Education Reform* 9, no. 2: 128–33.

An, S., Kulm, G., and Wu, Z. 2004. The pedagogical content knowledge of middle school mathematics teachers in China and the U.S. *Journal of Mathematics Teacher Education* (in press).

An, S., Kulm, G., Wu, Z., Ma, F., and Wang. 2002. The impact of cultural differences on middle school mathematics teachers' beliefs in the U.S. and China. Paper presented at ICMICS Conference, Hong Kong, November 2002.

Ashlock, R. B. 1994. *Error patterns in computation*. Upper Saddle River, N.J.: Merrill.

Ashmore, R. A., and Cao, Z. 1997. *Teacher education in the People's Republic of China*. Bloomington, Ind.: Phi Delta Kappa Educational Foundation.

Bishop, A. J. 1992. International perspectives on research in mathematics education. In D. A. Grouws, ed., *Handbook of mathematics teaching and learning*, 710–23. New York: Macmillan.

Boaler, J. 2000. Exploring situated insights into research and learning. *Journal for Research in Mathematics* 31: 113–19.

Cai, J. 2000. Mathematical thinking involved in U.S. and Chinese students' solving of process-constrained and process-open problems. *Mathematical Thinking and Learning* 2, no. 4: 309–40.

———. 2001. Improving mathematics learning: Lessons from cross-national studies of Chinese and U.S. students. *Phi Delta Kappan* 82, no. 5: 400–404.

Campbell, J. R., Hombo, C. M., and Mazzeo, J. 2000. *NAEP 1999 trends in academic progress: Three decades of student performance*. Washington, D. C.: U. S. Department of Education.

Carpenter, T. P., and Lehrer, R. 1999. Teaching and learning mathematics with understanding. In E. Fennema and T. A. Romberg, eds., *Mathematics classrooms that promote understanding*, 19–32. Mahwah, N.J.: Lawrence Erlbaum.

Carroll, W. M. 1999. Using short questions to develop and assess reasoning. In *NCTM 1999 yearbook: Developing mathematical reasoning in grades K–12*, 247–53. Reston, Va.: National Council of Teachers of Mathematics.

Cooney, T. 1985. A beginning teacher's view of problem solving. *Journal for Research in Mathematics Education* 16: 324–36.

Cooney, T. J., and Shealy, B. E. 1997. On understanding the structure of teachers' beliefs and their relationship to change. In E. Fennema and B. S. Nelson, eds., *Mathematics teachers in transition*, 87–109. Mahwah, N.J.: Lawrence Erlbaum.

Darling-Hammond, L. 2000. Teacher quality and student achievement: A review of state policy evidence. *Education Policy Analysis Archives* 8, no. 1: 1–62.

Dossey, J. A. 1992. The nature of mathematics: Its role and its influence. In D. A. Grouws, ed., *Handbook of mathematics teaching and learning*, 39–48. New York: Macmillan.

Doyle, W. 1992. Curriculum and pedagogy. In P. Jackson, ed., *Handbook of research on curriculum*, 486–516. New York: Macmillan.

Elbaz, F. 1983. *Teacher thinking: A study of practical knowledge*. London: Croon Helm.

Ernest, P. 1989. The impact of beliefs on the teaching of mathematics. In *Mathematics teaching: The state of the art*, 249–54. New York: Falmer.

Fennema, E., Carpenter, T. P., Franke, M. L., Levi, L., Jacobs, V. R., and Empson, S. B. 1996. A longitudinal study of learning to use children's thinking in mathematics instruction. *Journal for Research in Mathematics Education* 27, no. 4: 403–34

Fennema, E., and Franke, M. L. 1992. Teachers' knowledge and its impact. In D. A. Grouws, ed., *Handbook of mathematics teaching and learning*, 147–64. New York: Macmillan.

Fennema, E., and Romberg, T. A. 1999. *Mathematics classrooms that promote understanding*. Mahwah, N.J.: Lawrence Erlbaum.

Fisher, C. 1990. The research agenda project as prologue. *Journal for Research in Mathematics Education* 21: 81–89.

Gutek, G. L. 1995. *A history of the western education experience*. Prospect Heights, Ill.: Waveland.

Jiang, Z., and Eggleton, P. 1995. A brief comparison of the U.S. and Chinese middle school mathematics program. *Schools Science and Mathematics* 95, no. 4: 187–94.

Kagan, D. M. 1992. Implications of research on teacher beliefs. *Educational Psychologist* 27: 65–90.

Kaiser, G. 1999. International comparisons in mathematics education under the perspective of comparative education. In G. Kaiser, E. Luna, and I. Huntley, eds., *International comparisons in mathematics education*, 1–15. Philadelphia: Falmer.

Kerslake, D. 1986. *Fractions: Children's strategies and errors*. Windsor, U.K.: NFER-Nelson.

Kilpatrick, J. 1994. History of mathematics education. In T. Husen and T. N. Postlethwaite, eds., *International encyclopedia of education*, 3643–47. New York: Elsevier Science.

Kulm, G., Capraro, R. M., Capraro, M. M., Burghardt, R., and Ford, K. 2001. Teaching and learning mathematics with understanding in an era of accountability and high-stakes testing. Paper presented at the research presession of the 79th annual meeting of the National Council of Teachers of Mathematics, Orlando, Fla., April.

Lapointe, A. E., Mead, N. A., and Askew, J. M. 1992. *Learning mathematics*. Princeton, N.J.: Educational Testing Service.

Lave, J. 1988. *Cognition in practice*. Cambridge: Cambridge University Press.

Li, J., and Chen, C. 1995. Observations on China's mathematics education as influenced by its traditional culture. Paper presented at the meeting of the China-Japan-U.S. Seminar on Mathematical Education, Hongzhou, China.

Li, W. 1999. *A history of mathematics*. Beijing: China Higher Education Press.

Ma, L. 1999. *Knowing and teaching elementary mathematics*. Mahwah, N.J.: Lawrence Erlbaum.

Malloy, C. E. 1999. Developing mathematical reasoning in the middle grades: Recognizing diversity. In *NCTM 1999 yearbook: Developing mathematical reasoning in grades K–12*, 13–21. Reston, Va.: National Council of Teachers of Mathematics.

Mathematical Sciences Education Board. 1989. *Everybody counts: A report to the nation on the future of mathematics education*. Washington, D.C.: National Academy Press.

———. 1990. *Reshaping school mathematics*. Washington, D.C.: National Academy Press.

Mullis, I. V., Martin, M. O., Gonzalez, E. J., Gregory, K. D., Garden, R. A., O'Connor, K. M., Chrostowski, S. J., and Smith, T. A. 2000. *TIMSS 1999: International mathematics report*. Chestnut Hill, Mass.: Boston College.

National Center for Education Development Research (NCEDR). 1999. *National Center for Education Development Research in ten years, 1986–1996.* Beijing: Department of Foreign Affairs Office.

National Center for Education Statistics. 1999. *Highlights from TIMSS: The Third International Mathematics and Science Study, 1999.* No. 1999–081. Washington, D.C.: U.S. Department of Education.

———. 2000. *National Assessment of Educational Progress mathematics study 2000.* http://nces.ed.gov/nationsreportcard/mathematics.

National Commission on Excellence in Education. 1983. *A nation at risk: The imperative for educational reform.* Washington, D.C.: U.S. Government Printing Office.

National Council of Teachers of Mathematics (NCTM). 1989. *The curriculum and evaluation standards for school mathematics.* Reston, Va.: NCTM.

———. 2000. *Principles and standards for school mathematics.* Reston, Va.: NCTM.

National Research Council. 2001. *Adding it up: Helping children learn mathematics.* Edited by J. Kilpatrick, J. Swafford, and B. Findell. Washington, D.C.: National Academy Press.

Nespor, J. 1987. The role of beliefs in the practice of teaching. *Journal of Curriculum Studies* 19: 317–28.

Noddings, N. 1995. *Philosophy of education.* Boulder, Colo.: Westview.

Pepper, S. 1996. *Radicalism and education reform in twentieth-century China.* Cambridge: Cambridge University Press.

Pinar, W. F., Reynolds, W. M., Slattery, P., and Taubman, P. M. 1995. *Understanding curriculum.* New York: Peter Lang.

Romberg, T. A., and Kaput, J. J. 1999. Mathematics worth teaching, mathematics understanding. In E. Fennema and T. A. Romberg, eds., *Mathematics classrooms that promote understanding,* 3–17. Mahwah, N.J.: Lawrence Erlbaum.

Shulman, L. 1985. On teaching problem solving and solving the problems of teaching. In E. A. Silver, ed., *Teaching and learning mathematical problem solving: Multiple research perspectives,* 439–50. Hillsdale, N.J.: Lawrence Erlbaum.

———. 1986. Those who understand: Knowledge growth in teaching. *Educational Researcher* 15, no. 2: 4–14.

———. 1987. Knowledge and teaching: Foundations of the new reform. *Harvard Educational Review* 57, no. 1: 1–22.

Silver, E. A. 1998. *Improving mathematics in middle school: Lessons from TIMSS and related research.* Washington, D.C.: U.S. Department of Education.

Smith, M. K. 1994. *Humble pi*. New York: Prometheus.

Sowder, J. T., Philipp, R. A., Artrong, B. E., and Schappelle, B. P. 1998. *Middle-grade teachers' mathematical knowledge and its relationship to instruction*. Albany: State University of New York Press.

Spring, J. 1998. *Education and the risk of the global economy*. Mahwah, N.J.: Lawrence Erlbaum.

State Education Commission, People's Republic of China. 1989. *Chinese mathematics textbook*, volume 10. Beijing: State Education Commission.

Stevenson, H. W., Lee, S. Y., Chen, C., Lummis, M., Stigler, J. W., Fan, L., and Ge, F. 1990. Mathematics classrooms in Japan, Taiwan, and the United States. *Children Development* 58: 1272–85.

Stigler, J. W., and Hiebert, J. 1999. *The teaching gap*. New York: Free Press.

Stigler, J. W., and Perry, M. 1988. Cross-cultural studies of mathematics teaching and learning: Recent findings and new directions. In D. Grouws and T. Cooney, eds., *Effective mathematics teaching directions,* 194–223. Reston, Va.: National Council of Teachers of Mathematics.

Su, Z. X. 1995. A critical evaluation of John Dewey's influence on Chinese education. *American Journal of Education* 103, no. 3: 302–25.

Thompson, A. G. 1992. Teachers' beliefs and conceptions: A synthesis of the research. In D. A. Grouws, ed., *Handbook of mathematics teaching and learning,* 127–46. New York: Macmillan.

Tymoczko, T. 1986. *New directions in the philosophy of mathematics*. Boston: Birkhauser.

Wang, Q. 1994. *The history of elementary mathematics education*. Shandong, China: Shandong Publisher.

Whitehead, A. N. 1925. *Science and the modern world*. New York: Free Press.

Willoughby, S. S. 1990. *Mathematics education for a changing world*. Alexandria, Va.: Association for Supervision and Curriculum Development.

Wong, N. Y., and Wong, W. Y. 2002. The "Confucian heritage culture" learner's phenomenon. *Asian Psychologist* 3, no. 1: 78–82.

About the Author

Shuhua An is an assistant professor of mathematics education in the College of Education, California State University, Long Beach, and a former teacher in Texas and China. She received her Ph.D. in mathematics education from Texas A&M University in College Station, Texas.